Mind Control

Andrew Parry

Published by Andrew Parry, 2024.

MIND CONTROL

First edition. October 26, 2024.

ISBN: 979-8227076939

Written by Andrew Parry.

Table of Contents

Introduction: The History of Mind Control across Cultures

Mind control, often referred to as brainwashing, is not a new phenomenon. Throughout history, leaders, religious figures, and influential individuals have sought ways to manipulate the minds of others, whether to solidify power, spread beliefs, or shape societal behavior. In ancient times, and continuing into the present day, various cultures have utilized different forms of persuasion, coercion, and psychological influence to guide the thoughts, beliefs, and actions of the masses.

Looking back, the earliest forms of mind control can be found in the religious practices of ancient civilizations. The Egyptians, for instance, established a strong priesthood that interpreted divine messages for the populace. Through elaborate rituals, grand architecture, and mysterious symbols, they maintained an aura of divine authority. This spiritual hierarchy ensured the people's obedience to both the religious system and the ruling class. Beliefs in the gods, the afterlife, and divine punishment were powerful tools for controlling the behaviors and even thoughts of the population.

In Ancient Greece and Rome, leaders employed orators and philosophers to shape public opinion. Public speeches and philosophical dialogues were not just methods of communication but tools of influence. In many cases, these skilled orators could sway the masses, ignite revolutions, or calm a riotous crowd. Mind control was embedded in the rhetoric, where emotional appeals—fear, pride, and loyalty—were strategically used to manipulate the audience's perception and actions.

Fast forward to the Middle Ages, and the Christian Church stood as one of the most significant examples of mind control through religious dogma. The Church held immense power, both politically and spiritually, controlling nearly every aspect of life in Europe. Through the concept of sin, salvation, and divine retribution, people's thoughts and actions were heavily influenced. Fear of excommunication or eternal damnation was enough to ensure compliance. The Inquisition, a grim manifestation of this control, targeted heretics and dissenters, using torture and punishment to enforce religious orthodoxy. This period exemplifies how belief systems were crafted and enforced to maintain societal order through fear and manipulation.

Religious mind control wasn't limited to Christianity. The Islamic empires, stretching from the Middle East to Spain, also wielded religious authority to unify vast and diverse territories under one banner. The concept of the Caliphate, a religious-political system, ensured that Islamic law and doctrine controlled both the public and private lives of individuals. Any deviation from the prescribed beliefs was met with harsh consequences, often leading to a form of ideological subjugation where free thought was discouraged.

In more recent history, the 20th century gave rise to the most infamous examples of mind control through political regimes. Dictators like Adolf Hitler, Joseph Stalin, and Mao Zedong used a mix of propaganda, censorship, and fear to control entire populations. Hitler's Nazi regime is perhaps the most striking example. Through carefully orchestrated propaganda led by Joseph Goebbels, the Nazi party infiltrated every aspect of German life. Hitler was presented as a savior, while Jewish people, communists, and other minorities were demonized.

Nazi propaganda created a narrative that justified persecution, war, and genocide. The manipulation was so effective that even otherwise rational individuals became complicit in horrific atrocities.

In the Soviet Union, Stalin used a similar combination of propaganda and fear. The media was state-controlled, and any form of dissent was met with brutal repression. Stalin's purges, where millions were executed or sent to labor camps, served as a reminder of what happened to those who did not fall in line. The control extended into every household through informants, state surveillance, and forced loyalty to the Communist Party. Stalin's regime exemplified how a totalitarian government could completely dominate not only the actions of its citizens but also their very thoughts and beliefs.

China, under Mao, also demonstrated large-scale political mind control. The Cultural Revolution aimed to completely reshape Chinese society and eradicate all traditional and capitalist influences. Young people were indoctrinated through the Red Guard, and those who defied the new socialist vision were publicly humiliated, imprisoned, or executed. Propaganda posters, parades, and state-sponsored rallies worked in tandem to enforce loyalty to Mao's vision of a new China.

Mind control, however, is not only the domain of totalitarian states or ancient religions. In democratic societies, more subtle forms of influence exist. In the United States, during the Cold War, mind control took on a new form with the CIA's infamous MKUltra program. This secret project explored the potential of using psychological manipulation, drugs, and other experimental methods to control human behavior. Though officially terminated in the 1970s, the revelations surrounding MKUltra opened a dark chapter in the story of governmental control and manipulation.

The media, too, plays a significant role in shaping minds today. Governments and corporations utilize the media to promote ideologies, sell products, and influence voters. News networks, social media platforms, and advertising agencies have mastered the art of subtle persuasion, using everything from fearmongering to aspirational messaging to steer public opinion and consumer behavior.

In the 21st century, China's surveillance state represents perhaps the most technologically advanced form of mind control. Through the use of a social credit system, facial recognition, and constant surveillance, China is able to monitor and manipulate the behavior of its citizens. Those who conform to state expectations are rewarded, while those who do not are punished—sometimes without their knowledge. It's a modern, insidious form of control that operates less on fear and more on a constant awareness of being watched, where even private thoughts may have public consequences.

As we reflect on these historical examples, it becomes clear that mind control is not a relic of the past but an evolving phenomenon that has taken on new forms with the rise of technology. Whether through religious doctrine, political propaganda, or modern-day media manipulation, mind control continues to shape societies across the globe. What began as coercion through fear and violence has transformed into more sophisticated, subtle methods, but the outcome remains the same: control over the hearts and minds of individuals. This book will explore how mind control has been employed throughout history, the mechanisms behind it, and the ongoing challenges we face in understanding and resisting its influence today. From ancient priests to modern surveillance states, the story of mind control is the story of power and its ability to dominate the human spirit.

Ancient Civilizations and Early Forms of Brainwashing

In ancient civilizations, mind control, though not defined by the modern term, was a deeply rooted concept woven into the very fabric of societal control. These early forms of brainwashing were often intertwined with religious practices, cultural traditions, and the ruling powers of the time. The idea of influencing and controlling the thoughts, beliefs, and actions of large groups of people was an essential tool for maintaining power, ensuring loyalty, and suppressing dissent.

One of the earliest examples of mind control can be found in Ancient Egypt. The pharaohs were not only political rulers but were also seen as gods on earth. This divine status was reinforced through elaborate rituals, monumental architecture, and symbols that connected the pharaohs directly to the gods. The construction of the pyramids and other temples served as more than just architectural marvels—they were instruments of mind control. The immense scale of these structures was a constant reminder of the divine authority of the pharaoh, reinforcing his god-like image in the minds of the people. Through religion, the pharaohs could demand absolute loyalty and obedience. The fear of angering the gods, or worse, being excluded from the afterlife, was a potent psychological tool to keep the populace under control.

In Mesopotamia, a similar dynamic played out, with rulers positioning themselves as chosen by the gods to lead and protect the people. The priests, acting as intermediaries between the gods and the people, played a crucial role in this form of mind control. By controlling access to religious knowledge and interpreting divine will, priests could manipulate the population's beliefs and actions. Religious festivals and rituals were key events where communal worship reinforced the authority of both the gods and the ruling class. Fear of divine punishment for disobedience or failure to adhere to religious laws was a powerful motivator for compliance.

The Babylonians took mind control to another level through their famous legal code, the Code of Hammurabi. While it is widely considered a monumental achievement in law, it was also a sophisticated method of control. The laws dictated strict punishments for disobedience, and the concept of justice was often framed as divinely inspired. This created a system where fear of legal consequences was tied directly to moral and religious fear. The Code of Hammurabi, while seemingly a legal framework, was a psychological tool to ensure the compliance of a vast population, many of whom were illiterate but were influenced by the public inscriptions and the punishments they observed.

In Ancient Greece, philosophers and orators became masters of shaping public opinion and influencing thought. Socrates, Plato, and Aristotle explored the nature of belief, knowledge, and persuasion. However, it was the Sophists who refined rhetoric, the art of persuasion, into a tool of influence. Sophists would teach the wealthy and influential citizens of Athens how to sway crowds, influence decisions in courts, and win political debates, often with little regard for truth but with an emphasis on effect. Public oration in Athens became a means of controlling the narrative, and in many ways, an early form of what we might now call psychological manipulation. Through carefully constructed arguments, emotional appeals, and the manipulation of public sentiment, leaders could control the direction of civic decisions, wars, and policies.

The Roman Empire, with its vast territories and diverse populations, relied heavily on methods of psychological control to maintain order and unity. One of the most effective tools was the use of spectacles, such as gladiator games and public executions. These events were more than mere entertainment; they were displays of power meant to instill fear and awe in the populace. The idea that rebellion or disobedience could lead to a public and humiliating death kept people in line. Additionally, the deification of Roman emperors after their death (and sometimes even during their reign) played into the idea that the emperor was not just a political figure but a divine one, deserving of absolute loyalty.

Roman law also reinforced this control. Much like in Babylon, Roman legal systems were tied closely to moral and religious beliefs. The Pax Romana, or Roman Peace, was a period where the empire enforced strict legal and social codes to prevent uprisings and maintain control. Those who broke the law were not only punished physically but also often subjected to public shame, a psychological deterrent that discouraged others from following in their footsteps. Moving to the East, the Chinese empires utilized Confucian philosophy as a means of controlling thought and behavior. Confucianism promoted strict social hierarchies and loyalty to the emperor as a divine mandate. The idea of filial piety, or respect for one's elders and superiors, was ingrained in every aspect of Chinese society, from the family unit to the emperor himself. This philosophical system was a form of mind control that operated through moral and ethical teachings, creating a society where questioning authority was seen as a moral failing, not just a legal one. The emperor was seen as the "Son of Heaven," and any dissent against him was viewed as a disruption of the natural order.

The use of symbols, language, and ritual to maintain control over populations was not unique to any one civilization. Across the Americas, the Maya, Aztecs, and Inca empires developed intricate systems of control through religious sacrifice, divine kingship, and fear of supernatural punishment. In the Aztec Empire, for instance, human sacrifice was not only a religious act but also a psychological weapon. The brutal public spectacles of sacrifice served as a reminder of the gods' power and the emperor's connection to them. This instilled fear and awe, ensuring that the people remained compliant with the social and religious order.

The use of language as a tool for control also emerged in these early civilizations. In many ancient societies, the ruling class or priesthood controlled literacy and education. By limiting who could read and write, these elites controlled the flow of information and maintained their grip on power. The knowledge of religious texts, legal codes, and historical records was confined to a small group of individuals who used this monopoly to shape society's beliefs and behaviors. This control of language and knowledge was a subtle but powerful form of mind control that allowed these civilizations to maintain stability for centuries. In essence, early forms of brainwashing in ancient civilizations were built around the intersection of religion, fear, and control. The use of divine authority, monumental architecture, public spectacles, and strict legal codes created environments where individual thought and dissent were discouraged or even impossible. These systems of control ensured that the population remained loyal and obedient, often out of fear of divine or legal retribution. While these ancient forms of brainwashing lacked the technological sophistication of modern methods, their psychological impact was no less profound, and their legacy of control through fear and belief continues to echo in modern societies.

The Dark Art of Persuasion: Religious Influence on Belief Systems

Religious influence on belief systems has long been a powerful force, shaping entire societies and civilizations throughout history. The dark art of persuasion, as applied through religion, represents one of the most profound and far-reaching forms of mind control. Religions, through their doctrines, rituals, and hierarchical structures, have been able to mold individual and collective thought in ways that ensure not only adherence to faith but also obedience to political and societal systems. By positioning themselves as the ultimate arbiters of morality and truth, religious institutions have wielded their authority to control not only actions but thoughts, beliefs, and even personal identities.

At the heart of religious persuasion lies the promise of salvation and the fear of damnation. This duality—a reward for faithfulness and a punishment for disobedience—creates a psychological framework that is incredibly effective for mind control. People, deeply concerned with the afterlife and the state of their souls, are often willing to comply with religious teachings even when those teachings contradict personal desires, logic, or societal norms. The ability to control a person's deepest fears and aspirations is one of the most potent forms of persuasion, as it taps into the existential questions of life and death, meaning and purpose.

Take, for example, Christianity's role in medieval Europe. The Church, during the Middle Ages, held immense power not only over the religious lives of the people but over political and social structures as well. The Church's teachings about sin, repentance, and eternal salvation or damnation formed a psychological grip on the population. The doctrine of original sin, for instance, taught that all humans were born with a sinful nature and required the grace of God, dispensed through the Church, to achieve salvation. This idea permeated every level of life, from the peasant to the king. Through the fear of hellfire and eternal suffering, the Church controlled people's thoughts and actions, guiding them to follow religious dictates without question.

Religious persuasion was also deeply embedded in the sacraments and rituals of the Church. From baptism to last rites, every significant life event was marked by religious ceremony, reinforcing the idea that the Church held the keys to one's spiritual well-being. Priests, as intermediaries between God and humanity, held tremendous power over individuals. Confession, for example, required people to divulge their sins to a priest, who would then provide absolution. This practice not only reinforced the Church's authority over the moral and ethical lives of individuals but also created a system of surveillance, where people's inner thoughts and actions were monitored by religious authorities. Through confession, the Church exerted a form of control that reached into the very minds of the faithful, ensuring that guilt and fear kept them obedient.

OTHER RELIGIONS HAVE employed similar methods of mind control through persuasion. In Islamic empires, the concept of Sharia law, which is based on both the Quran and the Hadith (the sayings and actions of the Prophet Muhammad), provides a comprehensive guide for living a righteous life. Sharia governs not only religious practices but also personal behavior, business dealings, family relations, and criminal law. The blending of religion with everyday life ensures that individuals are constantly reminded of their duties to God and society. The fear of divine punishment, in the form of eternal damnation, and the promise of paradise for the faithful create a potent framework for controlling behavior.

Beyond fear and punishment, religions also offer powerful symbols of hope and redemption, which can be equally persuasive. The idea of an afterlife where one is rewarded for obedience and faith is a deeply motivating concept. In Christianity, the promise of heaven serves as a powerful tool for ensuring compliance with the Church's teachings. In Buddhism, the concept of nirvana—the ultimate release from the cycle of suffering—acts as an incentive for followers to adhere to the prescribed path of ethical living, meditation, and wisdom.

Religions have also historically used their sacred texts as tools of persuasion. The Bible, the Quran, the Torah, and other holy books are often regarded as the literal word of God or divinely inspired scripture. The authority of these texts is rarely questioned by the faithful, allowing religious leaders to interpret and manipulate their contents to serve specific agendas. Those in power have long understood that control over religious texts equates to control over the people. In medieval Europe, for instance, the Bible was written in Latin, a language known primarily by the clergy. This linguistic barrier meant that the interpretation of scripture was entirely in the hands of the Church, allowing religious authorities to frame religious teachings in ways that served their interests. Similarly, in the Islamic world, the interpretation of the Quran has often been controlled by religious scholars and clerics, allowing them to influence the way the text is understood and applied.

The power of religious persuasion also lies in its ability to form communities of believers. Religious identity often becomes synonymous with personal identity, making it difficult for individuals to separate their faith from their sense of self. This communal aspect of religion reinforces conformity to the group's beliefs and practices. Those who deviate from accepted religious norms risk being ostracized, shamed, or even persecuted. The fear of social exclusion, combined with the fear of divine punishment, creates a potent mix that compels individuals to align their thoughts and actions with the religious majority.

The power dynamics within religious hierarchies further contribute to this form of mind control. Religious leaders, seen as chosen or anointed by divine powers, often hold unquestioned authority. The loyalty and reverence given to these leaders can sometimes cross into dangerous territory, where followers are manipulated into accepting harmful practices or extremist ideologies. Cults, both ancient and modern, provide a stark example of how religious persuasion can be used for darker purposes. Leaders like Jim Jones of the People's Temple or David Koresh of the Branch Davidians were able to persuade their followers to commit extreme acts, including mass suicide, through a combination of fear, manipulation, and promises of divine rewards.

Religious influence is also particularly strong when combined with political power. Throughout history, rulers have aligned themselves with religious institutions to solidify their control over populations. By claiming divine sanction for their rule, kings, emperors, and even modern political leaders have used religion as a means to legitimize their authority. In ancient Egypt, the pharaohs were considered gods on earth, and in medieval Europe, kings ruled by divine right, with the Church's blessing. This intertwining of religious and political authority further deepens the influence of religion on belief systems, as questioning political authority becomes equivalent to questioning divine will.

In modern times, we still see the dark art of religious persuasion playing a significant role in shaping belief systems and societal norms. In some countries, religious fundamentalism is used to justify laws that restrict freedom of thought, speech, and personal choice. Religious extremism, in both the Islamic and Christian worlds, has led to violence, oppression, and the suppression of dissenting ideas. Whether through the fear of divine punishment, the promise of eternal salvation, or the influence of charismatic religious leaders, the methods of religious mind control remain as effective today as they were in ancient times.

Religious institutions, while often providing moral guidance and community, have also proven throughout history to be effective tools of persuasion and mind control. The combination of fear, hope, authority, and social conformity has allowed religions to mold the thoughts, beliefs, and behaviors of billions of people across the globe. Understanding these mechanisms is essential for recognizing the broader patterns of influence that have shaped human history and continue to affect modern societies.

Political Control through Fear: Dictatorship and Propaganda

Political control through fear has long been a cornerstone of dictatorships and authoritarian regimes. The use of fear, coupled with the strategic dissemination of propaganda, allows rulers to dominate both the public and private lives of citizens, suppress dissent, and maintain absolute power. Dictatorships thrive on creating environments where fear is not just a tool, but a pervasive force that infiltrates every aspect of life. By controlling the narrative through propaganda, leaders craft a reality that aligns with their interests, creating a system where loyalty is often less a matter of choice and more a matter of survival.

At the heart of any dictatorship is fear. Fear of punishment, fear of isolation, fear of death. These regimes utilize fear to subdue and control, turning citizens into subjects and ensuring that obedience becomes the only viable option. One of the most famous examples of political control through fear can be found in the reign of Joseph Stalin in the Soviet Union. Stalin's purges, where millions of perceived enemies of the state were executed or sent to the Gulag, created an atmosphere of terror. Anyone, at any time, could be accused of treason, espionage, or counter-revolutionary activities. The mere suspicion of disloyalty was enough to warrant arrest, and the state used this fear to keep citizens in line. Public trials and executions were often staged as spectacles, reinforcing the consequences of disobedience and ensuring that fear of the regime was deeply embedded in the minds of the populace.

In Nazi Germany, Adolf Hitler's regime similarly relied on fear as a primary tool of control. The Gestapo, Hitler's secret police, were instrumental in spreading fear through the population. The Gestapo could arrest anyone suspected of opposing the regime, and they operated outside the bounds of the legal system, ensuring that no one was safe from their reach. Neighbors, coworkers, and even family members were encouraged to report suspicious behavior, turning communities into networks of informants. This culture of surveillance and fear was further exacerbated by the state's use of concentration camps, where political prisoners, dissidents, and marginalized groups were sent to face horrific conditions or death.

Beyond the direct use of fear, dictatorships also rely heavily on propaganda to control the narrative and shape public perception. Propaganda is the art of manipulating information to serve the interests of those in power. It is not simply about spreading lies but about crafting a particular version of reality that aligns with the regime's goals. Dictatorships use propaganda to create enemies, both internal and external, to justify the need for harsh control measures. In many cases, this involves dehumanizing certain groups, whether they be political opponents, ethnic minorities, or foreign nations, and presenting them as existential threats to the safety and security of the state.

The Nazi regime's propaganda, led by Joseph Goebbels, is a prime example of this technique. Through films, posters, and speeches, the Nazis portrayed Jews, communists, and other marginalized groups as subhuman threats to the purity of the Aryan race. This dehumanization served to justify the regime's atrocities, including the Holocaust, as necessary actions for the survival of the nation.

Nazi propaganda also glorified Hitler, portraying him as a messianic figure who would lead Germany to greatness. The constant bombardment of propaganda ensured that the German population was not only fearful of external and internal enemies but also indoctrinated into a belief system that venerated their leader and his cause.

Similarly, in North Korea, the regime of the Kim dynasty has mastered the art of propaganda. From a young age, North Koreans are taught that their leaders, particularly Kim Il-sung, Kim Jong-il, and Kim Jong-un, are god-like figures. The state controls all media, ensuring that only the regime's narrative reaches the population. Through statues, songs, and state-controlled education, the Kims are presented as infallible leaders, responsible for the country's survival in the face of constant threats from the outside world. North Korean citizens are taught to view the rest of the world, particularly the United States and South Korea, as enemies who seek to destroy their way of life. This external threat, combined with the regime's brutal repression of dissent, creates an environment where fear and loyalty to the regime are deeply intertwined.

China offers a more modern example of political control through fear and propaganda, particularly under the rule of the Chinese Communist Party (CCP). While the Chinese government may not rely as heavily on overt terror as past dictatorships, it has developed a more sophisticated system of control that blends fear, surveillance, and propaganda. The state's social credit system, for instance, is a tool of political control that monitors citizens' behavior and rewards or punishes them accordingly. This system creates a pervasive sense of being watched, where even minor infractions can lead to severe consequences, such as restrictions on travel, education, or employment opportunities. The fear of losing social standing, coupled with the knowledge that one's every action is under scrutiny, ensures compliance with state mandates.

In addition to surveillance, the Chinese government has perfected the use of propaganda to maintain its control. State-controlled media presents a narrative of national unity, economic prosperity, and the benevolence of the CCP. Dissenting voices are suppressed, and information that contradicts the state's version of events is censored. The CCP's narrative of China as a global power under constant threat from foreign adversaries, especially the United States, is used to justify its authoritarian policies. This combination of fear and controlled information creates an environment where citizens are encouraged to support the regime, not necessarily out of genuine belief, but out of fear of the consequences of dissent.

Propaganda doesn't just create enemies; it also creates a sense of identity and belonging. Dictatorships often use nationalistic propaganda to foster a sense of pride and unity. By presenting themselves as protectors of the nation, dictators cast themselves as the only ones capable of defending the people from external and internal threats. This narrative of protection often goes hand in hand with the portrayal of enemies—whether they are political rivals, foreign powers, or marginalized groups—who are blamed for the country's problems. This us-versus-them mentality is essential in dictatorships because it simplifies complex societal issues into easily digestible narratives that reinforce the leader's legitimacy.

Modern examples of propaganda and fear-based control are not limited to dictatorships. Even in ostensibly democratic countries, propaganda can be used to manipulate public opinion and stoke fear to serve political ends. The use of fear to justify mass surveillance, restrict civil liberties, or marginalize certain groups can be seen in countries around the world. The war on terror, for instance, has been used by various governments to justify intrusive surveillance measures, indefinite detention, and the erosion of civil rights, all in the name of national security.

Fear remains one of the most effective tools for controlling populations because it taps into a primal instinct for survival. When combined with propaganda that manipulates perceptions and shapes belief systems, it becomes an incredibly powerful mechanism of control. Whether through violent repression or more subtle forms of surveillance and censorship, dictatorships have long relied on these dark arts to maintain their grip on power.

As we look to the future, it is important to recognize that while the forms of political control through fear and propaganda may evolve with technology, the underlying principles remain the same. The ability to control a population by manipulating their emotions and controlling the narrative is a time-tested strategy, one that will likely continue to be used by authoritarian regimes and even democratic governments in new and perhaps more insidious ways. Understanding these methods is crucial for recognizing and resisting them, and for ensuring that fear and propaganda do not override freedom and truth.

The Science behind Brainwashing: How It Alters the Mind

Brainwashing, also known as coercive persuasion, is a method of psychological manipulation that aims to alter a person's beliefs, behaviors, and perceptions. While it may seem like a concept rooted in the world of totalitarian regimes, cults, or sinister mind control experiments, brainwashing has a basis in psychological science. The process works by exploiting the vulnerabilities in human cognition, emotions, and social dependency to reshape thoughts and actions. In this chapter, we will explore the science behind brainwashing—how it works, the psychological mechanisms it exploits, and the profound impact it has on the human mind.

At its core, brainwashing disrupts a person's sense of self, identity, and reality. The process typically involves three main stages: breaking down the individual's sense of autonomy and confidence, introducing new ideologies or behaviors, and reinforcing these new beliefs through isolation, repetition, or control. To understand how brainwashing works, it is important to look at how the mind functions in terms of cognitive dissonance, social influence, and emotional regulation.

Cognitive dissonance is one of the key psychological principles that make brainwashing possible. Cognitive dissonance occurs when a person holds two conflicting beliefs, ideas, or values at the same time, which creates psychological discomfort. For example, if a person has a deeply held belief that their government is trustworthy, but is confronted with evidence of corruption, they will experience cognitive dissonance. This discomfort can be a powerful motivator for change. In brainwashing, the manipulator often seeks to create or amplify this dissonance by challenging the subject's existing beliefs and making them feel that their worldview is fundamentally flawed.

When a person is in a state of cognitive dissonance, they will typically seek to resolve it in one of three ways: by changing their beliefs to align with the new information, by dismissing the new information, or by rationalizing the conflict. A skilled manipulator will exploit this vulnerability, ensuring that the only path to psychological comfort is by adopting the new beliefs or behaviors being presented. Over time, the victim's sense of reality begins to erode, making them more susceptible to accepting alternative viewpoints that may seem unthinkable under normal circumstances.

Another essential element of brainwashing is social influence, particularly the impact of authority figures and group dynamics on human behavior. Psychologists have long studied how people's thoughts and actions are influenced by those around them, particularly in situations where they feel unsure, isolated, or threatened. In environments where brainwashing occurs, the presence of a controlling authority figure or a dominant group can exert tremendous pressure on an individual to conform. Cult leaders, political dictators, and other figures who seek to control others often present themselves as having exclusive access to truth, wisdom, or salvation, which sets them apart from ordinary individuals. Their authority, combined with an isolated or controlled environment, makes it difficult for individuals to resist the influence being exerted on them.

The famous experiments conducted by social psychologist Stanley Milgram in the 1960s, which involved participants administering what they believed to be electric shocks to others at the instruction of an authority figure, demonstrated just how powerful authority can be in shaping behavior. Milgram's findings revealed that people are often willing to perform actions that go against their personal beliefs and ethical standards when directed by someone in a position of power. This principle is frequently leveraged in brainwashing scenarios, where authority figures use their perceived legitimacy to erode personal boundaries and replace an individual's sense of right and wrong with the group's or leader's dictates.

Isolation is another critical factor in brainwashing. When individuals are cut off from alternative viewpoints, support systems, or familiar environments, their ability to resist manipulation weakens significantly. Cults and authoritarian regimes often isolate their victims, either physically or psychologically, by controlling access to outside information or by fostering distrust of outsiders. This isolation breaks down resistance, as the person becomes more reliant on the brainwashing authority for understanding and interpreting the world.

In addition to isolation, repetition plays a crucial role in reinforcing new beliefs and behaviors. The human brain is wired to respond to repeated stimuli by forming stronger neural connections, a process known as neuroplasticity. When ideas, behaviors, or phrases are repeated over and over, they become ingrained in the mind, forming new patterns of thought. For example, many authoritarian regimes use repetitive slogans, propaganda, and rituals to instill loyalty and obedience. Similarly, cults will repeat mantras or doctrine to solidify the group's belief system. Over time, this repetition can override a person's original beliefs, making the new ideology feel more natural and automatic.

Emotional manipulation is another critical component of brainwashing. The human mind is profoundly influenced by emotions, especially fear, guilt, and shame. Brainwashing techniques often focus on inducing strong emotional reactions in the victim, either through direct threats or by exploiting insecurities and fears. Fear is a particularly powerful tool, as it can override rational thought and make people more susceptible to suggestion. In brainwashing scenarios, fear might be induced through threats of punishment, exile, or harm to loved ones. For example, in cults, followers may be told that leaving the group will result in divine retribution or social ostracism, while in political brainwashing, individuals may fear imprisonment or even death if they dissent.

Guilt and shame are also frequently used in brainwashing. Victims may be made to feel responsible for their past actions or beliefs, often through the manipulation of their moral or ethical values. Once the manipulator has successfully instilled a sense of guilt, they present the new ideology or behavior as the only way to achieve redemption. This exploitation of emotional vulnerability makes it harder for the victim to resist the manipulator's influence.

NEUROLOGICALLY, BRAINWASHING can have significant effects on the brain's structure and function. The prolonged stress and emotional manipulation involved in brainwashing can affect the brain's limbic system, which regulates emotions, and the prefrontal cortex, which is responsible for decision-making and self-regulation. Under constant stress, the brain's ability to process information logically diminishes, and the individual becomes more reliant on instinctual and emotional responses, which are easier for the manipulator to control.

The effect of brainwashing on memory is another crucial aspect. Victims often experience memory distortion, where their recollection of past events is altered to fit the new narrative imposed by the manipulator. This process, known as confabulation, occurs when the brain attempts to make sense of conflicting information by creating false memories or adjusting existing ones. Over time, the victim's sense of self and identity becomes intertwined with the manipulated beliefs, making it increasingly difficult to separate truth from fiction.

One of the long-term effects of brainwashing is learned helplessness, a condition where the individual feels powerless to change their situation. After repeated attempts to resist or challenge the new ideology are met with punishment or failure, the victim may come to believe that resistance is futile. This psychological state makes it even harder to break free from the control, as the individual loses the will or ability to take independent action.

In conclusion, the science behind brainwashing is rooted in the manipulation of psychological vulnerabilities. By exploiting cognitive dissonance, social influence, isolation, emotional manipulation, and repetition, brainwashing techniques reshape a person's sense of reality, eroding their autonomy and replacing their beliefs with those of the manipulator. Understanding these mechanisms is essential to recognizing how brainwashing occurs and the profound impact it can have on individuals and societies. While the process is often associated with authoritarian regimes, cults, or extreme situations, the underlying principles of brainwashing can be seen in more subtle forms of influence in everyday life, making awareness and critical thinking key tools for resisting manipulation.

Subliminal Messaging: Hidden Influences on the Subconscious

Subliminal messaging is one of the most subtle yet effective forms of psychological manipulation. Unlike overt brainwashing or propaganda, which is designed to be recognized and absorbed consciously, subliminal messaging targets the subconscious mind, slipping past our mental defenses without us even being aware of it. These hidden influences can shape our thoughts, behaviors, and preferences in ways we might not fully understand or recognize. Whether through media, advertising, or even politics, subliminal messaging has been used to influence human behavior for decades, often raising ethical concerns about its use and effectiveness.

At its core, subliminal messaging refers to stimuli that are below the threshold of conscious perception. This means that while we may not be consciously aware of these messages, our brain can still process and store them. The idea is that the subconscious mind, which operates on a different level than our conscious awareness, can absorb these hidden cues and act on them in ways that influence our thoughts and actions. In practice, this can take many forms—flashing images on a screen too quickly for the conscious mind to register, embedding hidden words or sounds in audio, or using subtle imagery and symbolism to trigger emotional or cognitive responses.

The idea of subliminal messaging first gained widespread attention in the 1950s, when a market researcher named James Vicary claimed to have conducted an experiment in a New Jersey movie theater. Vicary said that he inserted the phrases "Drink Coca-Cola" and "Eat Popcorn" into a film at intervals that were too brief for the audience to consciously notice. According to Vicary, these subliminal messages led to a significant increase in the sales of both products during the film's screening. Although Vicary later admitted to fabricating his results, the public's interest in the potential of subliminal messaging to influence behavior took root, and the concept has persisted ever since.

The science behind subliminal messaging, however, is more complex than simple cause-and-effect relationships. While subliminal stimuli can influence thoughts and behaviors, the extent of their power is still debated. Research shows that subliminal messaging can have an effect, but its potency depends on a variety of factors, including the individual's receptiveness, the type of stimulus used, and the context in which it is presented. For example, some studies suggest that subliminal messages are more likely to work when they align with an individual's existing desires or needs, such as being more receptive to an advertisement for food when already hungry.

One of the most common ways subliminal messaging is used is through advertising. Companies have long sought ways to embed hidden messages in their marketing to make products more appealing without overtly pushing them. This can take the form of imagery that is designed to evoke certain emotions or desires. For example, sexual imagery is often used in advertising, even when the product being sold has little or no connection to sexuality. These images may be subtle, such as shapes or symbols that resemble sexual organs, or they may be embedded in more obvious ways, but the effect is the same—they trigger subconscious associations that make the product more desirable.

Color psychology is another tool used in subliminal messaging. Colors are known to evoke certain emotions and reactions. Red, for instance, is associated with passion, energy, and urgency, while blue is often linked to calmness, trust, and stability. Advertisers may use specific color schemes to subliminally influence how consumers feel about a product or brand, encouraging them to make decisions based on emotional reactions they may not fully understand. Similarly, sounds and music are often used to create subconscious associations. A catchy jingle can lodge itself in a person's mind, subtly reinforcing brand recognition and loyalty over time.

Subliminal messaging has also found its way into the realm of politics. Politicians and their campaigns use techniques designed to influence voters without their full awareness. This can be done through imagery, music, or even the timing and wording of political ads. In the 2000 U.S. presidential election, for example, a political ad aired by the campaign of George W. Bush flashed the word "RATS" on the screen for a fraction of a second during a critique of his opponent, Al Gore. Although the ad's creators claimed the word's appearance was accidental, it sparked debate about whether it was an attempt at subliminal messaging to associate negative emotions with Gore's campaign. While the impact of that specific case remains inconclusive, it highlights the potential for subliminal techniques to be used in political messaging.

One of the reasons subliminal messaging is so effective is that the subconscious mind plays a significant role in decision-making processes. While we often like to think of ourselves as rational beings who make choices based on logical evaluation, much of what we do is driven by subconscious impulses. These impulses are shaped by past experiences, emotions, and external stimuli that we may not consciously recognize. By tapping into these underlying processes, subliminal messaging can nudge people toward making decisions that align with the desired outcomes of the message sender, whether that's purchasing a product, supporting a political candidate, or forming opinions on social issues.

However, the use of subliminal messaging is not without controversy. Many people view it as a form of manipulation that violates personal autonomy, particularly when used in commercial or political settings. Critics argue that because subliminal messages bypass the conscious mind, they rob individuals of the ability to make fully informed decisions. This has led to legal restrictions on subliminal advertising in some countries. For example, the United States Federal Communications Commission (FCC) prohibits the use of subliminal techniques in broadcast advertising. Despite these regulations, questions remain about how often subliminal messaging is used covertly and whether it truly can be controlled or detected.

There is also an ethical dimension to the use of subliminal messaging in entertainment and media. Films, television shows, and music often contain hidden messages or symbols that are designed to evoke certain emotional or psychological responses. While these might be used for artistic purposes, they can also serve more manipulative ends. The blurring of the line between art and influence raises questions about the power of media to shape societal norms and values without viewers or listeners fully realizing it.

The entertainment industry has long been fascinated by the idea of subliminal messaging, sometimes blurring the lines between reality and fiction. The 1970s saw the release of films like *The Exorcist* and *The Texas Chain Saw Massacre*, which reportedly used subliminal images or sounds to heighten fear and unease in the audience. These hidden elements were meant to amplify the emotional experience of the film without viewers consciously recognizing what was happening. While the effectiveness of these techniques has been debated, they demonstrate the potential for subliminal messaging to create powerful psychological effects.

Another area where subliminal messaging has been explored is in self-help and personal development. Audio recordings and visual aids that claim to use subliminal techniques to help people quit smoking, lose weight, or improve self-esteem have been popular for decades. These programs usually involve playing messages or sounds that are meant to bypass the conscious mind and influence behavior at a deeper level. While there is limited scientific evidence to support the effectiveness of these products, they remain popular, suggesting that many people believe in the power of subliminal influence on their subconscious minds.

Despite its mysterious nature, the science of subliminal messaging is rooted in well-established psychological principles. The brain's ability to process stimuli at both conscious and subconscious levels is well documented, and researchers continue to study the ways in which hidden messages can shape our thoughts and actions. However, the ethical implications of using these techniques for commercial, political, or personal gain remain a point of contention. As technology advances and the methods for delivering subliminal messages become more sophisticated, it is crucial to maintain a balance between persuasion and manipulation, ensuring that individuals retain their autonomy and ability to make informed decisions.

In conclusion, subliminal messaging represents a powerful tool for influencing the subconscious mind. By bypassing conscious awareness, it can shape perceptions, behaviors, and decisions in ways that are often subtle and difficult to detect. Whether used in advertising, politics, or entertainment, subliminal techniques continue to raise questions about the limits of influence and the ethics of covert persuasion. Understanding how subliminal messaging works is key to recognizing when and how it is being used, empowering individuals to make more informed choices in a world where hidden influences abound.

Psychological Manipulation: How Leaders Mold Thought

Psychological manipulation is one of the most powerful tools that leaders, particularly those in positions of political or religious authority, use to mold the thoughts and behaviors of their followers. Unlike overt forms of control, psychological manipulation is subtle, often going unnoticed as it influences individuals on a deeply emotional and cognitive level. Leaders who master these tactics can effectively shape public opinion, create loyalty, and suppress dissent, all while maintaining the appearance of benevolence or rightful authority. By understanding how leaders use psychological manipulation, we can better recognize these tactics and protect ourselves from undue influence.

One of the most effective methods of psychological manipulation is the use of fear. Fear is a primal emotion that triggers the brain's fight-or-flight response, often bypassing rational thought in favor of immediate survival. Leaders throughout history have harnessed fear to control their populations, manipulating it to maintain their power. Fear can come in many forms, from the fear of physical harm to the fear of social ostracism or political instability. By presenting themselves as protectors from a perceived threat, leaders position themselves as necessary figures, securing loyalty and obedience.

Dictators and authoritarian leaders often use fear to create a sense of dependency among their people. For example, Stalin's reign in the Soviet Union relied heavily on the use of fear to maintain control. The constant threat of purges, executions, and forced labor camps meant that dissent was not only dangerous but nearly unthinkable. People feared not only for their own lives but for the safety of their families and loved ones. This widespread fear ensured that Stalin's grip on power was rarely challenged, as even those who disagreed with his policies were too frightened to act. In this way, fear becomes a psychological prison that suppresses critical thinking and opposition.

In modern times, fear-based psychological manipulation is often more subtle but no less effective. Leaders may stoke fears of terrorism, economic collapse, or social upheaval to justify repressive policies or increased control over the population. By presenting themselves as the only ones capable of protecting the nation from these threats, they ensure that any opposition to their authority is viewed as dangerous or even treasonous. This form of manipulation is particularly potent because fear tends to narrow a person's focus, making it harder to question the validity of the leader's claims or consider alternative perspectives.

Another key tool of psychological manipulation is the creation of an enemy or scapegoat. Leaders often use this tactic to unite their followers under a common cause while deflecting attention away from their own shortcomings or controversial policies. By blaming an external group—whether it's a political opposition, a minority population, or a foreign power—leaders can channel public anger and frustration toward a target, diverting it away from themselves. This strategy not only solidifies the leader's power but also fosters a sense of belonging and loyalty among followers, who feel they are part of a larger mission or struggle.

Adolf Hitler's use of scapegoating is one of the most infamous examples of this tactic. Hitler blamed Germany's economic troubles and political instability on the Jewish population, creating an enemy that he claimed was responsible for all of the country's woes. By dehumanizing Jewish people and other minority groups, Hitler was able to unite much of the German population behind his regime, deflecting blame for the country's struggles away from his own policies and toward an external group. This manipulation of thought not only justified the horrific atrocities of the Holocaust but also ensured that Hitler's rise to power was seen as a necessary step in protecting Germany from its enemies.

Psychological manipulation also relies heavily on the use of authority and the power of suggestion. Leaders often present themselves as infallible figures who have access to knowledge, wisdom, or divine guidance that ordinary people do not. By positioning themselves as experts or chosen leaders, they can manipulate their followers into accepting their ideas without question. This dynamic creates a relationship where followers defer to the leader's judgment, even when it conflicts with their own values or common sense.

The famous experiments conducted by psychologist Stanley Milgram in the 1960s demonstrated just how powerful authority can be in manipulating thought and behavior. In these experiments, participants were instructed by an authority figure to administer what they believed were increasingly painful electric shocks to another person. Despite the apparent distress of the "victim" (who was actually an actor), many participants continued to obey the authority figure's instructions, even when it went against their personal beliefs. Milgram's findings revealed the extent to which people are willing to obey authority, even to the point of causing harm to others, when they believe they are following legitimate orders.

Leaders who understand this dynamic can manipulate their followers by presenting themselves as the ultimate authority, whether through charisma, expertise, or divine right. In religious contexts, for example, leaders often claim that their authority comes directly from a higher power, making their instructions unquestionable. Cult leaders are notorious for using this type of psychological manipulation to convince followers to perform extreme acts, such as giving up their possessions, cutting ties with family members, or even participating in mass suicide.

In addition to authority, repetition is another key element of psychological manipulation. The more a message is repeated, the more likely it is to be accepted as truth. This is known as the "illusory truth effect," a cognitive bias that makes people more likely to believe information if they hear it frequently, regardless of its accuracy. Leaders use this tactic by repeating key phrases, slogans, or ideas over and over again until they become ingrained in the public's consciousness.

Propaganda, particularly in authoritarian regimes, often relies on repetition to create a shared narrative that reinforces the leader's authority and legitimacy. In North Korea, for example, the government constantly reinforces the idea that the Kim family is divinely chosen to lead the country. Through songs, posters, and speeches, this message is repeated so frequently that it becomes a core belief for many citizens, shaping their worldview in ways that make dissent or rebellion nearly unthinkable.

The repetitive nature of the message ensures that it is internalized, making it difficult for individuals to question or reject the narrative.

In addition to repetition, psychological manipulation often involves controlling the flow of information. By limiting access to alternative viewpoints or suppressing dissenting voices, leaders can create an environment where only their version of reality is presented. This control over information is often achieved through censorship, propaganda, and the suppression of free speech. In extreme cases, such as in North Korea or under Stalinist regimes, the media is entirely state-controlled, ensuring that only approved narratives are disseminated to the public.

In more subtle forms, modern leaders may use social media algorithms, disinformation campaigns, or biased news outlets to shape public opinion and suppress opposition. By controlling the narrative, these leaders can manipulate their followers into believing that their version of events is the only valid one. This creates a closed system of thought, where critical thinking is discouraged, and the leader's authority goes unchallenged.

Another powerful tool of psychological manipulation is the use of emotional appeals. Leaders often tap into deeply held emotions such as pride, fear, guilt, or hope to manipulate thought. Emotional appeals bypass logical reasoning and speak directly to a person's core beliefs and values. By appealing to emotions, leaders can create a sense of urgency or moral imperative that compels individuals to act in ways they might not otherwise consider.

For instance, nationalistic leaders often use pride and fear to manipulate their followers. By evoking pride in the nation's history, culture, or achievements, they create a sense of collective identity that binds followers to the leader and the state. At the same time, they may stoke fear by warning of external threats, such as foreign enemies or internal "traitors," convincing the public that drastic measures are necessary to protect the nation. This emotional manipulation creates an environment where loyalty to the leader is equated with loyalty to the country, and any opposition is viewed as a betrayal.

In conclusion, psychological manipulation is a powerful tool used by leaders to mold thought, shape behavior, and maintain control. By exploiting fear, authority, repetition, emotional appeals, and the control of information, leaders can create environments where critical thinking is suppressed, and obedience is seen as the only viable option. While these tactics are often associated with authoritarian regimes, they can be found in more subtle forms in democracies and other political systems as well. Understanding how these methods work is essential for recognizing when we are being manipulated and for safeguarding our autonomy and freedom of thought.

The Cult of Personality: Leaders Who Mastered Mind Control

The concept of the *cult of personality* is one of the most striking and enduring examples of how leaders use mind control to dominate entire societies. A cult of personality occurs when a leader uses mass media, propaganda, and other means to create an idealized, heroic, and often god-like image of themselves. Through this image, they cultivate extreme loyalty and devotion, often convincing people that they alone possess the vision, wisdom, or strength necessary to guide the nation or group. Leaders who master this technique don't just inspire obedience—they create followers who are deeply convinced of their leader's infallibility, even in the face of evidence to the contrary. These leaders blur the lines between reality and myth, between themselves as human beings and the near-deity figures they portray.

One of the most famous examples of the cult of personality is Joseph Stalin, who ruled the Soviet Union with an iron fist from the 1920s until his death in 1953. Stalin mastered the art of presenting himself as both the protector of the Soviet people and the personification of Communist ideology. His image was carefully constructed through propaganda that portrayed him as a father figure, a hero of the revolution, and an infallible leader. Statues of Stalin were erected throughout the Soviet Union, and his image appeared on posters, in newspapers, and on the walls of schools, factories, and homes. The media celebrated his every decision as a stroke of genius, even when those decisions led to famine, mass executions, or widespread suffering.

This carefully cultivated image created a psychological environment where dissent was not only dangerous but also unthinkable. The Soviet people were taught to believe that Stalin was the embodiment of the state and the Communist Party—criticizing him was akin to betraying the nation itself. Even those who suffered under his brutal purges often continued to believe in his leadership, convinced that the arrests and executions were necessary sacrifices for the greater good. Stalin's cult of personality was so effective that, for many years after his death, millions of Soviet citizens continued to revere him, despite overwhelming evidence of his cruelty and mismanagement.

Another prime example of a leader who mastered the cult of personality is Adolf Hitler, the Führer of Nazi Germany. Hitler's ability to use mind control and manipulation to rally an entire nation behind his radical ideology was unparalleled. His speeches were masterful performances, designed to appeal to the emotions and subconscious desires of his audience. Hitler presented himself as the savior of the German people, offering hope in a time of economic collapse, political instability, and national humiliation after World War I. Through his powerful oratory and the Nazi propaganda machine led by Joseph Goebbels, Hitler was able to convince millions of Germans that he alone had the strength and vision to restore Germany to its former glory.

THE NAZI REGIME UTILIZED mass rallies, films, and other forms of propaganda to reinforce Hitler's image as an almost supernatural figure. The famous Nuremberg rallies, for instance, were meticulously staged to portray Hitler as the central, messianic figure leading a united and powerful Germany. His likeness appeared on posters and in school textbooks, and Nazi slogans like "Heil Hitler" became everyday greetings, further ingraining his presence into the daily lives of Germans. As Hitler's power grew, so did the myth of his infallibility, leading to a dangerous blind loyalty that allowed him to implement catastrophic policies, including the genocide of millions during the Holocaust.

Mao Zedong, the founding father of the People's Republic of China, is another leader who mastered the cult of personality. Mao's image was omnipresent throughout China during his reign, especially during the Cultural Revolution, when his control over the country reached its peak. The "Little Red Book," a collection of Mao's quotations, became a symbol of loyalty, and millions of Chinese citizens were expected to carry it and study it as though it were a sacred text. Mao was portrayed as the ultimate revolutionary, the visionary who had liberated China from colonialism and feudalism. His portraits hung in every public building, and his thoughts were taught as absolute truths.

What made Mao's cult of personality particularly powerful was its emotional and psychological grip on the Chinese people. His leadership was associated with China's national identity, and to question Mao was to question the revolution and the country itself. During the Cultural Revolution, Mao encouraged radical youth groups, known as the Red Guards, to attack intellectuals, destroy cultural relics, and purge the country of perceived enemies. In doing so, he created a climate of fear and fervent loyalty where dissent was equated with treason. Even as China descended into chaos, Mao's status as a god-like figure remained intact.

North Korea's Kim dynasty provides a contemporary example of the cult of personality in action. Beginning with Kim Il-sung and continuing with his son Kim Jong-il and grandson Kim Jong-un, the North Korean regime has cultivated an intense personality cult around the ruling family. In North Korea, the Kims are not merely political leaders; they are portrayed as deities. The North Korean media refers to them as the "Great Leader," the "Dear Leader," or the "Supreme Leader," and their images dominate public spaces in the form of statues, murals, and portraits. Schoolchildren are taught to revere the Kim family from a young age, and the regime carefully controls information, ensuring that only positive portrayals of the leadership reach the public.

What makes the North Korean cult of personality so effective is the extreme isolation of the country. Most North Koreans have no access to information from outside the country, and any criticism of the regime is met with harsh punishment, not just for the individual but often for their entire family. This creates a closed loop where the population is fed a constant stream of propaganda reinforcing the leadership's god-like status while being deprived of any alternative perspective. The Kim family's cult of personality has persisted for decades, even as North Korea has faced economic collapse, famine, and international isolation.

Cults of personality are not limited to authoritarian regimes. In democratic societies, political leaders sometimes use similar techniques, though in less overt ways, to build personal brands that garner extreme loyalty. For example, in modern politics, leaders often use social media to cultivate a persona that resonates deeply with their followers, blurring the line between politician and celebrity. While democratic leaders may not always use the same level of coercion, they can still create strong emotional bonds with their supporters that mimic the devotion seen in more extreme personality cults.

One of the reasons cults of personality are so powerful is that they tap into the human need for a figure of authority and stability, especially in times of crisis. When people feel uncertain, afraid, or insecure, they often look to strong leaders who project confidence and certainty. Leaders who master the cult of personality exploit these vulnerabilities by presenting themselves as the solution to all problems, the embodiment of the nation, or the savior from external threats. This psychological manipulation creates a dependency on the leader, making it difficult for followers to imagine life without them.

The effectiveness of a cult of personality also lies in its ability to reshape reality. Through constant propaganda, leaders who build these cults create a new version of history, one that centers on their achievements, wisdom, and vision. Followers are encouraged to view the leader as indispensable, and any challenges to their authority are seen as attacks on the nation or the people themselves. This manipulation of reality makes it nearly impossible for individuals to critically assess the leader's actions, as they are conditioned to view everything through the lens of loyalty and devotion.

In conclusion, the cult of personality is a powerful form of mind control that allows leaders to dominate the thoughts, emotions, and actions of entire populations. By using propaganda, fear, repetition, and emotional manipulation, these leaders create a public image that transcends reality, making them appear infallible, heroic, and even divine. Whether through totalitarian regimes or more subtle democratic techniques, the cult of personality remains a potent tool for those who seek to control the minds of others. Understanding how these leaders manipulate their followers is crucial for recognizing and resisting the allure of charismatic authority, ensuring that personal autonomy and critical thinking are preserved in the face of powerful manipulation.

Fear and Obedience: Stalin's Iron Grip on the Soviet Union

Joseph Stalin's reign over the Soviet Union from the mid-1920s until his death in 1953 is one of the most infamous examples of how fear and obedience can be used to control an entire nation. Stalin's iron grip on the Soviet Union was maintained not only through political maneuvering and brute force but also through the psychological manipulation of the Soviet population. By instilling a pervasive sense of fear, Stalin was able to suppress dissent, eliminate rivals, and ensure near-total obedience from the millions of people under his rule. His methods of control, rooted in the calculated use of fear, are a chilling demonstration of how psychological manipulation can shape the thoughts and behaviors of an entire society.

Stalin's rise to power was marked by his ability to eliminate political opposition while consolidating authority within the Communist Party. After Lenin's death in 1924, Stalin quickly maneuvered to push aside rivals such as Leon Trotsky, using a combination of political intrigue and fear to weaken their support. Once in power, Stalin transformed the Soviet Union into a totalitarian state where dissent was not just dangerous but often fatal. Through a series of purges, show trials, and forced confessions, Stalin removed any perceived threats to his leadership, including high-ranking members of the Communist Party, military officers, and intellectuals. The Great Purge of 1936-1938 is perhaps the most notorious example of this tactic, during which an estimated 700,000 people were executed and millions more were sent to labor camps, known as gulags.

Fear was Stalin's primary weapon, and it was used to great effect at every level of Soviet society. The purges, which often targeted individuals with no clear evidence of wrongdoing, created a sense of paranoia that extended across the population. Anyone could be denounced as an enemy of the state, and accusations were often based on nothing more than rumor, personal grudges, or fabricated evidence. The randomness of the purges heightened the atmosphere of terror, as people came to realize that loyalty to the regime or even innocence offered no protection. Friends, neighbors, and even family members were encouraged to report any suspicious behavior, further deepening the culture of fear and mistrust. This system of surveillance and denunciation ensured that no one felt safe, and that obedience to Stalin was seen as a matter of survival.

Stalin's use of fear went beyond the physical threat of imprisonment or execution—it also permeated the psychological lives of Soviet citizens. The regime's propaganda reinforced the idea that Stalin was the protector of the Soviet Union and that any disloyalty to him was tantamount to treason against the nation. This psychological manipulation created a deep sense of dependency on Stalin's leadership, as people were conditioned to believe that only through absolute obedience could the country remain strong and safe. Stalin's image was everywhere—on posters, in schools, in factories—reminding people of his omnipresent power. Through propaganda, he was portrayed as a fatherly figure, a wise and benevolent leader who knew what was best for the Soviet people.

However, this carefully constructed image of Stalin as a paternal protector was juxtaposed with the brutal reality of his regime. The NKVD, Stalin's secret police, were responsible for enforcing his rule through terror. They carried out mass arrests, executions, and deportations with ruthless efficiency. The NKVD operated largely in secrecy, which only added to the climate of fear, as no one knew when or where they might strike next. People lived in constant fear of a knock on the door in the middle of the night, when they could be taken away without warning, never to be seen again. The lack of transparency and the arbitrary nature of the arrests further cemented Stalin's control, as people learned that resistance was futile.

The labor camps, or gulags, played a central role in Stalin's reign of terror. Millions of people were sent to these camps, often for minor infractions or simply for being perceived as enemies of the state. Conditions in the gulags were brutal—forced labor, inadequate food, and harsh weather led to the deaths of many prisoners. The fear of being sent to a gulag was enough to ensure compliance from most of the population. Even those who were not directly threatened by the purges or labor camps lived in fear of being associated with someone who was. The collective punishment system meant that entire families could suffer for the actions of one individual, which discouraged any form of dissent or resistance.

In addition to physical fear, Stalin used psychological manipulation to control thought. The Soviet government tightly controlled the flow of information, censoring any news or literature that could undermine Stalin's rule. Through this control of information, Stalin was able to shape the narrative of Soviet life, presenting the regime as prosperous, just, and invincible, despite the widespread suffering. Soviet citizens were bombarded with propaganda that celebrated Stalin's achievements, particularly in the areas of industrialization and the military. Even though these "achievements" often came at great human cost—such as the forced collectivization of agriculture, which led to the deaths of millions in the man-made famine known as the Holodomor—Stalin's propaganda machine portrayed them as triumphs for the Soviet people.

The cult of personality surrounding Stalin was another key element in his psychological control over the Soviet population. Stalin's image was elevated to near-mythical status, and any criticism of him was treated as heresy. Schools taught children to revere Stalin, and public events celebrated his leadership. Statues of Stalin were erected in cities and towns across the Soviet Union, and his name was attached to various projects and places. This deification of Stalin created a situation where people came to view him not just as a political leader but as an essential part of Soviet life itself. Questioning Stalin's policies or leadership was akin to questioning the very foundations of the Soviet state, and this emotional and psychological attachment further solidified his control.

ONE OF THE MOST INSIDIOUS aspects of Stalin's rule was the way in which fear and obedience became internalized within the Soviet population. Over time, many people no longer needed to be directly threatened to comply with Stalin's policies—they had absorbed the lessons of fear so deeply that obedience became automatic. This psychological conditioning was reinforced through constant surveillance, propaganda, and the knowledge that disobedience could lead to devastating consequences not just for the individual but for their family and community. People learned to self-censor, to avoid discussing anything that could be construed as critical of the regime, and to demonstrate outward loyalty at all times.

Stalin's use of fear to maintain control was not without its consequences. While his brutal methods ensured compliance, they also stifled creativity, innovation, and open discourse. The fear of reprisal meant that even well-intentioned officials and intellectuals were reluctant to propose new ideas or challenge ineffective policies. This atmosphere of fear and conformity hindered the development of Soviet society in many ways, contributing to inefficiencies, corruption, and stagnation.

In the end, Stalin's iron grip on the Soviet Union, forged through fear and obedience, left a lasting legacy of trauma and repression. Millions of lives were destroyed through his purges, labor camps, and forced policies, and the psychological scars of his reign endured long after his death. Stalin's methods of control, though extreme, illustrate the profound power of fear in shaping human behavior and the terrifying effectiveness of psychological manipulation when wielded by a leader with absolute authority.

In conclusion, Stalin's reign over the Soviet Union was defined by his mastery of psychological manipulation, particularly through the use of fear and obedience. By creating a climate of terror, controlling information, and cultivating a cult of personality, Stalin was able to maintain absolute power for decades. His rule serves as a stark reminder of how leaders can use fear to break the will of a population, suppress dissent, and secure unwavering loyalty, often at great human cost. Understanding the mechanisms behind Stalin's control is crucial for recognizing the dangers of unchecked power and the lasting impact of fear-based rule on societies.

Hitler's Propaganda Machine: Controlling a Nation

Adolf Hitler's rise to power and the subsequent control he maintained over Nazi Germany was not achieved solely through military might or political maneuvering. A crucial component of his dominance was the extensive use of propaganda to manipulate the minds of the German population. Hitler's propaganda machine, meticulously overseen by his Minister of Propaganda, Joseph Goebbels, became one of the most infamous and effective tools of mass manipulation in modern history. Through carefully crafted messages, mass media, and psychological manipulation, Hitler was able to create a national narrative that justified his policies, demonized his enemies, and ultimately led to the devastation of World War II and the Holocaust.

Propaganda was a key element of Hitler's political strategy from the very beginning. In *Mein Kampf*, Hitler explicitly discussed the power of propaganda in shaping public opinion and consolidating political power. He understood that to control a nation, one must first control the narrative that people believe in, shaping their understanding of reality itself. This belief in the power of propaganda became central to the Nazi Party's rise to power and its ability to sustain control over the German populace.

When the Nazis came to power in 1933, they wasted no time in taking control of all forms of communication within Germany. Under the leadership of Joseph Goebbels, the Ministry of Propaganda systematically took over newspapers, radio stations, films, and other forms of media. Goebbels was a master of manipulation and understood how to craft messages that resonated with the public on both emotional and intellectual levels. He and his team shaped an entire reality for the German people, presenting Hitler as a messianic figure, portraying Jews and other minority groups as dangerous enemies, and glorifying the Nazi ideology as the salvation of the German nation.

One of the primary tools of Nazi propaganda was the media, particularly radio and film. Radio was especially effective in reaching the masses. In 1933, the Nazis introduced the "Volksempfänger," a cheap radio that could be easily afforded by most Germans, ensuring that Nazi propaganda broadcasts reached virtually every household in the country. These radios were designed to only pick up German stations, further ensuring that the public could not access alternative viewpoints. Through constant broadcasts of Hitler's speeches, Nazi slogans, and patriotic music, the regime was able to create an atmosphere of constant ideological reinforcement. Radio became a direct line from the regime to the German people, where Goebbels could carefully control every word and message that reached the public ear.

Film was another powerful tool in the Nazi propaganda machine. Goebbels understood the emotional impact of visual media and used it to present the Nazi worldview in a compelling and often entertaining way. Films like *Triumph of the Will* (1935) by Leni Riefenstahl were used to glorify Hitler and the Nazi Party, presenting them as the embodiment of German strength, unity, and destiny. This film, which documented the 1934 Nuremberg Rally, showcased Hitler as a god-like figure, with carefully staged scenes of adoring crowds, military parades, and Nazi symbols. The sheer scale of these rallies and their portrayal on film created a sense of awe, inspiring a kind of emotional and psychological reverence for Hitler's leadership.

Films also played a role in dehumanizing the groups that the Nazis considered enemies of the state. Anti-Semitic films like *The Eternal Jew* (1940) were designed to portray Jewish people as a subhuman race, using grotesque stereotypes to incite fear and hatred among the German population. By constantly reinforcing these messages through film, the

Nazis were able to build a narrative that dehumanized entire groups of people, laying the psychological groundwork for the atrocities of the Holocaust.

Print media was another crucial element of Nazi propaganda. Newspapers, magazines, and pamphlets were filled with articles glorifying the regime and its policies, while demonizing Jews, communists, and other perceived enemies. The Nazis shut down any newspaper or media outlet that didn't align with their message, ensuring that the press became a mouthpiece for Nazi ideology. Editors and journalists who didn't conform were often imprisoned or killed, further tightening the regime's control over the written word. Nazi propaganda infiltrated even the educational system, where textbooks were rewritten to promote Nazi ideals, and schoolchildren were taught to view Hitler as a national savior.

The content of Nazi propaganda was carefully crafted to appeal to the emotions, fears, and aspirations of the German people. One of the central narratives was the idea of *Volksgemeinschaft*, or "people's community." This concept was designed to create a sense of unity and collective identity among Germans, promoting the idea that they were part of a superior race destined to lead the world. It played on feelings of nationalism, pride, and belonging, giving people a reason to support the regime and its radical policies. The Nazi Party presented itself as the protector of this community, while minorities, political enemies, and foreign nations were depicted as threats to its survival.

Fear was another key component of Hitler's propaganda machine. The Nazis were adept at stoking fears of communism, Jewish influence, and foreign powers, presenting these groups as existential threats to the German way of life. By creating a constant sense of danger, the regime was able to justify its increasingly draconian policies, including the expansion of police powers, the suppression of civil liberties, and eventually, the mass imprisonment and extermination of millions. Hitler's speeches were filled with dire warnings about the collapse of the German nation if these threats were not dealt with, effectively manipulating the German people into supporting policies they might otherwise have opposed.

Hitler himself was a masterful orator, and his speeches played a central role in Nazi propaganda. His speeches were broadcast across the nation, reaching millions of listeners through radio and loudspeakers in public squares. Hitler understood the emotional power of words and used his speeches to manipulate the fears, hopes, and anxieties of his audience. He often presented himself as a victim of injustice, whether it was the Treaty of Versailles or the supposed global Jewish conspiracy, which allowed him to position himself as the only person capable of saving Germany from its enemies. His fiery rhetoric, combined with carefully staged public appearances, created a psychological bond between Hitler and the German people, making it difficult for many to question his leadership.

THE NAZIS ALSO USED symbols and imagery as part of their propaganda machine. The swastika, the uniformed SS and SA troops, and the rigidly choreographed Nazi rallies all created a visual representation of order, power, and unity. These symbols became synonymous with the regime and reinforced the sense that the Nazi Party was an unstoppable force, destined to lead Germany to greatness. The use of grand architecture, such as the design of the Nuremberg Rally grounds, further cemented this image, turning political events into monumental spectacles that left a lasting impression on those who attended or saw them in propaganda films.

The propaganda machine was so pervasive that it infiltrated nearly every aspect of daily life in Nazi Germany. Youth organizations like the Hitler Youth and the League of German Girls were used to indoctrinate young people from an early age, ensuring that future generations would be loyal to the regime. Through these organizations, children were taught to idolize Hitler, internalize Nazi ideology, and prepare for military service or roles in Nazi society. The goal was to shape the minds of young Germans so completely that they would become lifelong supporters of the regime, unquestioning in their loyalty to the Führer.

The power of Nazi propaganda was not just in its ability to spread lies or promote ideology—it was in its ability to create an alternate reality, one in which the German people were constantly bombarded with a singular narrative that glorified the regime, vilified its enemies, and justified the most horrific acts as necessary for the survival of the nation. By controlling the media, education, and culture, Hitler and Goebbels were able to shape the thoughts, emotions, and beliefs of an entire nation, paving the way for some of the darkest chapters in human history.

In conclusion, Hitler's propaganda machine was a highly effective and insidious tool of mind control, one that allowed him to shape the thoughts and actions of millions of people. Through the manipulation of media, the use of fear, and the glorification of Nazi ideology, Hitler was able to create a national narrative that justified war, genocide, and dictatorship. The lessons of Nazi propaganda remain relevant today, serving as a stark reminder of the dangers of unchecked power and the psychological manipulation of entire populations. Understanding the techniques used by the Nazi regime is crucial for recognizing the signs of propaganda and mind control in our own time and for safeguarding against the repetition of such atrocities.

The Modern Autocrat: Vladimir Putin's Control Techniques

Vladimir Putin, the modern autocrat at the helm of Russia since the late 1990s, has employed a wide array of control techniques to maintain his grip on power. His reign, marked by both strategic brilliance and ruthless authoritarianism, draws from a combination of traditional authoritarian methods and more sophisticated, modern-day tools of psychological manipulation and media control. Putin's control over Russia is not solely about overt repression, but also about managing perceptions, controlling information, and shaping the narrative to maintain his dominance.

Putin's path to power began in the late 1990s, a time of turmoil for Russia following the collapse of the Soviet Union. The country was in the midst of political and economic chaos, with a weakened central government and a disillusioned populace. Putin capitalized on this instability by presenting himself as a strongman capable of restoring order, rebuilding the economy, and reclaiming Russia's former greatness. This image has been a central pillar of his control techniques ever since—he has cultivated an aura of strength, stability, and national pride that resonates deeply with many Russians.

One of the key elements of Putin's control is the extensive use of state propaganda and media manipulation. Under his rule, the Russian media landscape has been transformed into a tightly controlled apparatus that serves to disseminate government-approved narratives and suppress dissenting voices. Independent media outlets have been systematically shut down, bought out, or coerced into aligning with the state's messaging. Major television networks, which are the primary source of news for most Russians, are either directly owned by the government or controlled by pro-Kremlin oligarchs. These media outlets promote a narrative of Putin as the indispensable leader of Russia, the guardian of its sovereignty, and the protector against both internal and external threats.

One of the most effective propaganda narratives Putin has cultivated is the idea of a resurgent, powerful Russia standing up to the West. Throughout his presidency, Putin has positioned himself as a defender of Russian interests against Western encroachment. Whether it's NATO expansion, economic sanctions, or criticisms of Russia's human rights record, Putin has portrayed these actions as part of a broader Western campaign to weaken or subjugate Russia. This narrative resonates deeply with many Russians, particularly those who feel a sense of nostalgia for the Soviet era or who believe that Russia should once again be a dominant global power. By stoking nationalism and portraying himself as the only leader capable of defending Russia from its enemies, Putin has been able to cultivate a strong sense of loyalty among much of the population.

Another key aspect of Putin's control techniques is his use of fear, much like the traditional autocrats who came before him. While Putin's regime is not as overtly brutal as some of the 20th-century dictatorships, fear remains an important tool in maintaining control. Political opposition in Russia is frequently met with harassment, imprisonment, and even assassination. High-profile opposition figures, such as Boris Nemtsov and Alexei Navalny, have faced intense repression. Nemtsov, a prominent critic of Putin, was assassinated in 2015 near the Kremlin, while Navalny, a leading opposition figure, survived a poisoning attempt in 2020, widely believed to have been orchestrated by the Russian state.

Putin's regime has also used the legal system as a weapon against political opponents, journalists, and activists. Laws against "extremism" or "foreign agents" are often broadly interpreted to target anyone seen as a threat to the Kremlin's control. These laws allow the government to discredit, imprison, or silence dissenting voices under the guise of maintaining national security. This legal repression, combined with the occasional high-profile use of force, sends a clear message to would-be opponents: dissent can come at a high personal cost.

The cultivation of a loyal oligarch class is another cornerstone of Putin's control techniques. After coming to power, Putin quickly consolidated control over the country's vast resources by either co-opting or eliminating the oligarchs who had risen to prominence in the 1990s. Those who refused to align with Putin, such as Mikhail Khodorkovsky, found themselves jailed or exiled, while others who were willing to support Putin's regime were rewarded with wealth, political influence, and business opportunities. This symbiotic relationship between the state and the oligarchs ensures that the most powerful economic actors in Russia have a vested interest in maintaining the status quo. These oligarchs, in turn, use their influence to help reinforce Putin's control, whether through funding state projects, controlling media outlets, or supporting pro-Kremlin political movements.

Control over regional governance has also been critical to Putin's dominance. Early in his presidency, he moved to centralize power by reducing the autonomy of Russia's regional governors, ensuring that they were either loyal to him or could be easily replaced if they became too independent. This centralization of power has allowed Putin to maintain a strong grip over the vast and diverse regions of Russia, preventing any local leaders from challenging his authority. By ensuring that political and economic power flows from Moscow, Putin has effectively neutered potential opposition from regional elites.

Putin's use of modern surveillance and technological control is another method that differentiates him from previous autocrats. The Russian government has invested heavily in its surveillance capabilities, particularly in monitoring the internet and social media. Putin's regime has implemented a series of laws that require internet service providers and social media companies to store data on Russian servers, making it easier for the state to access personal information and monitor online activity. Websites that are critical of the government are often blocked, and the government has attempted to create its own internet infrastructure that would allow it to sever the country from the global internet if necessary. This level of control over digital communications allows Putin to prevent the spread of dissent and track potential opposition before it can gain momentum.

In addition to surveillance, Putin has mastered the art of disinformation and psychological warfare, both within Russia and abroad. The Kremlin's disinformation campaigns are designed not only to manipulate public opinion but also to sow confusion and distrust in information itself. Russian state media often promotes conflicting narratives, making it difficult for the public to discern the truth. This tactic of "firehosing," in which numerous false or misleading stories are spread simultaneously, creates an environment where facts become irrelevant, and people are left disoriented and susceptible to further manipulation.

This strategy extends beyond Russia's borders as well. Putin's regime has become notorious for using disinformation as a tool of foreign policy, most notably in the 2016 U.S. presidential election, where Russian interference aimed to destabilize American democracy and discredit Western political systems. By sowing discord abroad, Putin not only weakens his foreign adversaries but also reinforces the narrative at home that Western democracies are corrupt, dysfunctional, and hypocritical.

Another element of Putin's control is the manipulation of historical narratives. The Kremlin has used selective interpretations of Russian history to cultivate a sense of pride and nostalgia, particularly around the Soviet Union's victory in World War II. This historical narrative portrays Russia as a heroic nation that has repeatedly been forced to defend itself from foreign aggression. By framing contemporary geopolitical conflicts in this historical context,

Putin justifies aggressive foreign policies, such as the annexation of Crimea or the military interventions in Syria and Ukraine, as necessary for Russia's security and honor.

Putin's control techniques also involve a delicate balancing act with Russian public opinion. While fear, repression, and propaganda are important tools, Putin has been careful to maintain a certain level of legitimacy among the Russian people. He has successfully portrayed himself as a protector of traditional values, a restorer of Russia's global status, and a leader who has brought stability and economic growth after the chaotic 1990s. This image has allowed him to retain popular support, particularly among older generations and those in rural areas. However, this support has been increasingly challenged by younger, urban Russians who are more exposed to alternative sources of information and are more likely to protest against the regime.

In conclusion, Vladimir Putin has mastered a complex array of control techniques that blend traditional authoritarian methods with modern propaganda, technology, and disinformation. His regime uses fear, loyalty, media control, surveillance, and nationalism to maintain its grip on power, shaping both the thoughts and actions of the Russian population. While his methods may differ from those of previous dictators, the underlying goal remains the same: to ensure obedience, eliminate opposition, and solidify his position as the unchallenged leader of Russia. As Putin continues to wield these tools of control, the world watches closely, recognizing the profound impact they have on both Russia and the international community.

Surveillance and Punishment: China's Social Credit System

China's Social Credit System is one of the most ambitious and comprehensive efforts to control a population through surveillance and punishment. This system, which the Chinese government has been developing and implementing since the early 2010s, is a technology-driven tool designed to monitor, rate, and regulate the behavior of citizens and businesses. By using a combination of advanced surveillance technologies, big data analytics, and a system of rewards and punishments, the Social Credit System aims to create a society in which every action and decision is tracked and evaluated. This system has raised significant concerns about privacy, freedom, and the extent to which a government can exert control over its people.

At its core, the Social Credit System is a method of rating individuals and entities based on their behavior. The Chinese government refers to it as a way to "build trust" in society by rewarding those who are "trustworthy" and punishing those who are not. Trustworthiness in this context refers not only to financial reliability, such as paying debts on time, but also to social behaviors like obeying traffic laws, respecting public order, or even showing loyalty to the government. Individuals and companies that receive high social credit scores are rewarded with privileges, while those with low scores can face a range of punishments, some of which can severely impact their lives.

The foundation of China's Social Credit System is its vast surveillance network, which has grown exponentially in recent years. China has installed millions of surveillance cameras equipped with facial recognition technology in cities across the country. These cameras, combined with AI-powered analytics, allow the government to monitor the movements and activities of individuals in real-time. The data collected from these cameras, along with data from social media, online transactions, and other digital platforms, feeds into the Social Credit System. The use of this data extends beyond public spaces—individuals' interactions on platforms like WeChat and Alipay are also monitored, providing a complete picture of their daily lives and social behavior.

Facial recognition technology plays a key role in this system. By identifying individuals in public spaces, authorities can track behavior such as jaywalking, littering, or participating in protests. For example, in some cities, jaywalkers are instantly recognized by cameras, and their images and identities are publicly displayed on large screens as a form of public shaming. Such violations can negatively impact a person's social credit score. In other instances, individuals caught breaking minor rules or engaging in behaviors deemed undesirable may be denied certain privileges, such as the ability to book flights or train tickets, or have their children barred from attending prestigious schools.

The punishments within the Social Credit System are wide-ranging, and they are designed to reinforce behavioral conformity and obedience to the state. One of the most common penalties for those with low social credit scores is the restriction of travel. Individuals with poor scores can be banned from buying high-speed train tickets, flying on planes, or staying at certain hotels. This punishment is particularly effective in a country as large as China, where fast transportation is often necessary for business or personal needs. By limiting travel, the government can effectively isolate individuals with low scores, reducing their ability to operate normally within society.

Another consequence of having a low social credit score is restricted access to financial services. People with poor scores may find it difficult to get loans, mortgages, or even insurance. Their ability to open bank accounts or use credit cards can be limited, making it harder for them to participate in the economy. In extreme cases, individuals with low scores may also be blacklisted, which means that their names are made public, and businesses or other entities are encouraged to avoid dealing with them. This kind of social ostracism adds another layer of pressure on individuals to conform to the rules and maintain a high social credit score.

On the other hand, those with high social credit scores enjoy a variety of benefits. High scorers may receive better interest rates on loans, access to premium services, and preferential treatment when applying for government jobs or social services. They may also be fast-tracked for bureaucratic approvals, making it easier for them to navigate China's often complex administrative systems. These rewards create a powerful incentive for citizens to align their behavior with the government's expectations, reinforcing a system of obedience and conformity.

While the Social Credit System is ostensibly designed to promote "trustworthy" behavior, its scope goes far beyond issues of public order or financial reliability. The system has become a tool for the government to enforce political loyalty and social control. Citizens are rated not only on their adherence to laws but also on their participation in activities that demonstrate loyalty to the Communist Party. For example, individuals who participate in government-sponsored events or show their support for Party policies may see their social credit scores increase, while those who express dissenting opinions, criticize the government, or engage in activism are likely to see their scores drop.

This integration of political loyalty into the Social Credit System has serious implications for freedom of speech and expression. In a country where censorship is already pervasive, the Social Credit System adds another layer of pressure on individuals to self-censor and avoid any behavior that could be perceived as critical of the government. By linking behavior to real-world consequences, the government can effectively silence dissent and discourage opposition, without needing to resort to more overt forms of repression such as imprisonment or violence.

The corporate sector is also subject to the Social Credit System, with businesses being rated on their compliance with government regulations and their corporate behavior. Companies with high social credit scores are rewarded with preferential access to government contracts, lower taxes, and other benefits, while those with low scores face penalties such as fines, restrictions on market access, or increased scrutiny from regulators. For foreign companies operating in China, this has created a challenging environment, as they must navigate the expectations of the Social Credit System while maintaining their own ethical standards and global reputations.

ONE OF THE MOST CONCERNING aspects of China's Social Credit System is its lack of transparency and due process. Individuals often do not know how their scores are calculated or how to contest inaccurate or unfair scores. The algorithms that determine social credit scores are opaque, and there is little accountability for errors or abuses. This creates an environment where the government has near-total control over citizens' lives, with little recourse for those who find themselves penalized by the system. The ability of the government to monitor, judge, and punish individuals without clear checks and balances raises serious questions about human rights and individual freedoms in China.

The Social Credit System is part of a broader trend in China toward using technology for social control. The Chinese government has embraced technology as a means of maintaining order, controlling information, and ensuring compliance with its policies. From internet censorship and surveillance to data tracking and facial recognition, China's use of technology for governance has created a highly controlled society where dissent is discouraged, and conformity is rewarded.

However, the Social Credit System also reflects a unique fusion of ancient Chinese concepts of social harmony and modern technology. The idea of social harmony, or "◇◇◇◇" (héxié shèhuì), is deeply rooted in Confucian philosophy, which emphasizes the importance of social order, respect for authority, and individual responsibility to the collective. In many ways, the Social Credit System is a modern extension of this traditional idea, using technology to enforce behavior that aligns with the government's vision of a harmonious society. However, the coercive nature of the system, combined with the state's increasing use of surveillance, raises concerns about whether this vision of harmony comes at the cost of personal freedom and autonomy.

In conclusion, China's Social Credit System represents a sophisticated and far-reaching method of controlling its population through a combination of surveillance, rewards, and punishments. By monitoring nearly every aspect of citizens' lives, from financial behavior to political loyalty, the system creates powerful incentives for conformity while punishing those who step out of line. As technology continues to evolve, the Social Credit System raises important questions about the balance between social order and individual rights, the role of technology in governance, and the future of privacy and freedom in an increasingly monitored world. The system, while unique to China in its scope and scale, may serve as a model—or a warning—for other governments considering similar methods of control.

The Tools of Political Manipulation: Lies, Fear, and Propaganda

Political manipulation is as old as politics itself. Throughout history, leaders and regimes have employed a variety of tools to maintain power, shape public opinion, and control populations. Among the most effective and commonly used tools are lies, fear, and propaganda. These methods work by distorting reality, controlling the flow of information, and playing on the psychological vulnerabilities of individuals and societies. While each tool can be powerful on its own, when used in combination, they form a formidable mechanism of control that can shape the beliefs, behaviors, and perceptions of entire nations. In this chapter, we will explore how lies, fear, and propaganda function as tools of political manipulation and how they have been employed by various regimes throughout history.

Lies are perhaps the most basic and direct form of political manipulation. A lie can take many forms: it can be a complete fabrication, a half-truth, or a distortion of reality. Lies are often used to mislead the public, to create scapegoats, or to justify policies and actions that would otherwise be unacceptable. In authoritarian regimes, lying is frequently used to maintain the appearance of control, stability, and legitimacy, even in the face of crises or failures.

One of the most well-known examples of lying as a political tool is the Nazi regime's use of what Adolf Hitler termed the "big lie." In *Mein Kampf*, Hitler wrote that people are more likely to believe a big lie than a small one because ordinary people "would sooner believe a great lie than a small one" due to their inability to conceive that anyone could have the impudence to distort the truth so brazenly. This strategy was employed to devastating effect during the Holocaust, as the Nazis systematically spread lies about the Jewish population, blaming them for Germany's economic and social problems. These lies were repeated so often, and in so many forms, that they became accepted as fact by much of the German population, laying the groundwork for widespread anti-Semitism and the atrocities that followed.

Similarly, lies have been used to justify wars and other aggressive actions throughout history. The Gulf of Tonkin incident during the Vietnam War, for example, was a fabricated event that the U.S. government used to justify increased military involvement in Vietnam. The incident, which involved an alleged attack on a U.S. naval vessel by North Vietnamese forces, was later revealed to have been exaggerated or even fabricated. Nonetheless, the lie served its purpose in rallying public and congressional support for the war effort.

In more recent times, political leaders have used lies and disinformation to create alternate realities that support their agendas. The use of "fake news," disinformation campaigns, and conspiracy theories has become a common tactic in modern politics. By spreading false information, political actors can sow confusion, discredit opponents, and shift public attention away from their own misdeeds. The internet and social media have made it easier than ever to spread these lies rapidly and widely, creating an environment where the truth becomes increasingly difficult to discern.

Fear is another powerful tool of political manipulation. Fear operates on a primal level, bypassing rational thought and triggering the brain's fight-or-flight response. Political leaders have long understood that by creating or amplifying fear, they can rally people to their cause, justify repressive measures, and suppress dissent. Fear can take many forms: fear of external enemies, fear of internal threats, fear of economic collapse, or fear of social unrest. By manipulating fear, leaders can create a sense of urgency and danger that allows them to consolidate power and control over a frightened population.

One of the most notorious examples of using fear as a political tool was the reign of Joseph Stalin in the Soviet Union. Stalin maintained his control over the Soviet population in large part by creating a climate of fear. The Great Purge of the 1930s, during which millions of Soviet citizens were arrested, executed, or sent to labor camps, was a deliberate effort to instill terror in the population. Stalin's secret police, the NKVD, were known for arresting people in the middle of the night, and individuals often disappeared without warning or explanation. This atmosphere of fear ensured that the Soviet people would not dare to challenge Stalin's rule, as the consequences of dissent were too horrifying to contemplate.

Fear has also been used to justify war and aggressive foreign policies. In the lead-up to the Iraq War in 2003, the U.S. government, under President George W. Bush, used fear to build public support for the invasion of Iraq. The Bush administration repeatedly claimed that Iraq possessed weapons of mass destruction (WMDs) and that these weapons posed an imminent threat to the United States and its allies. These claims, which were later proven to be false, created a climate of fear that made the public more receptive to the idea of war. Fear of terrorism, which had already been heightened by the attacks of September 11, 2001, further contributed to the public's willingness to support military action. This manipulation of fear not only justified the invasion but also paved the way for broader expansions of government surveillance and restrictions on civil liberties through the Patriot Act.

Fear can also be used to suppress internal dissent. Authoritarian regimes frequently portray political opponents, dissidents, or minority groups as dangerous threats to national security or social stability. In doing so, they justify repressive measures such as censorship, surveillance, and imprisonment. In China, for example, the government has used fear to justify its crackdown on the Uyghur Muslim population in Xinjiang. By portraying Uyghurs as potential terrorists and separatists, the Chinese government has been able to justify the construction of mass internment camps and the implementation of invasive surveillance measures. The fear of terrorism and instability is used to legitimize these human rights abuses in the eyes of the Chinese public and the international community.

Propaganda is the third key tool of political manipulation, and it often works hand-in-hand with lies and fear. Propaganda is the deliberate dissemination of information, ideas, or rumors intended to influence public opinion and behavior. While propaganda can take many forms, it is most effective when it plays on emotions and reinforces existing beliefs. Through repetition and emotional appeal, propaganda can shape how people perceive reality, solidify their loyalty to a regime or cause, and marginalize or dehumanize enemies.

In Nazi Germany, propaganda was a cornerstone of Hitler's control over the German people. Joseph Goebbels, Hitler's Minister of Propaganda, created a massive propaganda apparatus that included films, newspapers, radio broadcasts, and public rallies. The messages were simple and repetitive: Hitler was Germany's savior, Jews and communists were the enemies of the people, and Germany was destined for greatness under Nazi rule. Through relentless repetition and emotional appeals, these messages became deeply ingrained in the German consciousness, making it difficult for individuals to think critically or question the regime.

Propaganda is not confined to authoritarian regimes. Democracies have also used propaganda to manipulate public opinion, particularly during times of war. During World War I, the British and American governments used propaganda to demonize the German enemy and rally support for the war effort. Posters, films, and speeches portrayed Germans as barbaric and inhumane, reinforcing the belief that the war was a just cause. In World War II, the United States government employed similar tactics to build public support for the war and to encourage citizens to contribute to the war effort through rationing, buying war bonds, and joining the military.

Modern propaganda has evolved to take advantage of new technologies and platforms. Social media, in particular, has become a powerful tool for disseminating propaganda. Political campaigns, governments, and interest groups use social media to target specific demographics with tailored messages designed to evoke emotional responses. Algorithms used by platforms like Facebook and Twitter amplify these messages, creating echo chambers where individuals are exposed only to information that reinforces their existing beliefs. This creates a fertile ground for propaganda, as people become more isolated from alternative viewpoints and more susceptible to manipulation.

The combination of lies, fear, and propaganda is a potent formula for political control. By distorting reality, amplifying fears, and shaping the narrative, political leaders can maintain power, justify repressive measures, and manipulate public opinion. These tools are particularly effective when they are used together, as they reinforce one another in a cycle of manipulation. Lies create the foundation for fear, fear justifies authoritarian measures, and propaganda ensures that these measures are accepted and even embraced by the population.

In conclusion, lies, fear, and propaganda are central tools in the arsenal of political manipulation. They have been used by regimes throughout history to control populations, shape public opinion, and justify actions that might otherwise be unacceptable. These tools work by distorting reality, creating enemies, and playing on the emotions of the public. Whether through disinformation campaigns, fearmongering, or the relentless dissemination of propaganda, political manipulation remains a powerful force in both authoritarian and democratic systems. Understanding how these tools work is essential for recognizing and resisting manipulation, and for safeguarding the truth, freedom, and critical thinking in the face of powerful forces of control.

The Role of Media in Modern-Day Mind Control

In today's world, media is one of the most powerful forces shaping public opinion, influencing behaviors, and, in many ways, controlling how we perceive reality. The role of media in modern-day mind control is not always overt, but it is deeply pervasive. Media in all its forms—television, radio, newspapers, social media, and digital platforms—can subtly and not-so-subtly manipulate how we think, feel, and react to the world around us. By controlling the flow of information, reinforcing certain narratives, and appealing to emotional and psychological vulnerabilities, media has the potential to serve as a tool for mass manipulation and mind control.

In democratic societies, the media is often seen as a pillar of free speech and a safeguard of democracy. Ideally, it serves as a watchdog, holding those in power accountable and providing the public with accurate and balanced information. However, in practice, media outlets are often influenced by political, economic, or corporate interests, which can shape the content they produce and the narratives they promote. As a result, media can become a powerful tool for those seeking to manipulate public opinion, whether they are governments, corporations, or other influential groups.

One of the most effective ways the media exerts control is through the agenda-setting theory. This theory suggests that while the media may not always tell people what to think, it is incredibly effective at telling them what to think about. By deciding which issues to highlight, how much attention to give them, and in what context to present them, media outlets can shape the public's perception of what is important. For example, by focusing heavily on certain issues—like crime, immigration, or terrorism—media can make these topics seem more pressing or urgent than they may actually be, prompting the public to prioritize them when forming opinions or making decisions, such as during elections.

Media also shapes thought through framing, which refers to the way information is presented. The framing of a story—how it is written, the language used, the imagery chosen, and the angle from which it is approached—can significantly influence how the public interprets that story. For example, a protest might be framed as a peaceful demonstration of democratic rights, or it might be presented as a dangerous and violent riot. The choice of frame affects how the audience feels about the event and how they respond to it. Through consistent framing, media can shape the narratives that govern public discourse.

One of the more concerning aspects of modern media's role in mind control is the rise of echo chambers and filter bubbles, particularly in the digital space. With the advent of social media and algorithm-driven newsfeeds, individuals are increasingly exposed only to information that aligns with their existing beliefs and opinions. Algorithms prioritize content that generates engagement, which often leads to the amplification of sensationalist, emotionally charged, or polarizing content. This creates a feedback loop where users are constantly fed information that reinforces their worldview, while opposing viewpoints are filtered out. As a result, people become more isolated in their beliefs, less exposed to alternative perspectives, and more susceptible to manipulation by those who control the content in their bubble.

Social media platforms, in particular, have been criticized for their role in fostering these echo chambers and enabling the spread of misinformation. The platforms' algorithms are designed to maximize user engagement by showing users content they are most likely to interact with. This has led to the rise of "clickbait" headlines, emotionally charged posts, and sensationalist news stories that may not be entirely accurate but are highly engaging. Furthermore, disinformation campaigns, often driven by political actors or foreign governments, have found fertile ground on social media. By spreading false information or manipulating trending topics, these campaigns can shape public opinion, stoke division, and even influence elections.

A powerful example of media's role in mind control through social media occurred during the 2016 U.S. presidential election. Russian interference, through social media disinformation campaigns, highlighted how vulnerable the digital media ecosystem is to manipulation. Russian operatives used fake accounts, bots, and targeted ads to spread misleading information, inflame political tensions, and create confusion among voters. The impact of these campaigns was profound, with many people exposed to false information that influenced their political views and voting decisions. This example shows how media, particularly social media, can be weaponized as a tool of political mind control on a massive scale.

Traditional media—television, newspapers, and radio—also continues to play a significant role in shaping public opinion and controlling narratives. One of the most effective ways this is done is through the creation of fear. Sensationalized news coverage of crime, terrorism, and other threats can create a heightened sense of fear and insecurity in the population. This fear can then be used to justify policies, laws, or government actions that might otherwise be unpopular or seen as infringing on civil liberties. Fear-based media, particularly when it is focused on foreign threats, immigrants, or marginalized groups, can lead to increased support for authoritarian measures, restrictions on personal freedoms, and even acts of violence.

News media's use of selective reporting is another way in which it shapes public perception and controls thought. By selectively choosing which stories to report on, which voices to elevate, and which facts to emphasize, media outlets can skew the public's understanding of events. For example, in conflict reporting, media coverage might focus heavily on one side's perspective while downplaying or ignoring the views of the other side, leading to a biased interpretation of the conflict. Similarly, by focusing on certain events while ignoring others, media can make some issues seem more significant than they are, while others fade into obscurity.

A critical aspect of media's role in modern mind control is its ability to create and sustain myths and narratives that serve specific political or corporate interests. For example, the myth of the "American Dream"—the idea that anyone who works hard enough can achieve success—has been perpetuated by media for generations. This narrative, while inspiring, also serves to obscure systemic inequalities and deflect attention from structural issues like poverty, racism, and income inequality. By focusing on individual success stories, the media reinforces the idea that failure is a personal shortcoming rather than the result of broader societal problems. This kind of narrative serves the interests of those in power by shifting responsibility away from the government or corporations and onto individuals.

The media's relationship with governments and corporations often leads to conflicts of interest that influence reporting. In many countries, media outlets are owned by a small number of powerful corporations, and these corporations often have close ties to political leaders or business interests. This concentration of media ownership can result in biased reporting that reflects the interests of those in power rather than providing an objective view of events. In some cases, governments use media outlets as direct propaganda tools, spreading misinformation or one-sided narratives to maintain control over the population. This is particularly evident in authoritarian countries where state-run media dominates, but it can also be seen in more subtle forms in democratic societies where media outlets may self-censor or promote government-friendly narratives to avoid conflict with political leaders.

Another area where media plays a role in modern-day mind control is in consumer behavior. Advertising, which is a major part of media revenue, is designed to manipulate consumer desires and behaviors. Through carefully crafted messages, images, and emotional appeals, advertising convinces people to buy products they don't need, aspire to lifestyles they can't afford, or associate happiness and success with material consumption. This form of media manipulation is so pervasive that it shapes entire cultures, creating societies where consumerism is viewed as the path to fulfillment and success.

Moreover, the rise of influencer culture on social media platforms has further blurred the lines between advertising, media, and personal identity. Influencers, who often have millions of followers, are paid to promote products and brands, but their content is often presented as authentic, personal recommendations rather than traditional advertisements. This subtle form of manipulation makes it more difficult for consumers to recognize when they are being sold to, and it creates an environment where personal identity and self-worth are increasingly tied to consumer choices.

The media's role in shaping political discourse, social values, and consumer behavior cannot be overstated. Whether through traditional outlets or new digital platforms, media serves as a powerful tool for controlling the narrative and influencing how people think, feel, and act. While it can be a force for good, providing information, education, and entertainment, it can also be a tool of manipulation that serves the interests of powerful political, corporate, or ideological actors.

In conclusion, the media plays a central role in modern-day mind control by controlling the flow of information, shaping narratives, and appealing to emotional and psychological vulnerabilities. Through agenda-setting, framing, selective reporting, and the creation of echo chambers, media outlets can manipulate public opinion and shape perceptions of reality. As technology continues to evolve and media consumption becomes increasingly digital, the potential for media manipulation grows, making it more important than ever for individuals to critically evaluate the information they receive and seek out diverse sources of news and perspectives. Understanding the tools and techniques used by the media to influence thought is essential for resisting manipulation and maintaining a free and informed society.

Controlling the Narrative: State Censorship and Media Control

Controlling the narrative is one of the most powerful forms of political manipulation, and nowhere is this more evident than in state censorship and media control. In authoritarian regimes, and even in some democracies, governments exert control over media outlets and information flow to ensure that only their version of reality reaches the public. Through censorship, propaganda, and manipulation of media channels, state authorities can shape public opinion, suppress dissent, and maintain a firm grip on power. By controlling what people see, hear, and read, they control what people think. In this chapter, we will explore how state censorship and media control are used as tools of modern-day mind control, examining both the mechanisms of control and their profound impact on societies.

State censorship is the deliberate suppression of information, ideas, or speech that is deemed threatening or undesirable by the government. This can include censoring news, political opinions, cultural content, or any information that might challenge the state's authority or undermine its narrative. In many countries, state censorship is used to protect the ruling elite from criticism, to prevent the spread of dissenting ideas, and to create a controlled, uniform version of events that supports the government's agenda. The effectiveness of state censorship lies in its ability to manipulate the public's understanding of reality by controlling the information they can access.

One of the most notorious examples of state censorship is in China, where the government exercises strict control over the media and the internet through its sophisticated censorship apparatus, often referred to as "The Great Firewall of China." The Chinese Communist Party (CCP) closely monitors all forms of communication, from traditional print and broadcast media to digital platforms and social media. Through the Central Propaganda Department, the government determines what can and cannot be reported in the news, ensuring that only stories favorable to the state make it to the public. Journalists and editors who fail to comply with the state's directives risk losing their jobs, being imprisoned, or facing other forms of punishment.

One of the key strategies employed by the Chinese government is the censorship of information related to sensitive political topics, such as the Tiananmen Square Massacre, human rights abuses, or pro-democracy movements. The government goes to great lengths to erase these topics from public discourse, scrubbing mentions from social media, banning books and films that reference them, and blocking access to foreign news sources that report on them. By keeping the public in the dark about these issues, the state is able to maintain a narrative of stability and control, where the CCP is seen as a benevolent protector of the Chinese people, rather than a repressive regime.

China's control of the narrative extends into the digital realm through its tight regulation of the internet. The Great Firewall blocks access to many Western websites, such as Google, Facebook, Twitter, and major international news outlets. This prevents Chinese citizens from accessing alternative viewpoints and uncensored news.

Domestic platforms like WeChat and Weibo are heavily monitored, and content that is critical of the government is quickly removed by state censors or the platforms themselves, which are legally required to comply with government regulations. In recent years, the CCP has even increased its use of artificial intelligence and machine learning to automate the process of identifying and censoring "subversive" content online.

In addition to outright censorship, the Chinese government uses more subtle forms of media control to shape public opinion. This includes promoting pro-government messages through state-run media outlets such as CCTV and the People's Daily, which reach millions of viewers and readers across the country. These outlets present a carefully curated version of reality, where the Chinese government is portrayed as strong, wise, and indispensable. News reports emphasize economic growth, social stability, and national achievements, while downplaying or ignoring stories that might reflect poorly on the government. The goal is not only to suppress dissent but also to instill a sense of national pride and loyalty to the state, reinforcing the government's legitimacy.

Other authoritarian regimes, such as North Korea, Russia, and Iran, also use state censorship and media control to maintain power. In North Korea, for example, the government controls all media outlets, and citizens are completely cut off from the outside world. The state-run news agency, KCNA, broadcasts only positive stories about the regime, portraying the Kim dynasty as infallible and god-like. North Koreans are taught to believe that their country is a paradise compared to the rest of the world, and they are kept in the dark about the extreme poverty and human rights abuses within their own borders. The Kim regime uses this control of information to ensure that there is no space for dissent or alternative viewpoints, effectively turning North Korea into one of the most tightly controlled societies in the world.

In Russia, the media landscape is dominated by state-run or state-aligned outlets that serve as mouthpieces for the Kremlin. Under Vladimir Putin's leadership, independent media has been systematically dismantled, with critical journalists often facing harassment, imprisonment, or even assassination. The Russian government controls television, which remains the primary source of news for most Russians, and uses it to shape the public's perception of both domestic and international events. Through media control, Putin has cultivated a narrative of Russia as a strong, independent nation under constant threat from the West, while portraying himself as the protector of Russian values and sovereignty. This narrative helps justify aggressive foreign policies, such as the annexation of Crimea or military interventions in Syria, as necessary defenses against external enemies.

State censorship is not limited to authoritarian regimes; even democratic governments can engage in media manipulation, although the methods are often more subtle. In some democracies, governments use legal means to suppress certain types of speech or media content, especially during times of crisis. For example, during wars or national security emergencies, democratic governments may impose restrictions on the press, censoring reports that could undermine military efforts or stoke public fear. While these measures are often justified as temporary responses to specific threats, they can also be used to suppress dissent or prevent criticism of government policies.

In addition to direct censorship, many democratic governments exert indirect control over media through ownership or influence over media companies. In countries like Hungary, Turkey, and India, governments have increasingly used their political and economic power to influence the media landscape, often by placing allies in key positions within media organizations or by buying out critical outlets. In these cases, the media is not overtly censored, but its content is shaped by the government's interests, ensuring that coverage remains favorable to those in power.

One of the most troubling aspects of state censorship and media control is its impact on free thought and critical thinking. When a government controls the narrative, it can prevent people from questioning authority, challenging the status quo, or forming independent opinions. In societies where censorship is pervasive, citizens may become passive consumers of information, accepting the state's version of events without skepticism or inquiry. Over time, this can create a culture of obedience and conformity, where people are discouraged from thinking critically or seeking out alternative perspectives.

The rise of digital media and the internet has complicated the issue of state censorship. On one hand, the internet provides a platform for alternative voices, independent journalism, and the free exchange of ideas. On the other hand, authoritarian governments have become increasingly adept at controlling digital spaces, using technology to monitor, censor, and manipulate online content. In some cases, governments have even developed their own alternatives to global digital platforms—such as China's WeChat and Russia's VKontakte—allowing them to maintain tight control over online discourse while limiting access to foreign influences. While digital platforms offer the potential for resistance against state censorship, they also present new opportunities for governments to control information. Social media companies, under pressure from governments, may be forced to comply with local laws and regulations that require them to censor content, hand over user data, or shut down accounts critical of the government. In some cases, social media platforms have been accused of prioritizing profits over the protection of free speech, agreeing to censorship requests in exchange for access to lucrative markets.

The consequences of state censorship and media control are profound. When governments control the narrative, they can shape public perception, limit dissent, and maintain power with little accountability. The suppression of free speech, access to information, and alternative viewpoints undermines democracy, human rights, and the potential for social and political progress. In authoritarian regimes, where dissent can be dangerous or deadly, censorship becomes a tool for maintaining totalitarian control. Even in more open societies, the influence of governments over media can erode trust in democratic institutions and create an environment where critical thinking is stifled. State censorship and media control are powerful tools for controlling the narrative, shaping public opinion, and maintaining political power. By restricting access to information, governments can manipulate how people think, feel, and act. Whether through direct censorship, control of media outlets, or digital surveillance, the suppression of free speech and the control of the narrative have far-reaching consequences for societies. As technology evolves, the battle over media control will continue to play a crucial role in determining the future of free expression, democracy, and human rights around the world. Recognizing and resisting the effects of state censorship is essential for preserving freedom of thought and ensuring that the truth can still be heard.

Advertising and Consumerism: How Companies Shape Our Desires

Advertising is one of the most powerful tools companies use to shape our desires, influence our decisions, and control our behaviors. It's not just about promoting a product or service; it's about creating needs where none existed, shaping aspirations, and embedding certain lifestyles or values into our psyche. Over time, advertising has evolved from merely informing consumers to manipulating their desires on a subconscious level. In the modern age, the intersection of advertising and consumerism has become a fundamental driver of our economic systems and social values, making it an essential tool in shaping personal identity, social behavior, and even collective consciousness.

At its core, advertising is designed to persuade people to take action—usually, that action involves purchasing a product or service. But the way this persuasion occurs goes far beyond simply showing the features and benefits of a product. Advertisers tap into human psychology, emotions, and social dynamics to create a sense of need, urgency, or desire that often transcends the actual utility of the product. In many cases, what's being sold is not just the product but an idealized version of life or personal identity. Through carefully crafted messages, visuals, and emotional appeals, advertisers create associations between products and deeper human needs, such as love, success, status, or happiness.

One of the most effective ways advertising shapes our desires is by linking products to emotional needs. For example, an advertisement for a luxury car doesn't just highlight the car's technical specifications or fuel efficiency. Instead, it portrays the car as a symbol of success, prestige, and achievement. The underlying message is that purchasing this car will elevate the consumer's social status and make them feel more powerful or respected. In this way, advertisers create an emotional connection between the consumer and the product, making the consumer feel that owning the car is not just a practical decision but a fulfillment of personal desires and aspirations.

Similarly, advertising often taps into our fears and insecurities to drive consumer behavior. Many beauty and personal care products, for instance, are marketed by exploiting consumers' anxieties about their appearance or self-worth. Advertisements for anti-aging creams, weight-loss supplements, or cosmetic surgeries often suggest that aging, gaining weight, or not looking a certain way is a problem that needs to be fixed. By framing these natural aspects of life as issues, advertisers create a sense of inadequacy in the consumer, who then feels compelled to purchase products to "correct" themselves. In this way, advertising plays on our vulnerabilities, shaping not just what we desire but how we feel about ourselves.

Another key tool of advertising is the creation of artificial scarcity or urgency. Limited-time offers, flash sales, and seasonal promotions all serve to create a sense of urgency in the consumer, encouraging impulsive buying behaviors. The fear of missing out (FOMO) is a psychological trigger that advertisers exploit to convince people that if they don't act quickly, they will lose the opportunity to obtain a desirable product or experience. This technique not only drives immediate sales but also reinforces a culture of instant gratification and consumerism, where people are conditioned to seek immediate pleasure rather than long-term satisfaction.

Advertising also plays a significant role in shaping social norms and collective values. By constantly bombarding the public with certain images, messages, and ideals, advertisers can influence what society deems desirable, acceptable, or fashionable. This is particularly evident in the way gender roles and beauty standards have been shaped by decades of advertising. For instance, the portrayal of women in many advertisements has historically reinforced narrow, unrealistic standards of beauty—thinness, youth, and flawless skin—leading to societal pressure for women to conform to these ideals. Similarly, advertisements aimed at men often emphasize strength, dominance, and material success, shaping cultural expectations of masculinity.

One of the most notable examples of how advertising shapes collective values is the commercialization of holidays and special occasions. Events like Christmas, Valentine's Day, and Mother's Day have been transformed from cultural or religious celebrations into major consumer-driven events. Advertisers have successfully embedded the idea that these occasions are incomplete without certain products—whether it's gifts, cards, or lavish meals. As a result, what were once personal or spiritual occasions have become significant drivers of consumer spending, reinforcing the idea that happiness and fulfillment come from material goods.

Consumerism, driven by advertising, has not only shaped individual desires but also created entire cultures of consumption. In many societies, particularly in Western nations, consumerism is deeply ingrained in the fabric of everyday life. People are often judged by what they own, the brands they wear, or the cars they drive. Advertisers play a critical role in perpetuating this culture by promoting the idea that personal identity and social status are tied to material possessions. Brands like Apple, Nike, and Louis Vuitton, for example, are not just selling products—they are selling a lifestyle and identity that consumers aspire to. Owning these brands becomes a symbol of personal achievement, creativity, or social belonging.

The relationship between advertising and consumerism is further intensified by the advent of digital media and targeted advertising. In the digital age, advertisers have unprecedented access to personal data, which allows them to target consumers with highly personalized ads based on their online behavior, search history, social media activity, and even location. This level of precision enables advertisers to shape desires and behaviors more effectively than ever before. For example, if someone searches for vacation destinations or luxury hotels, they may be bombarded with advertisements for travel packages, high-end resorts, or credit card offers tailored to affluent travelers. This creates a feedback loop where consumers are constantly exposed to ads that reflect and reinforce their existing desires and behaviors, pushing them further into the cycle of consumption.

Social media influencers have also become a key component of modern advertising strategies. These influencers, who have built large followings on platforms like Instagram, YouTube, and TikTok, often promote products and services to their audiences in a way that feels more authentic than traditional ads. By blending product promotion with personal content, influencers can make their followers feel as if they are receiving recommendations from a trusted friend rather than a corporation.

This level of trust makes influencer marketing highly effective, particularly among younger generations who are more skeptical of traditional advertising. However, it also blurs the line between genuine content and paid promotion, making it harder for consumers to recognize when they are being sold to.

Another aspect of modern advertising is its role in fostering planned obsolescence, a strategy where products are designed to have a limited lifespan or become outdated quickly, encouraging consumers to replace them frequently. This is particularly evident in industries like electronics and fashion, where new models or trends are introduced regularly to make older products seem obsolete. Advertisers play a crucial role in this process by promoting the latest models, technologies, or styles, creating a desire for constant upgrades and new purchases. This strategy drives continuous consumption and ensures that consumers remain locked in the cycle of buying new products, even when the ones they already own are still functional.

The environmental impact of consumerism, driven by advertising, is another critical issue. The constant push for more consumption has led to the depletion of natural resources, increased waste, and environmental degradation. Advertisers rarely highlight the environmental costs of their products, instead focusing on the immediate gratification or status that comes with ownership. However, the long-term effects of consumer-driven economies are becoming increasingly clear, with overconsumption contributing to climate change, deforestation, and the pollution of oceans and ecosystems.

In recent years, there has been growing awareness of the negative impact of consumerism, and some companies have responded by adopting more sustainable practices or promoting products with environmental benefits. However, even "green" advertising can be problematic, as it often involves "greenwashing," where companies exaggerate or misrepresent the environmental benefits of their products to appeal to eco-conscious consumers. In these cases, advertising still serves to drive consumption, albeit under the guise of sustainability.

Despite the pervasive influence of advertising, consumers are not entirely powerless. With increased access to information and greater awareness of the tactics used by advertisers, more people are beginning to question the consumerist mindset and seek alternatives to the constant cycle of buying and discarding. Movements like minimalism, slow fashion, and ethical consumerism encourage individuals to make more conscious choices about what they buy and why, prioritizing quality, sustainability, and personal values over trends or social status.

In conclusion, advertising plays a central role in shaping our desires, behaviors, and identities in the modern world. By tapping into emotional needs, fears, and social aspirations, advertisers are able to create demand for products that go far beyond their practical uses, embedding consumerism into the very fabric of society. As digital technology advances, the influence of advertising will only continue to grow, making it more important than ever for individuals to critically evaluate the messages they receive and make informed choices about what they consume. Understanding the psychological tactics used in advertising is the first step toward resisting manipulation and reclaiming control over our desires in a world driven by consumerism.

Brand Loyalty or Mind Control? The Psychology behind Marketing

Brand loyalty is often presented as a reflection of a company's ability to deliver consistent value, quality, and trustworthiness. Consumers, it is said, return to the same brands because they like the products and believe in what the company represents. But how much of this loyalty is truly based on rational choices? The truth is, brand loyalty is carefully cultivated using sophisticated psychological techniques designed to influence consumers' subconscious minds. Marketing strategies are not just about making people aware of products; they are about shaping desires, behaviors, and identities in ways that can resemble mind control. In this chapter, we will explore the psychology behind marketing and how brands create powerful, often irrational, loyalty in consumers.

At the heart of brand loyalty is the ability of marketers to forge emotional connections between the brand and the consumer. While consumers may believe that their purchasing decisions are based on logic—such as the price, quality, or features of a product—psychological research shows that emotions play a far more significant role in decision-making. Brands that tap into deep-seated emotions like love, pride, fear, or belonging can create loyalty that goes beyond rational thinking. In these cases, consumers aren't just buying a product; they are buying into an identity or a lifestyle that the brand represents.

One of the most common psychological techniques used in marketing is the creation of emotional resonance. This involves associating the brand with positive experiences, feelings, or aspirations. For example, Coca-Cola has long associated its brand with happiness, togetherness, and celebration. Its iconic advertisements often depict scenes of joyful moments—family gatherings, parties, or friends enjoying a summer day together, with a bottle of Coke at the center. The message is not just that Coke is a good-tasting beverage but that drinking Coke is tied to moments of joy and connection. Over time, these emotional associations become deeply embedded in the consumer's mind, creating a sense of loyalty to the brand that goes beyond the taste or price of the product.

Similarly, Apple has mastered the art of brand loyalty by positioning itself as a symbol of creativity, innovation, and individuality. Through its sleek designs, minimalist advertising, and iconic "Think Different" campaign, Apple has cultivated a sense of exclusivity and cultural cachet that appeals to consumers' desire to be seen as unique or forward-thinking. For many Apple users, owning an iPhone or MacBook is not just about the device's functionality—it's a statement about who they are. This emotional and psychological connection makes Apple users fiercely loyal, often willing to pay premium prices for new products, even when comparable alternatives exist at lower costs.

Another psychological principle that plays a significant role in brand loyalty is the concept of *cognitive dissonance*. This theory, developed by psychologist Leon Festinger, suggests that people experience discomfort when they hold two conflicting beliefs or attitudes. To resolve this discomfort, they will either change their behavior or justify their decisions to align with one belief or the other. Marketers use cognitive dissonance to their advantage by creating a situation where consumers feel the need to justify their continued loyalty to a brand, even in the face of contradictory evidence.

For example, if a loyal customer of a luxury car brand encounters negative reviews or hears about a major flaw in one of the brand's models, they may experience cognitive dissonance. Instead of switching to a different brand, the consumer might rationalize their continued loyalty by focusing on the brand's other positive attributes, such as its design or customer service. In this way, cognitive dissonance leads consumers to defend their loyalty to the brand, even when the product or service might not live up to expectations.

Social identity theory is another critical aspect of the psychology behind brand loyalty. According to this theory, people derive a significant portion of their identity from the groups they belong to, and this includes the brands they align with. When a consumer chooses a particular brand, they are not just making a purchase; they are affiliating themselves with the values, lifestyles, and even other consumers associated with that brand. This is why brands often focus on building communities around their products. For example, Harley-Davidson has created a community of devoted motorcycle enthusiasts who see their Harleys not just as a mode of transportation but as a symbol of freedom, rebellion, and brotherhood. These consumers are so loyal to the brand that they often get tattoos of the Harley-Davidson logo, further solidifying their identity as part of the Harley "family."

This sense of belonging and identity can be incredibly powerful in fostering brand loyalty. By making consumers feel like they are part of an exclusive group or community, brands can create a bond that is difficult to break. Consumers are not just loyal to the product; they are loyal to the lifestyle and the social connections that come with it. In many ways, this mirrors the dynamics of cults or tightly-knit social groups, where loyalty to the group is tied to the individual's sense of self and belonging.

Marketing also leverages *scarcity* and *exclusivity* to enhance brand loyalty. Scarcity, the perception that a product is rare or difficult to obtain, triggers a sense of urgency in consumers and increases the perceived value of the product. Brands like Supreme, which release limited quantities of their products in "drops," have mastered the use of scarcity to drive demand. Consumers rush to buy products not just because they want them but because they fear missing out. This fear of missing out (FOMO) is a powerful psychological trigger that drives impulsive purchases and reinforces loyalty. The consumer feels privileged to own something exclusive, which enhances their attachment to the brand.

Exclusivity works in a similar way, making consumers feel special or elite for choosing a particular brand. Luxury brands like Rolex, Gucci, and Louis Vuitton have built their entire identities around exclusivity, positioning their products as symbols of wealth, success, and status. By owning these brands, consumers signal to the world that they are part of an exclusive club. This exclusivity not only increases the desirability of the products but also fosters intense loyalty, as consumers want to maintain their status and continue being associated with these prestigious brands.

Rewards and loyalty programs are other tools used by companies to create a sense of commitment and dependence on a brand. Airlines, credit card companies, and retail chains offer loyalty programs that reward frequent customers with points, discounts, or perks. These programs tap into the psychological principle of *reciprocity,* the idea that people feel compelled to return a favor when they receive something.

When a customer receives rewards for their loyalty, they are more likely to feel a sense of obligation to continue supporting the brand. This is further reinforced by the *sunk cost fallacy,* where people are reluctant to abandon something they have invested time, money, or effort into, even if it no longer serves their best interests. Consumers who have accumulated rewards points or status in a loyalty program are less likely to switch to a competitor, even if the competitor offers a better deal.

The use of nostalgia is another psychological tool that brands leverage to foster loyalty. By evoking memories of the past, advertisers can create a strong emotional connection to a brand that transcends the product itself. For example, brands like Disney and Coca-Cola often tap into nostalgia by reminding consumers of their childhoods or previous happy experiences associated with the brand. These emotional connections can be powerful drivers of loyalty because they create a sense of continuity and comfort. Consumers feel that by purchasing these brands, they are reconnecting with cherished memories or reaffirming a part of their identity.

Digital marketing and social media have taken brand loyalty to new heights by allowing companies to engage with consumers on a more personal level. Through targeted ads, personalized content, and direct communication on social platforms, brands can create a sense of intimacy with their customers. Algorithms track users' online behavior and preferences, allowing brands to deliver highly personalized marketing messages that make consumers feel understood and valued. This sense of personalization creates a deeper connection between the consumer and the brand, reinforcing loyalty through the perception that the brand "knows" the customer on an individual level.

However, this hyper-personalized marketing also raises questions about the ethics of brand loyalty. When consumers are constantly bombarded with messages tailored specifically to their desires, fears, and behaviors, the line between persuasion and manipulation becomes blurred. Are consumers making informed, rational choices, or are they being subtly coerced into loyalty through psychological manipulation? When brands track our data, tailor their messages to our emotions, and use advanced behavioral science to keep us hooked, the concept of brand loyalty can start to feel more like mind control.

In conclusion, brand loyalty is not simply the result of rational decision-making; it is the product of carefully designed marketing strategies that tap into deep psychological principles. By creating emotional connections, fostering a sense of identity, leveraging scarcity and exclusivity, and using rewards and nostalgia, brands can cultivate loyalty that is deeply ingrained in consumers' minds. While this loyalty can benefit consumers by providing them with products and experiences they value, it can also raise ethical concerns about the extent to which marketers use psychological manipulation to drive consumer behavior. Understanding the psychology behind brand loyalty is essential for consumers to make more informed choices and resist the subtle forms of control that shape their preferences and decisions.

Indoctrination in Education: Shaping Minds from a Young Age

Education is one of the most powerful tools for shaping society, fostering knowledge, and developing critical thinking skills. However, when used as a means of indoctrination, it can become a subtle but effective way of controlling thought and behavior from a young age. Indoctrination in education refers to the process by which certain ideas, values, or ideologies are imposed upon students, often without room for questioning or critical analysis. This method of shaping minds can be intentional or unintentional, but its effects can last a lifetime, influencing how individuals see the world, understand their place in society, and engage with different viewpoints. In this chapter, we will explore how indoctrination occurs in educational systems, the techniques used to instill certain ideologies, and the long-term impact it can have on individuals and society.

Indoctrination in education often starts with the curriculum. What is taught in schools—and what is left out—can significantly shape a student's worldview. In many countries, governments or education authorities decide what is included in textbooks and lesson plans, which can be used to promote a particular version of history, politics, or social values. For example, in authoritarian regimes, school curricula are often designed to reinforce the legitimacy of the ruling party or government. By presenting a selective or distorted version of history, these regimes can cultivate loyalty and obedience among young people, who grow up believing that their government is just, strong, and indispensable.

In Nazi Germany, for instance, the education system was carefully controlled to indoctrinate young people into the ideologies of the regime. Textbooks were rewritten to glorify Adolf Hitler, promote Aryan racial superiority, and portray Jews as subhuman enemies. Subjects like history, biology, and geography were infused with Nazi ideology, teaching students that Germany was destined for greatness under Hitler's leadership and that the Jewish people and other minorities were to blame for the country's problems. The Hitler Youth, a paramilitary organization for young people, further reinforced this indoctrination by providing extracurricular activities that glorified militarism, obedience to authority, and loyalty to the Führer. By shaping young minds from an early age, the Nazi regime ensured that a generation of Germans would be loyal to the Nazi cause, even as the regime led the country to destruction.

Indoctrination in education does not always occur in such overt forms. In more subtle ways, many educational systems around the world impose particular values or worldviews on students without encouraging critical analysis or debate. Nationalism, for example, is often a central theme in school curricula. In some countries, students are taught to view their nation's history in a highly idealized way, focusing only on the positive achievements while downplaying or ignoring historical injustices, such as colonization, slavery, or war crimes. By presenting a one-sided version of history, these educational systems cultivate a sense of national pride and loyalty while discouraging students from questioning or critically examining their country's past.

This form of indoctrination can have long-lasting effects on how individuals perceive their role in the world. For example, students who are taught to view their country as always in the right may struggle to understand or empathize with other perspectives, leading to a narrow, insular worldview. They may also be less likely to question their government's policies, particularly in areas like foreign affairs or military interventions, because they have been conditioned to believe that their country's actions are always justified. In this way, educational indoctrination can stifle critical thinking and limit the ability of individuals to engage meaningfully with complex global issues.

Another area where indoctrination can occur in education is through the promotion of specific social, religious, or moral values. In some educational systems, particularly those influenced by religious institutions, students are taught to accept certain beliefs or practices as absolute truths, without room for questioning or alternative viewpoints. For example, in some religious schools, students may be taught that specific moral values—such as obedience to authority, adherence to traditional gender roles, or belief in a particular religious doctrine—are unquestionable. This form of indoctrination can have a profound impact on students' personal development, limiting their ability to explore different belief systems, challenge social norms, or develop independent moral reasoning.

The promotion of rigid gender roles is another common form of indoctrination in education. In many parts of the world, educational systems reinforce traditional gender norms by teaching boys and girls different expectations for behavior, achievement, and roles in society. Boys may be encouraged to pursue careers in science, technology, or leadership, while girls may be steered toward caregiving roles or less prestigious professions. This form of indoctrination can limit students' aspirations and reinforce societal inequalities, making it more difficult for young people to break out of prescribed gender roles as they grow older. By shaping children's understanding of what is "appropriate" for their gender, educational systems can perpetuate deeply ingrained social hierarchies and limit the potential for social progress.

A key aspect of indoctrination in education is the use of authority figures, such as teachers, to reinforce specific ideologies or beliefs. In many educational systems, teachers are seen as the ultimate authority in the classroom, and students are taught to accept what they are told without question. This dynamic can create an environment where students are discouraged from thinking critically or expressing dissenting views. In more extreme cases, teachers may be actively involved in promoting government propaganda or religious doctrine, shaping students' beliefs in ways that align with the dominant ideology. The power dynamic between teacher and student makes it difficult for young people to challenge or question what they are being taught, further entrenching the indoctrination process.

In addition to the curriculum and authority figures, school rituals and symbols can also play a role in indoctrination. National anthems, flag-raising ceremonies, and patriotic holidays are often part of the school experience in many countries, and while these rituals may seem harmless, they can reinforce a sense of loyalty to the state or nation that discourages critical engagement with national policies or history.

Similarly, in schools with a religious focus, daily prayers, religious symbols, and teachings can normalize certain beliefs or practices, making them seem like the only acceptable worldview. These rituals and symbols, repeated over time, can shape students' perceptions of what is "normal" or "correct," reinforcing the values or ideologies promoted by the educational system.

The media also plays a role in shaping education, especially in modern times when children are constantly exposed to information through television, the internet, and social media. In many cases, the media reinforces the narratives taught in schools, creating a broader environment of indoctrination. For example, in countries with tightly controlled media, the same version of history or politics taught in schools is often repeated in the news, entertainment, and cultural programs. This creates an echo chamber where students are exposed to the same ideas from multiple sources, making it more difficult for them to access alternative perspectives or develop critical thinking skills.

Even in more open societies, where media is not directly controlled by the state, the influence of corporate interests in education can contribute to subtle forms of indoctrination. For example, many educational materials, especially in science and technology fields, are sponsored or created by large corporations. These materials may present information in ways that align with the interests of the company, subtly promoting consumerism or corporate-friendly policies. In this way, corporate influence can shape students' understanding of the world in ways that serve specific economic interests rather than fostering independent thought.

While indoctrination in education can have powerful effects, it is important to recognize that not all education is inherently indoctrinative. A well-designed education system encourages critical thinking, open inquiry, and the exploration of multiple perspectives. Teachers and curricula that promote debate, discussion, and the questioning of assumptions can help students develop independent thought and resilience to indoctrination. For example, in systems that emphasize critical pedagogy, students are encouraged to question authority, examine power structures, and think critically about the world around them. This approach fosters a more open-minded and reflective form of education, allowing students to develop their own ideas and beliefs rather than simply adopting those imposed upon them.

In conclusion, indoctrination in education is a powerful tool for shaping minds from a young age. By controlling the curriculum, using authority figures to reinforce specific ideologies, and promoting rituals and symbols that encourage loyalty to the state, religion, or social norms, educational systems can influence how individuals see the world and their place within it. The effects of this indoctrination can last a lifetime, limiting critical thinking, stifling dissent, and reinforcing societal inequalities. However, education also has the potential to be a force for liberation, promoting independent thought, critical inquiry, and the exploration of diverse perspectives. Understanding how indoctrination occurs in education is the first step in recognizing and resisting its effects, ensuring that education serves as a tool for empowerment rather than control.

Religious Institutions: Mind Control through Doctrine and Faith

Religious institutions have been influential forces in human history, shaping cultures, values, and social structures. For billions of people, religion provides meaning, comfort, and moral guidance. However, it is undeniable that some religious institutions have also used their authority to exert control over the minds of their followers, often through the imposition of doctrine and faith. The power of religious institutions to guide and, in some cases, manipulate belief systems rests on their ability to tap into deeply personal, emotional, and existential aspects of human life. By controlling doctrine, dictating what is deemed sacred or sinful, and enforcing strict codes of behavior, some religious authorities have wielded a form of mind control over their followers. In this chapter, we will explore how religious institutions use doctrine and faith to shape thought, behavior, and social order, sometimes blurring the line between spiritual guidance and psychological manipulation.

The foundation of religious mind control lies in the authority of doctrine. Doctrines are the core beliefs and teachings of a religion, and they are often presented as divine truths that are beyond question. By defining what is true, sacred, and moral, religious institutions create a framework through which followers are expected to view the world. This framework can be deeply influential because it provides answers to some of life's most difficult questions: Why are we here? What is the purpose of life? What happens after death? These questions tap into existential fears and longings, and religious doctrines offer a sense of certainty and security in an otherwise uncertain world.

When religious doctrines are presented as absolute truths, they leave little room for doubt or alternative interpretations. Followers are taught that questioning or doubting the doctrine is not only wrong but potentially dangerous to their spiritual well-being. In many religions, doubt is framed as a form of moral weakness, a lack of faith, or even a sin. This discourages critical thinking and independent inquiry, as followers are conditioned to accept the teachings of the institution without questioning their validity. By framing doctrine as divinely inspired and infallible, religious institutions can control the thought processes of their followers, limiting their ability to explore other worldviews or ideas.

A prime example of this kind of control can be seen in the concept of religious orthodoxy. In many faiths, orthodoxy refers to the correct or accepted beliefs as defined by religious authorities. Followers are expected to adhere to these beliefs, and deviation from orthodoxy is often met with social, spiritual, or even physical consequences. In medieval Europe, the Catholic Church held immense power over the minds of its followers by enforcing strict adherence to its doctrine. Those who questioned the Church's teachings were labeled heretics, a designation that could lead to excommunication, persecution, or execution. The fear of being cast out of the religious community—and, by extension, the fear of eternal damnation—was a powerful tool for controlling the thoughts and behaviors of individuals.

One of the most effective ways religious institutions enforce doctrine is through the concept of faith. Faith, in the context of religion, is often defined as a deep trust or belief in something that cannot be proven or seen. It is presented as a virtue—something to aspire to and cultivate. By elevating faith to a central role in religious life, institutions encourage followers to accept beliefs and teachings without requiring empirical evidence or logical reasoning.

This acceptance of doctrine through faith can be a powerful form of psychological control, as it requires individuals to suspend their critical faculties and place their trust in religious authorities. Faith becomes a mechanism by which religious institutions can maintain control over their followers' minds, as any doubt or questioning is seen as a failure of the individual's spiritual commitment.

Religious institutions also use rituals, symbols, and traditions to reinforce doctrine and instill a sense of belonging and loyalty. Rituals—whether they are daily prayers, weekly services, or life-cycle events such as baptisms, weddings, and funerals—serve to reaffirm the teachings of the religion and create a shared experience among followers. These rituals often invoke powerful emotions, such as awe, reverence, or a sense of connection to the divine. By participating in these rituals, individuals internalize the teachings and values of the religion, further strengthening their commitment to the faith. The repetition of these rituals over time creates deep psychological associations between the act of worship and the religious doctrine, making it more difficult for individuals to question or abandon their beliefs.

Symbols play a crucial role in religious mind control as well. Religious symbols—such as the cross in Christianity, the crescent in Islam, or the lotus in Buddhism—carry deep emotional and spiritual significance. These symbols serve as constant reminders of the doctrines and teachings of the religion, and they reinforce the connection between the individual and the religious institution. The ubiquity of religious symbols in everyday life—from churches and mosques to clothing, jewelry, and art—creates an environment where the presence of religion is inescapable, making it difficult for individuals to distance themselves from the influence of their faith.

Religious institutions also exercise control through moral teachings and the concept of sin. Most religions provide a moral code by which followers are expected to live. These moral teachings often cover every aspect of life, from personal behavior and relationships to social and political matters. By defining what is right and wrong, sacred and sinful, religious institutions exert significant influence over the daily choices and actions of their followers. The fear of committing sin and the promise of eternal reward or punishment are powerful motivators that keep individuals in line with the teachings of the religion.

In many religions, the concept of sin is tied to feelings of guilt and shame, which can be used as psychological tools to enforce conformity. For example, in Christianity, the idea of original sin teaches that all humans are inherently sinful and in need of redemption. This doctrine instills a sense of unworthiness and guilt that can be exploited by religious authorities to maintain control. Followers are taught that they must seek forgiveness through the church or religious rituals to cleanse themselves of sin, creating a dependency on the institution for spiritual salvation. Similarly, in some Islamic teachings, the concept of *haram* (forbidden acts) is used to guide behavior, and the fear of sinning against God can create a sense of guilt that reinforces obedience to religious authority.

RELIGIOUS INSTITUTIONS often establish a clear hierarchy of authority that reinforces the idea that certain individuals—priests, imams, rabbis, or other religious leaders—have a special connection to the divine or are more spiritually enlightened than the average follower. This hierarchy reinforces the idea that followers must rely on these religious authorities for guidance, wisdom, and interpretation of doctrine. By placing themselves in a position of spiritual authority, religious leaders can exert significant influence over the beliefs and actions of their followers. In many cases, this hierarchy is used to suppress dissent and maintain control, as those who challenge religious authorities are seen as challenging the divine order itself.

One of the most troubling aspects of religious mind control is the use of fear to maintain obedience. Many religious doctrines emphasize the consequences of disobedience, including eternal punishment, excommunication, or spiritual abandonment. The fear of hell, damnation, or divine retribution can be a powerful psychological tool for keeping followers in line with religious teachings. This fear is often instilled from a young age, making it deeply ingrained in an individual's psyche. Religious institutions can use this fear to discourage questioning or rebellion, as followers are taught that doubting the faith or straying from the prescribed path will lead to dire spiritual consequences.

Cult-like religious groups often take mind control to extreme levels by isolating followers from the outside world and creating a closed, insular environment where dissent is not tolerated. In these groups, followers are often subjected to intense indoctrination, where they are bombarded with the group's teachings and cut off from alternative viewpoints. Cult leaders, who are often charismatic and manipulative, use psychological techniques such as love-bombing (excessive praise and attention) and gaslighting (manipulating followers into doubting their perceptions of reality) to control their followers. The sense of community and belonging within these groups can make it difficult for individuals to break free, even when they realize they are being manipulated.

Despite these concerns, it is important to recognize that not all religious institutions engage in mind control or manipulation. Many religions encourage critical thinking, questioning, and the exploration of faith. Religious traditions that emphasize personal spiritual development, ethical inquiry, and compassion for others can provide individuals with a strong sense of purpose and moral guidance without resorting to manipulation. In these cases, religion serves as a tool for personal growth and empowerment rather than control.

In conclusion, religious institutions have the potential to exert significant control over the minds of their followers through the use of doctrine, faith, rituals, and fear. By presenting their teachings as absolute truths and discouraging doubt or dissent, religious authorities can create a powerful form of psychological control that shapes how individuals think, feel, and behave. While religion can offer comfort, meaning, and community to many people, it is essential to recognize the ways in which it can also be used to manipulate and control. Understanding the techniques of religious mind control is crucial for individuals seeking to explore their faith freely and critically, ensuring that their beliefs are based on personal conviction rather than institutional pressure.

The Rise of Cults: Techniques Used to Enforce Belief

The rise of cults throughout history, particularly in the modern era, has fascinated and horrified observers alike. Cults are groups that often form around a charismatic leader or an ideology, employing highly manipulative techniques to control the thoughts, behaviors, and emotions of their members. What sets cults apart from traditional religious or social groups is their extreme level of control over followers and the psychological methods used to enforce absolute loyalty and belief. These techniques are often so powerful that individuals who join cults may abandon their previous lives, relationships, and even their sense of self in service to the group. In this chapter, we will explore the techniques used by cults to enforce belief, maintain control, and prevent members from leaving, shedding light on how these groups manipulate the human mind to create intense and often dangerous devotion.

One of the most fundamental techniques used by cults is the manipulation of a follower's sense of identity. Many people who join cults are seeking meaning, purpose, or a sense of belonging, often during times of personal crisis or vulnerability. Cult leaders capitalize on these emotional needs by presenting the group as a source of comfort, direction, and answers to life's big questions. By offering an identity that feels secure and purposeful, cults create an emotional bond with new members, gradually replacing their previous sense of self with the identity provided by the group. Over time, members come to see themselves primarily through the lens of the cult, losing their independence and adopting the group's worldview as their own.

At the heart of cult recruitment and indoctrination is the concept of *love-bombing*. This technique involves showering new recruits with attention, affection, and praise, making them feel valued and accepted in a way they may not have experienced before. Love-bombing creates an immediate emotional bond between the recruit and the cult, making them feel as though they have found a community that truly cares for them. This overwhelming display of affection serves to lower the recruit's defenses, making them more open to the group's teachings and less likely to critically assess the group's intentions or practices. Love-bombing is particularly effective because it creates a sense of euphoria and belonging, which can be difficult to resist or walk away from.

Another common technique used by cults to enforce belief is *isolation*. Once a new member is drawn into the group, they are often encouraged to cut ties with family, friends, and anyone who might challenge the cult's influence. This isolation serves two main purposes: first, it prevents the new member from being exposed to alternative perspectives or information that might contradict the cult's teachings. Second, it makes the member more dependent on the group for emotional and social support. In extreme cases, cults may relocate members to remote locations, cut off communication with the outside world, or create schedules that keep members constantly occupied with group activities. This isolation is a key factor in maintaining control over the member's thoughts and behaviors, as it limits their ability to critically evaluate the group or seek help from outside sources.

Cults also use *thought reform* or *brainwashing* techniques to control their followers' beliefs. Thought reform is a systematic process of breaking down a person's sense of reality and replacing it with the cult's ideology. This is often done through intense indoctrination sessions, where members are bombarded with the group's teachings and discouraged from questioning or doubting what they are told. Repetition is a key element of thought reform, as cults frequently use repetitive chanting, mantras, or lectures to reinforce their beliefs. Over time, this repetition dulls the member's ability to think critically, as their minds become conditioned to accept the group's teachings without question.

Confession and guilt are also powerful tools used by cults to enforce conformity. Many cults require members to regularly confess their perceived wrongdoings or failures, often in front of the entire group. This public confession creates a sense of vulnerability and dependence, as members are made to feel that they are constantly falling short of the group's expectations. The cult then presents itself as the only path to redemption or improvement, reinforcing the member's dependence on the group for guidance and salvation. This cycle of guilt and confession keeps members trapped in a loop of obedience, as they are continually seeking approval from the group and its leader.

Fear and intimidation are frequently used to maintain control over members and enforce loyalty. In many cults, members are taught to fear the outside world and anyone who might try to take them away from the group. The cult may frame the outside world as corrupt, evil, or filled with dangers that only the group can protect them from. This fear creates an "us versus them" mentality, where the cult is seen as the only safe haven in a hostile world. Cult leaders may also use fear of spiritual consequences, such as damnation or punishment in the afterlife, to keep members in line. In more extreme cases, physical intimidation or threats of violence are used to prevent members from leaving or questioning the leader's authority.

One of the most insidious techniques used by cults is *gaslighting*. Gaslighting is a psychological manipulation tactic where the leader or group makes the individual doubt their own perceptions, memories, or judgment. By constantly questioning or contradicting a member's version of reality, the cult leader can make the person feel confused, disoriented, and dependent on the group for a sense of stability. Gaslighting undermines the individual's ability to trust themselves, making them more likely to accept the cult's version of events, even if it contradicts their own experiences. This manipulation of reality is a powerful way to control thought, as it breaks down the individual's confidence in their own ability to discern truth from falsehood.

Cults also employ charismatic leaders who wield significant psychological influence over their followers. These leaders are often charming, persuasive, and appear to possess special knowledge or spiritual insight. They present themselves as messianic figures who offer the only path to salvation, enlightenment, or truth. The leader's charisma, combined with their ability to manipulate emotions and present an aura of authority, creates a deep sense of loyalty among followers. Members come to view the leader as infallible, and any criticism of the leader is seen as an attack on the group itself. This dynamic creates a hierarchy where the leader's words and actions are beyond question, further cementing their control over the group.

Information control is another critical component of cult mind control. Cult leaders often restrict access to information that might contradict the group's teachings or challenge the leader's authority. Members are discouraged from reading books, watching television, or consuming media that might present alternative viewpoints. In some cases, cults go as far as to censor or rewrite religious texts, historical accounts, or scientific facts to fit their own narrative. By controlling what information members can access, cults create an environment where the group's ideology becomes the only source of truth, making it difficult for members to break free from the group's influence.

Cults also use the concept of rewards and punishments to enforce belief and behavior. Members who are obedient and show loyalty to the group are often rewarded with praise, special privileges, or increased status within the group. Conversely, those who question the leader or fail to conform to the group's expectations may be punished with humiliation, isolation, or expulsion. These rewards and punishments create a powerful incentive for members to remain loyal and obedient, as they seek the approval of the leader and fear the consequences of disobedience.

The *sunk cost fallacy* also plays a significant role in keeping members trapped in cults. Once a person has invested significant time, energy, and emotional commitment to the group, it becomes difficult to walk away, even if they begin to see signs of manipulation or abuse. The fear of losing everything they have invested—their relationships within the group, their identity, or even their sense of purpose—makes it harder for members to leave, even when they recognize that the group is harmful. This psychological phenomenon helps explain why people often remain in cults long after they have begun to question the group's practices.

Finally, cults often create a sense of *apocalyptic urgency*, convincing members that the end of the world is near, and only the group can provide salvation. This tactic creates a sense of immediate, existential threat, making it difficult for members to think rationally or question the group's authority. Apocalyptic rhetoric heightens fear and dependence on the leader, as members are told that only by following the leader's guidance can they survive the impending catastrophe. This sense of urgency reinforces obedience and discourages members from leaving, as they are made to feel that their lives—and their souls—are at stake.

In conclusion, cults use a variety of sophisticated psychological techniques to enforce belief, maintain control, and manipulate their members. Through methods such as love-bombing, isolation, thought reform, fear, gaslighting, and information control, cult leaders can create an environment where followers become deeply dependent on the group and are unable to see the manipulation they are subjected to. While these techniques may vary from cult to cult, the underlying goal is the same: to control the minds of followers and maintain the power of the leader. Understanding how these techniques work is essential for recognizing the signs of cult manipulation and protecting individuals from falling into the trap of dangerous, controlling groups.

The Science of Fear: How Anxiety Is Used to Control Populations

Fear is one of the most powerful and primal emotions, deeply rooted in human survival mechanisms. It can override rational thought, influencing behavior in ways that serve to protect individuals from perceived threats. However, fear can also be manipulated by those in power to control large populations, suppress dissent, and manipulate public opinion. Throughout history, leaders, governments, and institutions have used fear to enforce obedience, justify oppressive policies, and maintain control over their citizens. In this chapter, we will explore the science of fear and examine how anxiety is strategically used to control populations, drawing on psychological, sociological, and historical perspectives.

At its core, fear is a biological response designed to keep us safe from danger. When confronted with a threat, the brain's amygdala activates the "fight-or-flight" response, releasing adrenaline and other stress hormones that prepare the body to either confront the threat or escape from it. This heightened state of arousal can cause people to act quickly and instinctively, often bypassing rational thought in favor of immediate action. While this response is beneficial in situations of real danger, it can also be exploited when fear is deliberately instilled by external forces—particularly by political or religious leaders seeking to maintain power.

Fear has long been recognized as an effective tool for controlling populations, and its manipulation can be seen across various historical contexts. One of the most notorious examples of fear-based control is found in totalitarian regimes, such as those led by Adolf Hitler, Joseph Stalin, and Mao Zedong. These dictators used fear of external and internal enemies to justify extreme policies, ranging from mass surveillance to purges, imprisonment, and genocide. By convincing their populations that they were under constant threat—whether from ethnic minorities, political dissidents, or foreign powers—these leaders were able to suppress opposition and consolidate their power. Fear was not only used to control behavior but also to mold public perception, creating an "us versus them" mentality that justified violence and repression.

One of the key reasons fear is such an effective tool of control is its ability to impair critical thinking. When people are afraid, their cognitive resources are focused on immediate survival rather than long-term analysis or rational decision-making. This makes individuals more susceptible to suggestion and less likely to question authority. Fear-based messaging can amplify this effect, as leaders or institutions repeatedly stress the dangers of a particular threat—whether real or imagined—until the population internalizes the belief that their safety depends on following the directives of those in power.

This manipulation of fear can be seen in modern political contexts as well. In the wake of the 9/11 attacks, for example, fear of terrorism was used by the U.S. government to justify a range of policies, including the Patriot Act, which expanded government surveillance powers, and the wars in Afghanistan and Iraq. The constant repetition of messages about the imminent threat of terrorism created a climate of fear, in which the public was willing to accept the erosion of civil liberties and the escalation of military interventions as necessary measures for their protection. The fear of terrorism not only shaped public opinion but also influenced voting patterns, political rhetoric, and the implementation of long-lasting policies that continue to affect society today.

The use of fear as a control mechanism is not limited to political regimes or warfare; it also plays a significant role in economic and social contexts. In consumer culture, fear is often exploited to drive purchasing behavior. Advertisers and marketers frequently use fear-based appeals to sell products, particularly in industries like insurance, pharmaceuticals, and security. For example, advertisements for home security systems often play on fears of burglary, while pharmaceutical ads may emphasize the risks of untreated medical conditions to encourage the purchase of medications. By invoking anxiety about potential dangers, companies can create a sense of urgency that pushes consumers to act.

Fear of social exclusion is another powerful form of anxiety that can be manipulated to control populations. Humans are social beings, and the desire to belong is a fundamental psychological need. Many social structures, including religious organizations, political parties, and even online communities, use the fear of exclusion or ostracism to enforce conformity. This can be seen in cases where dissenting views are punished by social rejection, shaming, or expulsion from a group. For example, in high-control religious groups or cults, members may be threatened with excommunication or isolation if they fail to adhere to the group's beliefs or practices. The fear of losing social support or community can be so overwhelming that individuals will suppress their doubts or critical thoughts, choosing obedience over the risk of isolation.

The media plays a crucial role in amplifying fear and anxiety on a societal level. Sensationalist news coverage often focuses disproportionately on negative or frightening events, such as crime, terrorism, pandemics, or economic crises. This "if it bleeds, it leads" approach to news reporting increases viewership but also contributes to heightened levels of public fear and anxiety. In the digital age, the constant barrage of alarming news, social media posts, and viral stories can create an atmosphere of perpetual crisis, making people feel as though danger is always imminent. This constant exposure to fear-based content can have a profound psychological impact, leading to chronic stress, anxiety, and a heightened sense of vulnerability.

A clear example of media-driven fear can be seen in the coverage of pandemics, such as the COVID-19 outbreak. During the height of the pandemic, media outlets frequently emphasized worst-case scenarios, death tolls, and the failures of healthcare systems. While accurate reporting on a public health crisis is necessary, the relentless focus on fear-inducing content can lead to panic and irrational behavior. For instance, the initial stages of the pandemic saw widespread hoarding of supplies like toilet paper, masks, and hand sanitizers, driven largely by fear of shortages rather than any actual scarcity. This panic buying was a direct result of the anxiety stoked by media coverage, which amplified fear and encouraged people to act out of self-preservation, often at the expense of rationality.

Governments also use fear to control populations through the threat of punishment or coercion. In authoritarian states, fear of arrest, imprisonment, or violence is often used to suppress dissent and maintain order. The secret police, surveillance programs, and harsh legal penalties create an environment where citizens are constantly aware that any action or statement could lead to severe consequences. Even in democratic societies, governments may use fear-based tactics to justify expanded policing, surveillance, or military intervention. The framing of certain groups—immigrants, minorities, or political opponents—as threats to national security or social order allows those in power to implement repressive measures without significant opposition.

Social fear can also be instilled through the manipulation of societal norms and expectations. Fear of deviating from social norms—whether related to race, class, gender, or sexual orientation—can be used to enforce conformity and marginalize those who do not fit into accepted categories. For example, fear of being labeled "unpatriotic" or "disloyal" can be used to suppress political dissent, while fear of social stigma can discourage people from expressing their true identities or beliefs. This form of fear is particularly effective because it is often internalized, making individuals police their own behavior to avoid the risk of social judgment or exclusion.

In psychological terms, fear can be understood through the framework of *classical conditioning*. This occurs when a neutral stimulus is repeatedly paired with a fear-inducing event, eventually causing the individual to associate the neutral stimulus with fear. In a political context, this can happen when certain symbols, words, or groups are consistently portrayed as dangerous or threatening. Over time, people begin to associate these symbols with fear, even in the absence of a direct threat. For example, during the Cold War, the constant portrayal of communism as an existential threat led many Americans to develop an automatic fear response to anything associated with communism, regardless of the actual context.

In addition to classical conditioning, *operant conditioning* also plays a role in how fear is used to control populations. In this psychological model, behaviors are shaped by rewards and punishments. When governments or institutions reward behaviors that align with their interests (such as obedience or compliance) and punish behaviors that challenge their authority (such as protest or dissent), they reinforce fear-based obedience. Over time, individuals learn that dissent carries a high risk, while compliance leads to safety or reward. This system of rewards and punishments serves to maintain control over the population by making the costs of rebellion seem too high to bear.

Fear can also be manipulated through *social learning theory*, which suggests that people learn behaviors by observing others. When people see that dissenters are punished or ostracized, they are less likely to challenge authority themselves. Similarly, when they see that those who comply with power structures are rewarded, they are more likely to follow suit. This observational learning is a subtle but effective way to enforce fear-based control, as individuals internalize the consequences of fear without needing to experience them directly.

Despite the effectiveness of fear as a tool for control, it is not without limits. Prolonged exposure to fear can lead to *fear fatigue*, where individuals become desensitized or apathetic in the face of constant threats. This can be seen in situations where governments or institutions overuse fear-based messaging, causing people to disengage rather than remain obedient. Additionally, fear can backfire if individuals begin to recognize that it is being used manipulatively. In some cases, awareness of fear-based control can lead to resistance, rebellion, or the formation of alternative movements that challenge the power structure.

In conclusion, fear is a potent and versatile tool for controlling populations, whether through political regimes, economic systems, social norms, or media narratives. By manipulating anxiety, those in power can influence behavior, suppress dissent, and justify repressive policies. Understanding the science of fear and how it is used to control populations is essential for recognizing when fear is being exploited for manipulation. By identifying fear-based tactics and their psychological effects, individuals and societies can resist manipulation and reclaim their autonomy, ensuring that fear does not become a means of control but a natural response to genuine threats.

Mind Control through Surveillance: The Power of Watching

Surveillance has always been a tool of power, used to monitor, control, and influence populations. With the rise of digital technology, the capacity for widespread, continuous surveillance has expanded dramatically, allowing governments, corporations, and other entities to watch individuals more closely than ever before. This constant observation not only tracks people's actions but also shapes their behavior, often without them realizing it. The mere awareness that one is being watched can lead to self-censorship, obedience, and conformity, making surveillance a powerful tool of mind control. In this chapter, we will explore the psychological effects of surveillance, how it is used to influence behavior, and its role as a modern tool of mind control.

The psychological impact of surveillance can be understood through a concept known as the *Panopticon*, a prison design proposed by the philosopher Jeremy Bentham in the late 18th century. The Panopticon was a circular prison with a central tower from which guards could observe every inmate. Crucially, the prisoners could not see the guards and were never sure if they were being watched at any given moment. The result was that prisoners began to regulate their own behavior as if they were constantly under surveillance. This idea of self-regulation under the threat of being watched is central to how surveillance works as a tool of control.

Modern surveillance operates on a similar principle. Whether through cameras in public spaces, online tracking, or government monitoring, people today live with the awareness that their actions may be observed, recorded, and analyzed. This creates a psychological pressure that influences behavior in profound ways. When people believe they are being watched, they are more likely to conform to social norms, obey laws, and avoid behaviors that could be considered rebellious or controversial. The feeling of being constantly monitored makes individuals less willing to engage in actions that might draw negative attention or repercussions, even if those actions are not inherently wrong or harmful.

Surveillance operates not only in the physical world but also in the digital realm. With the proliferation of smartphones, social media, and the internet, the digital footprints of individuals have become a rich source of data for surveillance. Governments, corporations, and other organizations can track online activities, location data, search histories, and even private communications. This type of surveillance, often justified under the guise of national security, consumer convenience, or targeted advertising, provides a window into people's habits, preferences, and behaviors, allowing those in power to predict, influence, and control actions in subtle ways.

One of the most insidious effects of surveillance is *self-censorship*. When individuals know they are being watched, they are less likely to express controversial or dissenting opinions, both online and in person. This can have a chilling effect on free speech and democratic participation, as people become fearful of voicing criticism of the government, corporations, or social norms. Even in societies where free speech is legally protected, the pervasive presence of surveillance can lead to a culture of self-silencing, where individuals avoid topics that might be seen as controversial or dangerous. Over time, this self-censorship weakens public discourse, as only the most mainstream or approved viewpoints are shared openly.

The use of surveillance as a tool of control can be seen in various political contexts, particularly in authoritarian regimes. For example, China's extensive surveillance network, which includes millions of cameras equipped with facial recognition technology, is used to monitor the movements and behaviors of its citizens. This surveillance infrastructure is a key component of China's Social Credit System, a program that tracks individuals' behaviors—such as paying bills on time, adhering to traffic laws, or posting politically acceptable content online—and assigns scores based on their perceived trustworthiness. Those with high scores are rewarded with privileges, while those with low scores face penalties, such as travel restrictions or limited access to social services. The awareness of constant surveillance and the potential consequences for non-compliance creates a powerful incentive for people to regulate their own behavior according to the government's standards.

Surveillance is also used to control political dissent. In many countries, activists, journalists, and opposition figures are closely monitored by the state. In some cases, their phones are tapped, emails intercepted, and movements tracked to prevent the organization of protests or political resistance. This type of surveillance goes beyond mere observation; it serves as a preemptive tool to suppress opposition and maintain the status quo. Knowing that they are under surveillance, potential dissidents are less likely to take action, fearing retaliation or arrest. This creates a climate of fear that discourages political participation and undermines democratic processes.

Even in democracies, where surveillance is often framed as a necessary tool for national security, it can have a profound impact on civil liberties. The post-9/11 era saw a significant expansion of government surveillance programs, particularly in the United States and Europe, where intelligence agencies were granted broad powers to monitor communications and track individuals in the name of preventing terrorism. Programs like the U.S. National Security Agency's (NSA) mass data collection efforts, revealed by whistleblower Edward Snowden, showed the extent to which governments were using digital surveillance to track not only potential terrorists but also ordinary citizens. While justified as a means of protecting national security, these surveillance programs raised concerns about privacy, civil liberties, and the potential for abuse.

In the digital age, corporate surveillance has become just as pervasive as government monitoring. Social media platforms, search engines, and tech companies collect vast amounts of data on their users, often without their explicit knowledge or consent. This data is used to create detailed profiles of individuals, which are then sold to advertisers or used to manipulate consumer behavior. Companies like Facebook, Google, and Amazon track everything from users' online shopping habits to their political views, search histories, and social connections. This information is used to serve personalized ads, recommend content, and, in some cases, influence voting behavior or public opinion.

Corporate surveillance is particularly concerning because it operates in the background of everyday life. Most people are unaware of the extent to which they are being tracked and how their data is being used. The algorithms that determine which ads users see, which news stories are promoted, and which products are recommended are often opaque, making it difficult for individuals to understand how their behavior is being shaped by the information they are exposed to. This creates a form of invisible manipulation, where companies use surveillance data to subtly nudge individuals toward certain behaviors, purchases, or beliefs without their conscious awareness.

The psychological impact of being under constant surveillance can lead to what is known as the *observer effect*. This effect occurs when individuals alter their behavior because they know they are being observed. While the observer effect can be beneficial in some contexts—such as promoting law-abiding behavior—it can also lead to increased anxiety, stress, and paranoia. People who feel they are constantly being watched may become hyper-vigilant, second-guessing their actions or avoiding certain behaviors out of fear of negative consequences. Over time, this can lead to a diminished sense of personal freedom, as individuals feel less in control of their own lives and more constrained by the expectations of those observing them.

In addition to shaping behavior, surveillance can also be used to influence thoughts and beliefs. The knowledge that one's online activity is being monitored, for example, can lead people to avoid searching for information on controversial topics or to censor their social media posts. This creates a feedback loop in which only certain viewpoints are expressed, while others are suppressed or avoided altogether. Over time, this can lead to a homogenization of thought, where individuals are less likely to encounter diverse perspectives and more likely to adopt the dominant narrative. In this way, surveillance not only controls behavior but also shapes the intellectual landscape of society.

Surveillance is not always about directly controlling individuals; it also serves as a tool for gathering data on populations to predict and influence future behavior. Through the use of predictive analytics and artificial intelligence, governments and corporations can analyze vast amounts of data to identify patterns, trends, and potential threats. This allows them to anticipate and prevent dissent, rebellion, or crime before it occurs—a concept often referred to as *pre-crime*. While predictive surveillance can have benefits, such as improving public safety or preventing terrorism, it also raises serious ethical concerns about privacy, autonomy, and the potential for abuse.

In some cases, surveillance can be used to enforce social control through *social surveillance*, where individuals monitor each other's behavior. This can be seen in authoritarian regimes that encourage citizens to report suspicious activity or dissenting behavior among their neighbors, colleagues, or family members. In this environment, the fear of being reported creates a sense of paranoia, where individuals are constantly aware that they could be under scrutiny from those around them. This type of surveillance not only isolates individuals but also fosters distrust within communities, making it more difficult for people to organize or resist.

Despite the pervasive nature of surveillance in modern society, it is important to recognize that surveillance is not always negative. When used responsibly and with proper oversight, surveillance can enhance public safety, prevent crime, and improve governance. For example, body cameras worn by police officers can provide transparency and accountability in law enforcement, while security cameras in public spaces can deter criminal activity. However, the key issue is ensuring that surveillance is used in a way that respects civil liberties and does not become a tool for unchecked control or manipulation.

In conclusion, surveillance has become a powerful tool of mind control in the modern age, shaping behavior, thoughts, and beliefs through the constant awareness of being watched. Whether through government monitoring, corporate data collection, or social surveillance, the knowledge that our actions are being observed can lead to self-censorship, obedience, and conformity. The psychological effects of surveillance, combined with the power of predictive analytics and data-driven manipulation, create an environment where individuals are increasingly controlled by unseen forces. As surveillance technology continues to evolve, it is crucial for societies to critically examine how it is used and to safeguard against its potential for abuse, ensuring that privacy, autonomy, and freedom remain protected in the face of constant observation.

Information Warfare: The Role of Technology in Manipulating Beliefs

Information warfare, in its modern form, represents one of the most pervasive and powerful ways to manipulate beliefs, shape public opinion, and influence entire populations. Through the use of technology, governments, corporations, and political actors have gained unprecedented access to the minds of individuals, allowing them to wage psychological battles on a global scale. Whether through social media, search engines, digital platforms, or targeted disinformation campaigns, technology has become the battlefield where control of narratives, beliefs, and worldviews is contested. In this chapter, we will explore the role of technology in information warfare, the techniques used to manipulate beliefs, and the consequences of living in a world where information is both weaponized and distorted.

At its core, information warfare involves the use of data, media, and communication tools to influence, deceive, or disrupt the beliefs of individuals or groups. This can be done for political, economic, or ideological purposes and is often aimed at sowing discord, undermining trust, or altering the course of public discourse. In the past, information warfare took the form of propaganda disseminated through newspapers, radio, and television. Today, however, the rise of the internet and digital technology has transformed the nature of these campaigns, making them more targeted, far-reaching, and difficult to detect.

One of the most effective tools in modern information warfare is *social media*. Platforms like Facebook, Twitter, Instagram, and YouTube have created vast networks where people can share news, opinions, and content instantaneously. While these platforms provide opportunities for open communication, they are also highly vulnerable to manipulation. The algorithms that govern social media prioritize content that generates high engagement, such as sensationalist headlines, emotional content, or provocative opinions. This makes these platforms fertile ground for disinformation, as manipulative actors can craft misleading or false information that spreads rapidly through networks, creating echo chambers where people are exposed only to content that aligns with their existing beliefs.

Disinformation, or the deliberate spreading of false information, is a key weapon in information warfare. Disinformation campaigns are designed to confuse, mislead, or divide the public by spreading falsehoods that appear credible or appealing. These campaigns can be orchestrated by state actors, political organizations, or even independent groups seeking to cause chaos or advance specific agendas. For example, during the 2016 U.S. presidential election, Russian operatives used social media platforms to spread disinformation aimed at influencing voter behavior and sowing division among Americans. Fake news stories, memes, and inflammatory posts were shared across platforms, targeting specific demographics with messages designed to amplify racial, political, and cultural tensions.

The power of disinformation lies not only in the content itself but in the way it is disseminated. Social media platforms use algorithms to prioritize content based on user preferences, which means that disinformation campaigns can be tailored to specific individuals or groups. By analyzing data such as browsing history, social connections, and online behavior, disinformation actors can create highly targeted messages that exploit the fears, biases, or desires of their audience. This level of precision allows disinformation to bypass traditional gatekeepers of information—such as journalists, editors, or fact-checkers—and reach people directly, making it more difficult to combat or debunk.

One of the most troubling aspects of information warfare is the creation of *echo chambers*, where individuals are exposed only to information that reinforces their preexisting beliefs. Social media algorithms are designed to show users content that they are most likely to engage with, based on their past behavior. This creates a feedback loop where people are continuously fed content that aligns with their views, while opposing perspectives are filtered out. Over time, this leads to the formation of ideological bubbles, where individuals become more entrenched in their beliefs and less likely to engage with different viewpoints.

Echo chambers are particularly dangerous in the context of political and social polarization. When people are exposed only to information that confirms their biases, they become more radicalized in their views, less tolerant of opposing opinions, and more likely to distrust information that challenges their worldview. This polarization can weaken democratic institutions, as it becomes increasingly difficult to find common ground or engage in constructive dialogue. Moreover, echo chambers create an environment where disinformation can thrive, as individuals are less likely to question the credibility of information that aligns with their beliefs.

Deepfakes and other forms of manipulated media represent another alarming development in the realm of information warfare. Deepfakes are videos or audio recordings that use artificial intelligence to create realistic but fake representations of people, often making it appear as though they said or did something they never did. These technologies are becoming increasingly sophisticated, making it difficult for even trained observers to distinguish between real and fake content. Deepfakes can be used to discredit public figures, spread false information, or incite violence. For example, a deepfake video showing a political leader making inflammatory statements could be used to spark unrest or disrupt an election, undermining trust in democratic processes.

The use of *bots* and *troll farms* further amplifies the power of information warfare. Bots are automated accounts that can generate content, share posts, and engage with users on social media. Troll farms, often state-sponsored, employ large numbers of individuals to create and spread content that aligns with specific political or ideological goals. These tools allow disinformation actors to flood social media platforms with content, creating the illusion of widespread support for certain viewpoints or ideas. This tactic, known as *astroturfing*, makes it appear as though there is grassroots support for a cause when, in reality, it is being manufactured by a small group of actors. This can shift public perception and make fringe ideas seem more mainstream than they actually are.

Psychographic profiling is another powerful tool in information warfare, allowing actors to tailor disinformation campaigns to specific psychological characteristics of individuals or groups. By analyzing vast amounts of data collected from online activity, marketers and political operatives can create detailed profiles of individuals, including their personality traits, values, fears, and aspirations. This data is then used to craft highly personalized messages designed to resonate with the target's psychological profile. The Cambridge Analytica scandal, in which the data of millions of Facebook users was harvested without their consent, highlighted the dangers of psychographic profiling in political campaigns. By using this data, actors can create content that triggers emotional responses, manipulates opinions, and influences behavior on a subconscious level.

In addition to the direct manipulation of information, *censorship* and *information control* are key components of information warfare, particularly in authoritarian regimes. Governments may block access to certain websites, restrict social media usage, or control the flow of news and information within their borders. China's Great Firewall, for example, restricts access to foreign websites and tightly controls what information can be shared online. In these environments, state-sponsored media becomes the primary source of information, and dissenting voices are silenced through censorship or punishment. By controlling what information people can access, these regimes can manipulate public opinion and maintain power by ensuring that only their narrative is heard.

Even in democratic countries, *media consolidation* can lead to a form of information control. When a small number of corporations own the majority of media outlets, they have significant power to shape public discourse and determine which stories are covered and how they are framed. This can lead to a narrowing of perspectives, where only certain viewpoints are given airtime while others are marginalized or ignored. In these cases, the diversity of information available to the public is diminished, making it easier for powerful actors to influence beliefs and opinions.

The *weaponization of conspiracy theories* is another tool used in information warfare. Conspiracy theories often tap into deep-seated fears, anxieties, and distrust of authority, making them highly effective at spreading disinformation and creating division. By promoting conspiracy theories, disinformation actors can destabilize trust in institutions, sow confusion, and undermine social cohesion. For example, the QAnon conspiracy, which falsely claims that a secret cabal of powerful elites is engaged in child trafficking and other crimes, has gained significant traction in the U.S. and elsewhere. By framing opponents as part of a vast, nefarious conspiracy, QAnon has radicalized individuals, encouraged political violence, and eroded trust in democratic institutions.

The consequences of information warfare are far-reaching. At the individual level, constant exposure to disinformation, fake news, and manipulative content can lead to confusion, anxiety, and a loss of trust in reliable sources of information. People may begin to question the credibility of all media, becoming more susceptible to conspiracy theories or alternative narratives that fit their emotional needs. At the societal level, information warfare can weaken democratic institutions, increase polarization, and undermine the rule of law. When large segments of the population are operating with different sets of "facts," it becomes increasingly difficult to engage in meaningful dialogue or reach consensus on important issues.

One of the most troubling consequences of information warfare is the erosion of *trust in truth itself*. As people become inundated with conflicting information and exposed to manipulative content, they may lose faith in the ability to discern objective truth. This creates an environment where disinformation flourishes, as people become more cynical and disengaged from traditional sources of knowledge. When truth becomes a matter of opinion or belief rather than fact, societies risk descending into chaos, where lies, rumors, and conspiracy theories hold as much weight as verified information.

In conclusion, technology has transformed the nature of information warfare, making it easier to manipulate beliefs, spread disinformation, and control public opinion on a global scale. Through social media, targeted disinformation campaigns, deepfakes, and psychographic profiling, powerful actors can wage psychological battles that shape how people think, feel, and behave. The rise of echo chambers, the weaponization of conspiracy theories, and the erosion of trust in truth all contribute to an environment where beliefs are easily manipulated. In this digital age, understanding the mechanisms of information warfare is critical for protecting individuals and societies from manipulation, ensuring that the flow of information remains free, diverse, and grounded in truth.

The Internet as a Tool for Manipulation and Control

The internet, often heralded as a tool for democratizing information and empowering individuals, has paradoxically become one of the most effective instruments for manipulation and control. While the internet provides unparalleled access to knowledge, communication, and opportunities for self-expression, it also serves as a powerful platform for governments, corporations, and bad actors to influence behavior, shape beliefs, and track every aspect of people's lives. This chapter will explore how the internet is used as a tool for manipulation and control, from subtle data collection practices to overt forms of censorship and social engineering, and examine the profound impact this has on individuals and societies.

One of the primary ways the internet is used for manipulation is through *data collection* and *surveillance*. Every time a person interacts with the internet—whether by browsing websites, engaging on social media, or making online purchases—they leave behind a digital footprint. This data can reveal intimate details about their habits, preferences, relationships, and even psychological profiles. Corporations, particularly tech giants like Google, Facebook, and Amazon, collect vast amounts of data from their users, often without their explicit consent. This information is then used for targeted advertising, but it can also be sold to third parties or used to influence behavior in ways that users may not fully understand.

The sheer volume of data collected allows these companies to create detailed profiles of individuals, including their interests, fears, and desires. By tracking everything from search history to location data, tech companies can predict future behavior and tailor content to keep users engaged, all while subtly influencing their decisions. This level of insight provides companies with an immense amount of power over individuals, allowing them to manipulate what people see, buy, and believe based on algorithmic predictions. While the primary goal of this data collection is often commercial, it can have far-reaching implications for personal autonomy and freedom.

One of the most insidious forms of manipulation facilitated by the internet is the use of *algorithms*. Algorithms are the invisible engines that power much of the internet, from search engine rankings to social media feeds. These algorithms determine what content is presented to users, creating a personalized digital ecosystem that is tailored to each individual's preferences and behavior. On the surface, this seems like a positive development—after all, who wouldn't want a customized experience? But the reality is that algorithms can be used to subtly shape people's perceptions of the world by prioritizing certain types of content over others.

For example, social media algorithms often prioritize content that generates strong emotional reactions—whether it's outrage, joy, or fear—because this type of content tends to increase engagement and keep users on the platform longer. This creates a feedback loop where sensationalist, polarizing, or emotionally charged content is amplified, while more nuanced or moderate perspectives are sidelined. As a result, users are often exposed to content that reinforces their existing beliefs and biases, leading to the formation of *echo chambers* where only one point of view is heard. Over time, this can have a radicalizing effect, as people become more entrenched in their opinions and less open to alternative viewpoints.

In political contexts, the manipulation of information through algorithms can have significant consequences. During elections, for instance, political campaigns and interest groups use the internet to target voters with specific messages designed to sway their opinions or influence their voting behavior. This practice, known as *microtargeting*, involves using data to identify specific segments of the population and deliver tailored ads or content to them. These messages can be finely tuned to exploit voters' fears, anxieties, or biases, making them more likely to support a particular candidate or cause. The precision of microtargeting makes it possible to influence behavior in ways that are difficult to detect or resist, especially when the messages being delivered are not easily visible to the broader public.

In addition to targeted manipulation, the internet is a fertile ground for *disinformation* and *fake news*. Disinformation campaigns, which involve the deliberate spread of false or misleading information, have become a central tool in modern information warfare. By using fake websites, social media accounts, and bots, bad actors can flood the internet with false narratives, often targeting specific individuals or groups. These campaigns are designed to sow confusion, distrust, and division, making it harder for people to discern what is true and what is false. The rapid spread of disinformation online is amplified by the algorithms that prioritize engagement, allowing fake news to go viral more easily than legitimate information.

The internet's architecture also allows for *astroturfing*, a technique used to create the illusion of grassroots support for a particular cause or position. Astroturfing involves using fake accounts or coordinated campaigns to simulate widespread public support for an idea, even when that support is manufactured. This can be particularly effective in political or social movements, where the appearance of popular backing can sway public opinion or influence policy decisions. By artificially inflating the visibility of a cause or movement, astroturfing manipulates perceptions of legitimacy and consensus, making it easier for bad actors to control narratives and shape public discourse.

Censorship is another tool of control that has become more pervasive with the rise of the internet. Governments around the world, especially in authoritarian regimes, use the internet to monitor, restrict, and suppress information that challenges their authority. In countries like China, Iran, and Russia, governments tightly control what content is accessible online, blocking websites, social media platforms, and news outlets that are critical of the state.

China's Great Firewall is one of the most well-known examples of internet censorship, where access to foreign websites is restricted and domestic platforms are heavily monitored and regulated. This form of control extends beyond merely blocking information—it also involves spreading state-approved narratives to shape public opinion and ensure conformity to the regime's goals.

Even in democratic countries, governments have been accused of using the internet to silence dissent. For example, during times of political unrest or protest, some governments have shut down the internet or restricted access to social media platforms to prevent organizers from mobilizing or sharing information. In such cases, the internet becomes a tool for suppressing free expression and controlling the flow of information, rather than empowering citizens.

Corporate interests also play a role in internet censorship and control. Major tech companies have the power to decide which content is allowed on their platforms and which is removed. While these decisions are often made in the name of protecting users from harmful or illegal content, they also raise questions about who gets to decide what is permissible and what is not. The de-platforming of controversial figures, the removal of politically sensitive content, and the suppression of certain viewpoints have sparked debates about the limits of free speech in the digital age. When a handful of companies control the platforms where the majority of people get their information, they wield significant power over what is seen, heard, and believed.

Surveillance capitalism is another way the internet is used to manipulate and control individuals. Coined by scholar Shoshana Zuboff, the term refers to the business model in which companies monetize the data they collect from users by selling it to advertisers or using it to predict and influence behavior. In this model, the internet is not just a tool for accessing information—it is a tool for extracting value from users by tracking their every move and turning their data into profit. This surveillance-based economy shapes the way platforms are designed, with an emphasis on keeping users engaged and collecting as much data as possible. In the process, users become the product, with their attention, preferences, and behaviors sold to the highest bidder.

The psychological impact of *constant connectivity* and *surveillance* cannot be overstated. As people spend more time online, they become increasingly aware that their actions are being tracked and analyzed. This awareness can lead to self-censorship, as individuals may avoid expressing certain opinions or engaging with certain content out of fear of being monitored or judged. This form of self-regulation mirrors the concept of the *Panopticon*, where the fear of being watched leads individuals to modify their behavior even when no one is actively observing them. Over time, this creates a culture of compliance and conformity, where people are less willing to challenge norms or take risks that could jeopardize their online reputation or privacy.

IN ADDITION TO SURVEILLANCE, *social engineering* is a technique that takes advantage of human psychology to manipulate people into revealing sensitive information or taking specific actions online. Phishing scams, for example, involve tricking individuals into clicking on malicious links or providing personal information by posing as legitimate organizations. These tactics exploit trust, fear, and urgency to manipulate individuals into compromising their own security. Social engineering can also be used to spread malware, steal data, or gain unauthorized access to networks, highlighting the darker side of online manipulation.

The consequences of the internet's role as a tool for manipulation and control are profound. On an individual level, the constant exposure to targeted content, disinformation, and surveillance can lead to increased anxiety, polarization, and a loss of personal autonomy. People may feel that their choices are being shaped by forces beyond their control, whether it's the algorithms deciding what they see or the data brokers tracking their every move. On a societal level, the manipulation of information and public opinion online can weaken democratic institutions, fuel social unrest, and erode trust in the media, government, and even truth itself.

However, it's important to recognize that the internet is not inherently good or bad—it is a tool, and how it is used depends on the intentions of those wielding it. While the internet can be exploited for manipulation and control, it also has the potential to be a force for empowerment, education, and social change. The challenge lies in developing systems of accountability, transparency, and regulation that protect individuals from exploitation while preserving the internet's role as a space for free expression and innovation.

In conclusion, the internet has become a powerful tool for manipulation and control, shaping beliefs, behaviors, and public discourse in ways that are often invisible to users. Through data collection, algorithmic manipulation, disinformation, censorship, and surveillance, governments, corporations, and bad actors have found new ways to influence and control populations. As individuals navigate the digital landscape, understanding how these tools are used is crucial for safeguarding autonomy, privacy, and freedom in an increasingly connected world. By recognizing the ways in which the internet is used to manipulate, individuals and societies can take steps to resist and reclaim control over their digital lives.

Social Media: Addiction, Influence, and the Manipulation of Thought

Social media has revolutionized how we communicate, access information, and interact with the world. It connects billions of people globally, offers platforms for self-expression, and provides unprecedented access to information. However, beneath the surface, social media has also become a tool for manipulation, influencing not only our behaviors and emotions but also shaping the very ways in which we think. The addictive nature of social media, combined with its capacity for amplifying influence and controlling thought, has profound implications for individuals and society at large. This chapter will explore how social media fosters addiction, manipulates thought, and influences our decisions, often in ways that are subtle, unconscious, and difficult to resist.

At the heart of social media's power is its addictive nature. Platforms like Facebook, Instagram, TikTok, and Twitter are designed to keep users engaged for as long as possible. This is achieved through a combination of psychological tactics that tap into our natural desires for social validation, connection, and novelty. Every "like," comment, or share triggers a release of dopamine, a neurotransmitter associated with pleasure and reward. This creates a feedback loop in which users feel a sense of gratification each time they receive positive interaction, leading them to return to the platform in search of more rewards. Over time, this pattern of behavior becomes addictive, with users feeling compelled to check their notifications, post updates, and engage with content, even when they have no conscious reason for doing so.

The addictive nature of social media is often compared to gambling or other forms of compulsive behavior. Much like a slot machine, social media platforms use variable reward schedules, meaning that users never know exactly when they will receive a "reward" (in the form of likes, comments, or new followers). This unpredictability heightens the compulsion to keep checking the platform, as users are drawn back by the possibility of receiving a gratifying interaction. The more time spent on social media, the more entrenched this cycle of behavior becomes, leading to a dependency that can be difficult to break.

While the addictive nature of social media is concerning in itself, the deeper issue lies in how these platforms influence and manipulate thought. Social media algorithms are designed to prioritize content that generates engagement, which means that posts that elicit strong emotional reactions—whether they provoke outrage, joy, or sadness—are more likely to be seen by a wider audience. This creates a digital environment in which emotionally charged content dominates, encouraging users to respond to information in emotional rather than rational ways.

The amplification of emotional content on social media has significant consequences for how people think and engage with information. By constantly being exposed to sensationalist or emotionally charged posts, users are more likely to adopt polarized opinions, react impulsively, and make decisions based on emotional rather than logical reasoning.

This is particularly evident in political and social discourse, where debates often become heated and divisive as opposing sides are pitted against each other by algorithms that prioritize confrontation and controversy. Over time, this leads to the formation of echo chambers, where users are only exposed to viewpoints that align with their existing beliefs, reinforcing biases and deepening ideological divides.

The creation of *echo chambers* is one of the most profound ways in which social media manipulates thought. In an echo chamber, users are surrounded by content that reinforces their worldview, while dissenting opinions are filtered out or minimized. This phenomenon occurs because social media platforms are designed to show users content that aligns with their preferences and past behavior. As a result, users are less likely to encounter diverse perspectives, making it easier for them to become entrenched in their beliefs. Over time, echo chambers can lead to the radicalization of thought, as users are repeatedly exposed to the same viewpoints, without being challenged by alternative perspectives.

The impact of echo chambers is particularly evident in the rise of *misinformation* and *conspiracy theories*. Social media platforms are fertile ground for the spread of false information, as emotionally charged or sensationalist content often goes viral before it can be fact-checked or debunked. Once misinformation enters an echo chamber, it can spread rapidly, as users share and amplify content that aligns with their pre-existing beliefs. This creates a dangerous feedback loop, where false information is validated by others within the echo chamber, making it more difficult for users to discern truth from fiction. In some cases, misinformation can lead to real-world consequences, such as political polarization, public health crises, and the erosion of trust in institutions.

The *attention economy* is another way in which social media manipulates thought. In this economy, attention is a commodity, and social media platforms compete for users' time and focus. To maximize engagement, platforms use algorithms to show users content that is most likely to keep them on the platform for longer periods. This often means prioritizing content that is not necessarily informative or beneficial but that captures attention through sensationalism, entertainment, or controversy. The result is that users are often drawn to content that is designed to grab their attention rather than content that challenges them to think critically or deeply about important issues.

Social media influencers play a key role in shaping thought on these platforms. Influencers are individuals with large followings who are able to sway the opinions, behaviors, and purchasing decisions of their audiences. While influencers can provide entertainment, education, or inspiration, they can also be used as tools for manipulation, either by promoting products, ideologies, or behaviors that serve specific interests. The relationship between influencers and their followers is built on trust and perceived authenticity, which makes it easier for influencers to shape the thoughts and behaviors of their audience without them realizing they are being influenced. This dynamic creates a new form of power, where individuals with large online platforms can exert significant control over public opinion and culture.

THE MANIPULATION OF thought on social media is not limited to influencers or algorithms; it is also facilitated by the *design* of the platforms themselves. Features like infinite scrolling, autoplay videos, and push notifications are all designed to keep users engaged for as long as possible. These design elements take advantage of cognitive biases, such as the tendency to seek immediate gratification or to avoid missing out (often referred to as FOMO, or the fear of missing out). By constantly presenting new content and triggering notifications, social media platforms create a sense of urgency and compulsion, making it difficult for users to disconnect or reflect on their usage.

In addition to these features, *social validation* plays a crucial role in shaping thought and behavior on social media. The desire for likes, comments, and shares drives much of the content creation and interaction on these platforms. Users often post content that they believe will receive positive feedback, which reinforces certain types of behavior and discourages others. Over time, the need for social validation can lead users to conform to the expectations of their online communities, shaping their opinions, interests, and even their self-image. This pressure to conform can be particularly strong among younger users, who may be more susceptible to peer influence and more likely to measure their self-worth through online interactions.

The *commodification of attention* on social media has profound implications for mental health. Studies have shown that excessive social media use is linked to higher levels of anxiety, depression, and feelings of inadequacy, particularly among teenagers and young adults. The constant comparison to others, the pursuit of social validation, and the pressure to present a curated version of oneself can take a significant toll on mental well-being. Moreover, the addictive nature of social media can lead to compulsive behaviors, where users feel unable to disconnect, even when they recognize the negative impact it is having on their lives.

Perhaps one of the most concerning aspects of social media's influence on thought is its ability to shape political behavior and democratic processes. Social media platforms have been used to spread political propaganda, influence elections, and manipulate public opinion on a global scale. Through micro-targeting, political campaigns and interest groups can deliver tailored messages to specific demographics, exploiting their fears, anxieties, or biases to sway their voting behavior. This level of precision in targeting makes it possible to influence elections without the broader public being aware of the manipulation taking place. The use of social media in political contexts has raised serious concerns about the integrity of democratic processes and the role of big tech companies in shaping political outcomes.

Despite the challenges posed by social media, it is important to recognize that these platforms are not inherently good or bad. They can be used to connect people, share knowledge, and drive social change. The key issue is how these platforms are designed and used, and whether individuals are aware of the ways in which they are being influenced. Understanding the psychological and technological mechanisms that drive social media addiction, influence, and manipulation is the first step in reclaiming control over how these platforms shape our thoughts and behaviors.

In conclusion, social media has become a powerful tool for influencing and manipulating thought. Through algorithms that prioritize emotional content, the creation of echo chambers, the spread of misinformation, and the commodification of attention, these platforms have a profound impact on how we think, feel, and behave. The addictive nature of social media, combined with its capacity for amplifying influence through influencers, political campaigns, and social validation, raises serious concerns about the role of these platforms in shaping public opinion, culture, and democratic processes. As individuals and societies grapple with the consequences of social media, it is crucial to develop strategies for critical engagement, digital literacy, and mental health awareness to ensure that these platforms are used responsibly and ethically.

The Use of Algorithms: How Your Online Experience Is Curated

The internet offers vast, seemingly endless opportunities for information, entertainment, and communication. However, much of what we see, read, and interact with online is not random or entirely self-directed; it is carefully curated by algorithms. These algorithms, often invisible to users, decide what content we are shown, how frequently we see it, and in what order it appears. Whether it's your social media feed, search engine results, or recommendations on streaming platforms, algorithms shape your online experience by personalizing it to suit your perceived preferences. In this chapter, we will explore how algorithms work, their impact on thought and behavior, and the broader implications of living in a world where technology silently guides much of what we see and do online.

At the core of every algorithm lies the goal of predicting user preferences and maximizing engagement. An algorithm is essentially a set of rules or calculations that takes input data—such as your browsing history, likes, shares, and searches—and uses it to generate outputs, typically in the form of recommendations or ranked content. The purpose of these algorithms, especially on platforms like Facebook, Google, YouTube, and Netflix, is to keep users engaged for as long as possible by presenting content that is most likely to capture their attention. The longer you stay on the platform, the more data is collected about you, and the more opportunities arise for advertising and monetization.

Algorithms rely heavily on *data tracking* to understand user behavior. Every click, like, comment, or search adds to a growing profile of who you are, what you like, and what will keep you engaged. Over time, these algorithms "learn" your habits and preferences using machine learning and artificial intelligence, becoming more accurate at predicting what you might want to see next. If you frequently engage with content about cooking, for instance, algorithms will prioritize showing you more food-related content. This creates a feedback loop where your preferences shape the content you are shown, and the content you are shown further reinforces your preferences.

However, this personalization comes at a cost: *filter bubbles* and *echo chambers*. When algorithms prioritize content based on what they think you want to see, they limit your exposure to diverse perspectives and ideas. Over time, you are shown more of the same types of content, while other viewpoints, topics, or news that challenge your existing beliefs are filtered out. This phenomenon, often referred to as living in a "filter bubble," can create a sense of tunnel vision, where you are only exposed to information that confirms your existing worldview. While this can make your online experience feel comfortable and familiar, it also narrows your understanding of the world and reduces opportunities for critical thinking.

Echo chambers—online spaces where like-minded people reinforce each other's beliefs—are closely tied to filter bubbles. Algorithms, by promoting content that aligns with your preferences, often lead you into virtual communities that share your views. In these environments, opposing perspectives are rarely encountered, and groupthink takes hold.

This can lead to polarization, where individuals become more extreme in their views due to constant validation from others within the echo chamber. On social media, this effect is magnified by the platform's structure, which rewards engagement with emotionally charged content. The more polarizing or sensational the content, the more likely it is to be shared and prioritized by the algorithm.

A key example of how algorithms curate online experiences is seen in *social media feeds*. On platforms like Facebook, Instagram, and Twitter, the content that appears in your feed is not chronological or random—it is selected by an algorithm that takes into account factors such as your past engagement, the popularity of posts, and the behavior of your social network. This means that your feed is not an unbiased stream of information; it is a curated selection designed to maximize your time on the platform. If you consistently engage with certain friends or types of content, those are prioritized, while posts from other friends or pages you don't engage with as often are less likely to appear. This can give the illusion that your online world is reflective of the real world, even though it is heavily filtered and shaped by algorithms.

Search engines, such as Google, also rely on algorithms to curate your online experience. When you type a query into Google, the results you see are not just based on relevance or accuracy but on a complex algorithm that takes into account hundreds of factors, including your location, search history, click patterns, and even the behavior of other users. This means that two people searching for the same term might see completely different results based on their individual profiles. While this personalization can be convenient, it also means that the information you receive is filtered through the lens of what Google thinks you want to see, rather than offering an objective view of the topic.

Another area where algorithms have significant influence is *content recommendations* on platforms like YouTube, Netflix, and Spotify. These platforms use algorithms to suggest videos, shows, or music based on your past behavior and the behavior of users with similar profiles. For example, if you frequently watch crime documentaries on Netflix, the algorithm will recommend more crime-related content, even if you might enjoy other genres. On YouTube, the recommendation algorithm has been criticized for promoting extreme or controversial content because it generates more engagement. Users who start watching relatively neutral content can quickly find themselves being recommended increasingly radical videos, leading them down a "rabbit hole" of extremism or conspiracy theories.

The impact of algorithmic curation on *news consumption* is another major concern. Many people now get their news primarily from social media or news aggregation sites that use algorithms to select stories. These algorithms prioritize news articles based on engagement metrics, such as clicks, shares, and comments, rather than journalistic quality or accuracy. As a result, sensationalist headlines, emotionally charged stories, and fake news are often promoted over more balanced or nuanced reporting. This has contributed to the spread of misinformation and the erosion of trust in traditional news sources. In an environment where clicks and shares determine which stories are seen, the line between legitimate news and clickbait becomes increasingly blurred.

One of the more troubling aspects of algorithmic curation is its *invisibility*. Most users are unaware of how algorithms shape their online experiences. Because algorithms operate in the background, it is easy to assume that the content we see is a reflection of reality or is organically presented to us. In reality, algorithms are actively shaping the information landscape in ways that can subtly manipulate our thoughts, preferences, and behaviors. This lack of transparency makes it difficult for users to critically assess the information they are consuming, leading to an environment where individuals are more susceptible to manipulation by the platforms themselves or by external actors using the platforms to push certain agendas.

In addition to filtering information, algorithms are also used in *advertising*, where they play a crucial role in determining which ads you see online. This practice, known as *targeted advertising*, allows companies to use data collected from your online behavior to show you personalized ads that are more likely to lead to a purchase. For example, if you frequently search for or browse clothing websites, you may notice ads for specific brands or products appearing on your social media feed or on unrelated websites you visit. While targeted advertising can be more relevant to individual users, it also raises privacy concerns, as it involves the collection and use of vast amounts of personal data without explicit user consent.

Algorithmic bias is another issue that arises from the use of algorithms in curating online experiences. Because algorithms are created by humans and trained on data sets that reflect human behavior, they can inadvertently reinforce existing biases. For example, if an algorithm is trained on data that reflects societal biases—such as racial or gender stereotypes—it may replicate or even amplify those biases in its recommendations. This has been seen in cases where search engine algorithms disproportionately show negative or stereotypical results for certain demographic groups or where social media algorithms prioritize certain voices over others, marginalizing minority perspectives.

Despite these challenges, algorithms are not inherently bad. They can improve user experience by making it easier to find relevant content, discover new interests, and navigate the vast amount of information available online. The problem arises when algorithms are used in ways that prioritize engagement or profit over the well-being and autonomy of users. Platforms that rely on algorithms to keep users hooked often sacrifice diversity of thought, critical inquiry, and personal agency in favor of maximizing time spent on their site.

The use of algorithms to curate online experiences raises important questions about *digital ethics* and the role of technology in shaping human thought. As algorithms become more sophisticated and play an increasingly central role in our lives, there is a growing need for transparency, accountability, and user awareness. Platforms must take responsibility for the impact their algorithms have on society, particularly in areas like news, politics, and public discourse. At the same time, individuals must become more informed about how algorithms work and develop the skills necessary to critically engage with the content they consume online. Algorithms play a powerful and largely invisible role in curating our online experiences. By tracking user behavior and predicting preferences, algorithms shape what we see, how we think, and how we interact with the digital world.

Manipulating Emotions: How Propaganda Appeals to Fear and Hope

Propaganda has been used throughout history as a powerful tool to shape public opinion, reinforce ideologies, and control populations. Its success hinges on its ability to manipulate emotions, particularly the primal forces of fear and hope. By appealing to these deep-seated emotions, propagandists can influence thought, behavior, and decision-making in ways that are often difficult to resist. Whether in times of war, political upheaval, or social change, propaganda taps into our most basic desires for safety, security, and a better future. In this chapter, we will explore how propaganda uses fear and hope to manipulate emotions, examining the psychological mechanisms behind this influence and the impact it has on individuals and societies.

At its most basic level, propaganda works by simplifying complex issues and presenting them in emotionally charged terms that appeal directly to the audience's instincts. The appeal to *fear* is one of the most effective tactics in this process. Fear is a primal emotion that triggers the brain's survival instincts, making people more susceptible to messages that promise protection or safety. When individuals are afraid, they are more likely to seek out information or solutions that reduce that fear, even if those solutions are irrational or harmful in the long term.

Fear-based propaganda often relies on the creation of an external threat, whether real or imagined, to generate a sense of urgency and vulnerability. This technique is particularly common in wartime propaganda, where governments and leaders depict enemies as existential threats that must be confronted. For example, during World War II, both the Axis and Allied powers used fear to galvanize their populations. Nazi propaganda portrayed Jews, communists, and other minority groups as dangerous internal enemies, using fear to justify extreme measures such as genocide. Similarly, Allied propaganda emphasized the threat posed by the Axis powers, portraying them as evil forces bent on world domination and the destruction of democracy.

Fear is not only used in times of war but also in political campaigns, where candidates or parties depict their opponents as dangerous or incompetent. By stoking fears of economic collapse, crime, or foreign invasion, politicians can rally support by presenting themselves as the only viable option to protect the nation. This tactic can be seen in modern elections, where fear-based rhetoric is often used to sway voters. In many cases, fear is amplified through the use of *dog whistles*—coded language that plays on existing anxieties about race, immigration, or social change without overtly expressing those ideas. This allows propagandists to tap into deep-seated fears while maintaining plausible deniability.

One of the reasons fear is such an effective tool in propaganda is that it activates the *fight-or-flight* response, which narrows our focus and reduces our ability to think critically. When we are afraid, our brains prioritize survival over analysis, making us more likely to accept simple, black-and-white explanations for complex problems. Propagandists take advantage of this by presenting their message in stark, emotionally charged terms, often framing the situation as a battle between good and evil, or between order and chaos. This reduces the need for nuanced debate and encourages people to act quickly, often without fully understanding the issue at hand.

Fear-based propaganda also exploits the human tendency toward *tribalism*, the instinct to identify with and protect one's own group while viewing outsiders with suspicion or hostility. By framing the situation as an "us versus them" conflict, propagandists can deepen divisions within society and create a sense of solidarity among those who feel threatened. This tactic is particularly effective in times of political polarization or social upheaval, where people are already primed to see the world in terms of opposing camps. By reinforcing these divisions and amplifying fear, propagandists can strengthen their hold on power while suppressing dissent.

In contrast to fear, the appeal to *hope* offers a more positive, yet equally manipulative, emotional strategy in propaganda. Hope is a powerful motivator, as it speaks to our desires for a better future, security, and personal fulfillment. When used effectively, hope-based propaganda can inspire loyalty, sacrifice, and perseverance, especially during times of crisis or uncertainty. Hope offers a vision of a brighter future, often tied to the leadership or ideology being promoted, and promises that following a particular path will lead to salvation, success, or national greatness.

Hope-based propaganda is often used to rally support for political leaders or movements by offering a utopian vision of the future. This vision may include promises of economic prosperity, social justice, or national renewal, depending on the specific goals of the propagandist. For example, during his rise to power, Adolf Hitler used hope-based propaganda to present the Nazi Party as the solution to Germany's economic woes, promising a return to national greatness after the humiliation of World War I. Similarly, political campaigns around the world frequently use slogans and imagery that emphasize hope for a better tomorrow, encouraging voters to believe that their chosen candidate or party will lead them to success.

Hope-based propaganda can also take on a religious or spiritual tone, especially when tied to ideologies that position leaders as saviors or messianic figures. Totalitarian regimes often use this form of propaganda to elevate their leaders to near-divine status, portraying them as the only ones capable of guiding the nation to prosperity and security. In these cases, hope is tied to personal loyalty to the leader, with promises of national salvation dependent on the people's unwavering support. This type of messaging can be seen in the cult of personality that surrounded figures like Stalin, Mao Zedong, and Kim Il-Sung, where the leader was portrayed as the embodiment of the people's hopes and aspirations.

However, the appeal to hope can be just as manipulative as the appeal to fear, particularly when it is used to distract from or cover up the negative aspects of a regime or movement. Hope-based propaganda often presents an overly simplistic or idealized view of the future, glossing over the complexities or potential dangers of the proposed path. By focusing on an idealized outcome, propagandists can avoid engaging with critical questions about how that future will be achieved, who will benefit, or what sacrifices may be required along the way. This can lead people to support policies or leaders that are ultimately harmful, based on the belief that the promised future justifies any means.

THE COMBINATION OF fear and hope in propaganda is especially powerful. Fear primes people to seek protection, while hope offers a clear path to safety or success. Propagandists often use these emotions together, first creating a sense of fear or insecurity and then offering hope as the solution. For example, during political campaigns, a candidate might emphasize the dangers facing the country—such as crime, economic instability, or foreign threats—before presenting themselves as the hopeful alternative who can fix these problems. This dual emotional appeal makes the message more persuasive, as it both frightens and reassures the audience in a single narrative.

A modern example of this dual approach can be seen in populist movements, which often use fear of "outsiders" or "elites" to generate anger and anxiety, while simultaneously promising that by reclaiming control or returning to traditional values, the people can achieve a better, more secure future. This message is particularly effective in times of economic hardship or social change, where people are already feeling vulnerable and uncertain about the future. By stoking these fears and offering a hopeful vision of reclaiming lost glory or security, populist leaders can consolidate power and deepen divisions within society.

The use of *symbols* and *imagery* is another key element of emotional manipulation in propaganda. Symbols—whether they be flags, emblems, or slogans—carry powerful emotional weight, evoking feelings of pride, loyalty, fear, or hope. These symbols often simplify complex ideas into easily digestible visuals that appeal to the emotions rather than the intellect. For example, propaganda posters during wartime often use symbols of national identity, such as flags or soldiers, to evoke feelings of patriotism and solidarity. By associating these symbols with positive emotions like hope or unity, propagandists can strengthen the emotional impact of their message without needing to rely on logical argumentation.

Repetition is another tactic used to reinforce emotional appeals in propaganda. By repeatedly exposing people to the same messages, slogans, or images, propagandists can condition their audience to associate certain emotions with specific ideas. Over time, this repetition can create automatic emotional responses, where people react with fear or hope whenever they are presented with the propagandist's message. This technique is especially effective when combined with other forms of media, such as radio, television, or social media, which can saturate the public sphere with emotionally charged propaganda on a continuous basis.

In the digital age, *social media* and *digital platforms* have amplified the emotional manipulation used in propaganda. Algorithms on social media prioritize content that generates strong emotional reactions, which means that fear-based and hope-based propaganda often goes viral more easily than more measured or nuanced content. This allows propagandists to reach wider audiences and intensify the emotional impact of their messaging. The speed at which propaganda spreads online also means that people have less time to critically evaluate the information they are exposed to, leading them to make decisions based on emotional impulses rather than rational analysis. Propaganda is a powerful tool for manipulating emotions, particularly through appeals to fear and hope. Fear-based propaganda exploits the instinct for survival, encouraging people to seek protection from perceived threats, while hope-based propaganda offers a vision of a better future that motivates loyalty and action.

Thought Control in the Workplace: Manipulation by Employers

The workplace, like any social environment, is a space where power dynamics, authority, and control come into play. While businesses and organizations are often viewed as spaces for professional growth and productivity, they can also serve as arenas for subtle or overt forms of thought control and manipulation. Employers have a vested interest in shaping the behaviors, attitudes, and even beliefs of their employees to align with organizational goals. This chapter will explore the various ways in which employers exert influence over their workforce, from corporate culture and loyalty programs to performance metrics and surveillance, and how these practices can be used to manipulate thought and behavior in the workplace.

One of the most pervasive forms of control in the workplace is the creation and enforcement of *corporate culture*. Corporate culture refers to the set of shared values, norms, and practices that define the environment and identity of an organization. While a strong corporate culture can foster collaboration, innovation, and a sense of belonging, it can also be used to exert control over employees by shaping how they think and behave. Through training programs, team-building exercises, mission statements, and company slogans, employers instill specific values that employees are expected to internalize. Over time, employees may begin to view their personal identity as closely tied to the organization, making it harder for them to question authority or act against company interests.

In many cases, corporate culture is framed as a positive force, emphasizing values such as teamwork, integrity, and customer service. However, these values can also serve as mechanisms of control. For example, an organization that prioritizes "teamwork" may discourage employees from voicing dissenting opinions or challenging management, under the guise of maintaining harmony. Similarly, an emphasis on "customer service" may be used to pressure employees into putting the needs of the company or its clients ahead of their own well-being. By presenting these values as non-negotiable elements of the company's identity, employers create an environment where employees feel compelled to conform, even when it conflicts with their personal values or interests.

The manipulation of thought through corporate culture often goes hand-in-hand with *corporate loyalty programs*. Many organizations reward loyalty to the company through bonuses, promotions, or recognition programs that celebrate employees who demonstrate unwavering commitment to the organization's goals. These rewards are framed as incentives for hard work, but they also serve to reinforce the idea that loyalty to the company is paramount. Over time, employees may become conditioned to equate loyalty with success, leading them to suppress any thoughts or actions that could be perceived as disloyal, such as questioning policies or seeking employment elsewhere.

IN SOME CASES, COMPANIES even create a sense of *family* or *community* within the workplace, blurring the lines between professional and personal life. By fostering close-knit relationships among employees and promoting the idea that the company is a "family," employers can increase emotional attachment to the organization. This can make it difficult for employees to leave the company, even when it is in their best interest to do so, because they feel a sense of loyalty and obligation to their colleagues. Additionally, framing the company as a family can be used to justify long hours, unpaid overtime, or sacrifices in work-life balance, as employees are expected to go "above and beyond" for the sake of the team.

Performance metrics are another tool used to control thought and behavior in the workplace. Many companies rely on quantifiable data—such as sales targets, customer satisfaction scores, or productivity metrics—to evaluate employee performance. While these metrics are often presented as objective measures of success, they can be used to manipulate employees into prioritizing company goals over their own well-being. For example, an employee who is constantly measured against high-performance targets may feel pressured to work longer hours, take fewer breaks, or engage in unethical behavior to meet those targets. The constant focus on performance metrics can create a culture of competition and fear, where employees are afraid of falling behind or being viewed as underperformers.

The use of *gamification* in the workplace is a more modern approach to controlling employee behavior through performance metrics. Gamification involves applying game-like elements—such as points, leaderboards, and rewards—to non-game activities, including work tasks. While gamification can make mundane tasks more engaging, it also subtly encourages employees to internalize company goals and compete with one another for rewards or recognition. Over time, employees may begin to view their worth and success through the lens of these gamified metrics, leading to a focus on short-term gains and task completion rather than critical thinking or innovation. In this way, gamification can create a sense of obligation to constantly perform and meet goals, even at the expense of creativity or work-life balance.

Surveillance in the workplace is another method used by employers to control thought and behavior. With advances in technology, many companies now use monitoring tools to track employee productivity, internet usage, location, and even communications. This surveillance is often justified as a way to ensure compliance with company policies or to protect against security risks. However, the constant awareness of being watched can have a significant psychological impact on employees, leading them to self-regulate their behavior even when they are not directly monitored. This sense of *panopticism*—where individuals modify their actions out of fear of being observed—creates an environment where employees are less likely to express dissent or take risks, as they feel that every move is being scrutinized.

Surveillance can extend beyond productivity tracking to more invasive practices, such as monitoring personal communications or using AI to analyze employee moods through email or messaging platforms. This type of surveillance goes beyond ensuring compliance with company policies—it creates a culture of control where employees feel that their every thought and emotion is being monitored. The fear of being watched can lead employees to suppress their true feelings, conform to company expectations, and avoid actions that could be perceived as rebellious or unproductive.

The rise of *remote work* during the COVID-19 pandemic has further expanded the reach of workplace surveillance. Many companies have implemented tools to monitor remote employees' screen time, keystrokes, and webcam activity to ensure that they are working productively from home. While these tools are often framed as necessary for maintaining accountability, they can also foster an environment of mistrust and micromanagement. The constant tracking of employees' activities can lead to feelings of anxiety and stress, as employees may feel that they are never truly "off the clock" and must always be performing at a high level to avoid being penalized.

Beyond surveillance, employers also exert control through *management techniques* that shape how employees think about their work and their role within the company. Many organizations use *motivational rhetoric* that encourages employees to adopt a specific mindset—often referred to as the "company mindset" or "growth mindset." This type of rhetoric is designed to make employees feel that they are part of something larger than themselves and that their personal success is tied to the success of the company. While this can foster a sense of purpose, it can also be manipulative, as it pressures employees to align their personal goals with the company's objectives.

Mandatory training sessions or workshops on topics like leadership, teamwork, or company values are another common method of thought control in the workplace. These sessions are often framed as opportunities for personal and professional development, but they can also be used to reinforce corporate ideology and expectations. By repeatedly exposing employees to the same ideas, employers can subtly condition them to adopt the company's way of thinking and suppress dissenting viewpoints. This type of training often emphasizes positive traits like adaptability, resilience, and loyalty, making employees more compliant with organizational changes or demands.

One of the more subtle forms of manipulation in the workplace is the use of *corporate jargon* or *buzzwords* to shape how employees perceive their work. Phrases like "synergy," "out-of-the-box thinking," "disruptive innovation," or "lean in" are often used to encourage certain behaviors or mindsets without directly stating what is expected. By framing work tasks or goals in these terms, employers can create an environment where employees feel that they must conform to the latest corporate trends or risk falling behind. This use of language subtly manipulates employees into thinking that success is defined by their ability to adapt to the company's evolving expectations, even when those expectations may not align with their personal values or career goals.

The pressure to conform to corporate expectations is also reinforced through *peer influence* in the workplace. In many organizations, employees are encouraged to engage in social activities, participate in team-building exercises, or join internal networks that foster a sense of camaraderie and loyalty to the company. While these activities can create positive social bonds, they can also be used to reinforce groupthink, where employees feel pressured to conform to the prevailing attitudes and behaviors of their colleagues. The desire to fit in or be seen as a "team player" can lead employees to suppress dissenting opinions, avoid conflict, and prioritize group harmony over critical thinking.

Burnout culture is another way in which employers manipulate thought and behavior in the workplace. In industries where long hours and high levels of productivity are glorified, employees may feel that they must constantly push themselves to work harder, even at the expense of their health and well-being. This culture of overwork is often reinforced by management, who may reward employees who put in extra hours or meet ambitious goals, while those who prioritize work-life balance are seen as less committed. By framing overwork as a badge of honor, employers manipulate employees into accepting unhealthy work habits as part of the company's identity.

Ultimately, the manipulation of thought in the workplace can lead to a sense of *learned helplessness*, where employees feel that they have no control over their work environment or career trajectory. The constant pressure to conform, meet targets, and align with corporate values can erode an employee's sense of agency, making them feel powerless to effect change or stand up for themselves. This can lead to feelings of frustration, disengagement, and burnout, as employees lose their sense of purpose and autonomy in the workplace.

In conclusion, thought control in the workplace is a pervasive issue that extends beyond traditional management practices. Through the use of corporate culture, performance metrics, surveillance, and motivational rhetoric, employers shape how employees think about their work, their role in the organization, and their relationship to the company. While these practices can foster productivity and loyalty, they also have the potential to manipulate and control employees in ways that undermine their autonomy, creativity, and well-being. Understanding the techniques used by employers to influence thought and behavior is essential for employees seeking to reclaim control over their work experience and navigate the complex power dynamics of the modern workplace.

Psychological Warfare: How Governments Use Fear to Subdue Citizens

Psychological warfare is the deliberate use of tactics designed to influence, manipulate, or control the thoughts and emotions of individuals or groups, typically to achieve a political, military, or ideological objective. Throughout history, governments have wielded psychological warfare to subdue their populations, often relying on fear as the most potent weapon. By instilling fear, governments can undermine resistance, suppress dissent, and create a compliant, submissive citizenry. This chapter will examine how governments use fear to subdue citizens, exploring the mechanisms behind these tactics, the psychological effects on individuals and societies, and the lasting impact of fear-based control.

Governments frequently employ fear to ensure obedience and loyalty, often framing external or internal threats as justifications for authoritarian measures. This tactic is effective because fear is a primal human emotion, designed to protect us from danger. When people are afraid, they are more likely to seek safety and security, even at the cost of their freedoms. Governments exploit this instinct by presenting themselves as the protectors, offering solutions to the dangers they emphasize—whether these dangers are real, exaggerated, or fabricated.

One of the most common forms of fear-based psychological warfare is the creation of an *external enemy*. Governments often depict other nations, ideologies, or groups as existential threats to the nation's security or way of life. By highlighting the danger posed by this enemy, leaders can rally citizens around a common cause, justify military action, and suppress internal dissent under the guise of national unity. This tactic has been used throughout history: from the Cold War's fear of communism, which justified widespread surveillance and intervention abroad, to the war on terror, where fear of terrorism has led to expanded government powers, surveillance, and restrictions on civil liberties in many democratic nations.

This fear of an external enemy often extends beyond military threats and can be used to foster xenophobia or nationalism. Governments may stoke fear of immigrants, refugees, or foreign influence, presenting these groups as cultural or economic threats. This fear-based narrative can galvanize support for restrictive immigration policies, isolationist foreign policies, and the curtailing of civil rights for minority groups within a country. By positioning themselves as defenders of the nation against an external enemy, governments can maintain control while distracting citizens from internal problems, such as corruption, economic hardship, or political dysfunction.

In addition to creating external enemies, governments also use fear to manage *internal threats*. One of the most pervasive forms of psychological warfare is the fear of punishment. In authoritarian regimes, fear of arrest, imprisonment, torture, or even death is used to keep citizens in line. The mere possibility of punishment for dissent is often enough to suppress criticism, protest, or any form of organized opposition. In these environments, people are often afraid to speak out, not only for fear of personal consequences but also for fear of putting their families and communities at risk.

The *secret police* or surveillance agencies, often seen in totalitarian regimes, play a crucial role in fostering fear. Governments establish these institutions to monitor, intimidate, and control the population, often without needing to overtly demonstrate their power. In countries like the former Soviet Union or Nazi Germany, secret police organizations such as the KGB and the Gestapo relied on informants and a culture of mistrust to keep citizens constantly aware that they could be watched at any moment. This sense of omnipresent surveillance—where no one knows exactly when or how they are being observed—creates an environment of *panopticism*, where individuals self-regulate their behavior out of fear of unseen authorities. Even in the absence of direct punishment, this psychological pressure ensures widespread compliance and submission.

In modern times, the use of *digital surveillance* has expanded the scope of governmental psychological control. Many governments use mass data collection, monitoring of online activity, and digital tracking to keep tabs on their citizens. This surveillance can extend to social media activity, emails, phone calls, and even location data, making citizens feel as though they are constantly being watched. In countries like China, the government's extensive surveillance system, including facial recognition technology and social credit scores, is used to monitor citizens' behavior and enforce social conformity. The awareness that their every move could be tracked creates a climate of fear where citizens are less likely to express dissent, engage in political activism, or question authority.

Another aspect of internal psychological warfare is the creation of a *climate of fear and uncertainty* through propaganda and media manipulation. By controlling the flow of information, governments can spread fear-inducing narratives that serve their interests. State-controlled media outlets are often used to amplify threats—whether they are economic crises, social unrest, or natural disasters—while presenting the government as the only force capable of addressing these issues. In such environments, citizens may feel overwhelmed by the constant barrage of fear-based messaging, making them more likely to submit to authoritarian measures in exchange for a sense of safety or stability.

The *fear of social exclusion* is another powerful tool used in psychological warfare. Humans are social beings, and the fear of being ostracized from the community is a potent motivator for compliance. In many authoritarian regimes, dissenters are not only punished by the state but are also shamed, demonized, or ostracized by society. The government often encourages citizens to report on each other, fostering a culture of mistrust where even family members may turn against each other. This social control mechanism ensures that individuals are less likely to challenge the government, as doing so could result in isolation, not just from the state, but from their social circles as well.

In some cases, governments use *fear to create divisions within society*, pitting different groups against each other to prevent unified opposition. By fostering divisions along racial, religious, or political lines, governments can distract citizens from the failings of those in power. This tactic is often seen in populist regimes, where leaders stoke fear of minority groups, immigrants, or political opponents to consolidate their own authority. By creating a sense of "us versus them," leaders can justify oppressive policies and maintain control over a fragmented society. Fear-based division not only weakens social cohesion but also reduces the likelihood of collective resistance against the government.

The use of *emergency powers* is another way in which fear is used to control citizens. During times of crisis—whether due to war, terrorism, or natural disasters—governments often expand their powers under the guise of protecting the public. These emergency powers may include curfews, restrictions on free speech, increased surveillance, or even martial law. While these measures are often justified as temporary necessities, they can become permanent fixtures of governmental control long after the crisis has passed. In this way, governments use fear to normalize authoritarian practices, gradually eroding civil liberties and democratic processes in the name of security.

Fear-based psychological warfare also extends to *economic control*. In some cases, governments use fear of economic instability or job loss to maintain compliance. In authoritarian regimes or politically volatile countries, citizens may fear that criticizing the government or participating in protests could result in economic reprisals, such as losing their jobs or facing financial penalties. This creates a sense of economic vulnerability, where individuals are less likely to engage in political activism for fear of damaging their livelihoods. The fear of financial instability can be just as effective in controlling citizens as the fear of imprisonment or punishment.

In more subtle forms, fear can be instilled through the manipulation of *national identity and pride*. Governments often use patriotic rhetoric to foster a sense of unity and loyalty, but this can also serve as a tool for psychological control. Leaders may frame dissenters or opposition groups as "unpatriotic" or as threats to the nation's values and identity. By equating loyalty to the government with loyalty to the country, they can suppress criticism and marginalize political opponents. This tactic creates a climate where citizens are reluctant to challenge the government for fear of being seen as traitors or enemies of the state.

The psychological effects of fear-based governance are profound and long-lasting. Individuals who live under constant fear may experience chronic stress, anxiety, and a sense of powerlessness. Over time, this can lead to a condition known as *learned helplessness*, where people come to believe that their actions have no impact on their circumstances and that resistance is futile. This mindset makes it easier for governments to maintain control, as citizens are less likely to mobilize or demand change when they feel that their efforts will be in vain. Learned helplessness can also contribute to a culture of apathy, where people disengage from political processes and accept the status quo, even if it is oppressive or unjust.

Despite the effectiveness of fear-based psychological warfare, it is not without risks. When governments rely too heavily on fear to control their populations, they can create an environment of widespread paranoia and mistrust. Over time, this can lead to social instability, as citizens may become disillusioned with the government's tactics or begin to seek alternative sources of power. In some cases, fear can fuel resistance, as oppressed groups band together to challenge the state. Revolutions, uprisings, and coups are often sparked when fear reaches a tipping point, and citizens decide that the risks of inaction outweigh the risks of rebellion.

In recent years, fear-based psychological warfare has taken on new dimensions with the rise of *cyber warfare* and *disinformation campaigns*. Governments and political actors now use online platforms and digital tools to spread fear and confusion on a global scale. Social media platforms, in particular, have become battlegrounds for fear-based propaganda, with bad actors spreading disinformation, conspiracy theories, and fake news to stoke fear and division within societies. These tactics are often used to weaken democratic institutions, undermine trust in government, and manipulate public opinion. By creating a climate of fear and uncertainty, disinformation campaigns can destabilize entire nations and make it easier for authoritarian regimes to consolidate power.

In conclusion, fear is one of the most powerful weapons in psychological warfare, and governments have long used it to subdue their citizens. Whether by creating external enemies, fostering internal divisions, or instilling a fear of punishment and surveillance, governments can manipulate emotions to control behavior and maintain power. The psychological effects of fear-based control can be devastating, leading to chronic anxiety, learned helplessness, and social division. While fear is a potent tool for maintaining order, it is also a double-edged sword, as it can ultimately fuel resistance and undermine the stability of the regimes that wield it. Understanding the mechanisms of fear-based psychological warfare is crucial for resisting manipulation and protecting individual freedoms in the face of governmental control.

The Influence of Public Figures and Celebrities on Public Opinion

Public figures and celebrities wield immense power when it comes to shaping public opinion. In today's media-saturated world, their influence extends far beyond entertainment, reaching into politics, social movements, consumer behavior, and even cultural norms. Through their massive followings, celebrities and other high-profile individuals can sway public sentiment, rally people behind causes, and amplify messages that shape societal discourse. This chapter will examine how public figures and celebrities influence public opinion, exploring the psychological mechanisms behind this phenomenon, the role of social media, and the potential consequences—both positive and negative—of this far-reaching influence.

At the heart of celebrity influence is the *psychological concept of identification*. People are naturally drawn to role models, and celebrities often fill that role because of their visibility, success, and perceived relatability. When individuals admire or aspire to be like a public figure, they are more likely to adopt that person's views, behaviors, and lifestyle choices. This identification is reinforced through repeated exposure to the celebrity's public persona, making fans feel a personal connection to someone they likely have never met. This sense of connection fosters trust, which makes the public figure's opinions, endorsements, and actions seem more credible and impactful.

One of the key ways public figures influence opinion is through *social endorsement*. Celebrities often use their platform to endorse products, political candidates, or social causes. These endorsements carry weight because fans see the figure as an authority or someone whose lifestyle they aspire to emulate. Companies and politicians alike recognize the power of celebrity endorsements, often seeking out high-profile partnerships to boost credibility, increase visibility, and enhance public appeal. For example, when a celebrity endorses a brand, that brand is often seen as more desirable, trustworthy, or trendy, leading to increased sales and public interest.

In politics, celebrity endorsements can have a similar effect. High-profile figures such as Oprah Winfrey, Taylor Swift, and LeBron James have used their platforms to support political candidates or movements, influencing the voting behavior of their followers. During election cycles, celebrities often speak out on social media or at rallies, leveraging their popularity to bring attention to issues and candidates. While some may argue that celebrities have no place in politics, the reality is that their voices can shape the way people think, vote, and engage with political discourse. In some cases, a celebrity endorsement can bring an issue into the mainstream that might otherwise have gone unnoticed.

Public figures also influence public opinion through the concept of *parasocial relationships*. These are one-sided relationships in which a person feels a strong emotional connection to a media figure despite having no real interaction with them. This phenomenon is particularly prevalent in the age of social media, where celebrities often share intimate details about their lives, creating a sense of familiarity and closeness with their followers. Fans come to view these figures as friends or confidants, making them more susceptible to influence. When a celebrity shares their views on social issues, personal struggles, or political stances, their followers are more likely to empathize with their perspective, feeling that they "know" the person behind the fame.

Social media has amplified the reach of celebrities and public figures, allowing them to connect directly with millions of people around the world. Platforms like Instagram, Twitter, TikTok, and YouTube have created a new kind of celebrity, where influencers and digital personalities often hold just as much sway as traditional movie stars or musicians. These social media platforms provide a space where celebrities can engage with their audience in real-time, creating a more personal and interactive form of influence. Unlike traditional media, where access to public figures was limited, social media allows for continuous engagement, making it easier for public figures to shape public opinion on a near-constant basis.

Through social media, public figures can craft and control their public image in ways that were not possible in the past. They can share their thoughts, opinions, and experiences directly with their audience, bypassing traditional media filters. This ability to self-represent allows celebrities to shape how they are perceived, which in turn influences how their opinions are received. A public figure who is seen as authentic, relatable, or genuine is more likely to sway public opinion than one who is viewed as out of touch or overly polished. Social media also allows celebrities to participate in real-time conversations about current events, often using hashtags or viral content to engage their followers and drive attention to causes or issues they care about.

The power of celebrities to influence public opinion is perhaps most visible in the realm of *social activism*. Celebrities often lend their voices to social movements, bringing awareness to causes such as racial justice, gender equality, climate change, or LGBTQ+ rights. By aligning themselves with these movements, public figures can mobilize large numbers of people to take action, whether through donations, protests, or social media campaigns. The visibility and attention that celebrities bring to social causes can be instrumental in driving change, as they have the ability to reach audiences that traditional activists may not be able to access as easily.

For example, during the Black Lives Matter movement, high-profile figures like Colin Kaepernick, Beyoncé, and Serena Williams used their platforms to speak out against racial injustice and police violence. Their involvement helped bring the movement into mainstream consciousness, encouraging widespread participation and media coverage. Similarly, environmental activists like Leonardo DiCaprio and Greta Thunberg have used their celebrity status to highlight the urgency of climate change, drawing attention to environmental policies and encouraging people to adopt more sustainable practices.

However, the influence of public figures on social movements is not without controversy. Some critics argue that celebrity involvement in activism can be shallow or performative, where figures engage with causes for publicity or self-promotion rather than genuine commitment. The term "slacktivism" is often used to describe superficial involvement in activism, where celebrities (and their followers) participate in social movements by posting hashtags or sharing content online without taking meaningful action. This raises questions about the authenticity of celebrity activism and whether it leads to real change or merely serves to boost the public image of the celebrity involved.

PUBLIC FIGURES CAN also wield influence in more subtle, cultural ways. Celebrities shape *fashion trends*, *lifestyle choices*, and *body image ideals*, which can have a profound impact on how people see themselves and others. The promotion of certain beauty standards, for example, can influence body image, particularly among younger audiences who look up to these figures. Celebrities like Kim Kardashian, Kylie Jenner, and influencers in the fitness and beauty industries have set standards of physical appearance that millions of followers attempt to emulate, often going to great lengths—such as cosmetic surgery or extreme diets—to achieve these looks. This raises concerns about the role of celebrities in perpetuating unrealistic beauty standards and the potential negative effects on self-esteem and mental health. Beyond beauty and lifestyle, public figures also influence *consumer behavior*. Many celebrities engage in product endorsements, advertising, or launching their own brands, effectively monetizing their influence. When a well-known figure endorses a product or service, it carries a sense of credibility and desirability. Whether it's an athlete promoting sportswear, a musician endorsing a beverage, or a social media influencer pushing beauty products, these endorsements can drive consumer choices in ways that traditional advertising cannot. People are more likely to trust a recommendation from someone they admire or follow closely, making celebrities and influencers highly effective marketing tools.

However, celebrity influence over public opinion also carries significant risks. When public figures espouse misinformation, conspiracy theories, or controversial opinions, their followers may adopt these views without critical thought. For instance, some celebrities have been criticized for promoting anti-vaccine rhetoric, conspiracy theories, or unproven health treatments, leading to confusion, distrust in science, and even public health risks. In the digital age, where false information spreads quickly, the influence of public figures can amplify dangerous ideas and contribute to societal harm. The phenomenon of *celebrity worship*—where fans place celebrities on a pedestal and view them as infallible—can exacerbate this issue. When people are overly invested in the lives and opinions of public figures, they may be less likely to critically evaluate the information they receive from them. This can lead to a blind acceptance of opinions or behaviors, even when they are harmful or misleading. The influence of celebrities on public opinion, therefore, raises important questions about responsibility, accountability, and the ethical use of their platforms.

While celebrities have the potential to drive positive change, their influence must be balanced with critical thinking and awareness. Public figures have the power to amplify important causes, shape cultural norms, and inspire action, but they also have a responsibility to use their platforms ethically and thoughtfully. As consumers of celebrity culture, it is important to recognize that while these figures can provide valuable perspectives and inspiration, they are not always experts or authorities in the fields they speak on. Public figures, like everyone else, are fallible, and their influence should be subject to the same scrutiny as any other source of information. Public figures and celebrities have an immense capacity to shape public opinion, influencing everything from politics and social movements to consumer behavior and cultural trends. Their ability to connect with audiences through social media, parasocial relationships, and endorsements makes them powerful agents of change—both positive and negative. While their influence can bring attention to important causes and inspire action, it can also perpetuate misinformation, unrealistic standards, and shallow activism.

The Role of Fear in Obedience: Why Threats Are So Effective

Fear is one of the most powerful emotions governing human behavior, and its ability to shape obedience is a cornerstone of control in both personal and societal contexts. Whether in governments, workplaces, or social structures, threats of punishment, danger, or loss can compel individuals to comply with authority or submit to rules, even when such obedience goes against their own best interests or ethical beliefs. This chapter will explore why fear is so effective in producing obedience, how threats work to influence behavior, and the psychological mechanisms that make fear such a potent tool for control. At its most basic level, fear is a survival mechanism. When we perceive a threat—whether physical, emotional, or social—our bodies and minds enter a state of heightened alertness designed to protect us from harm. The *fight-or-flight* response kicks in, driven by the amygdala, the part of the brain that processes emotions. Adrenaline surges, preparing us to either confront the threat or escape from it. In situations of fear, rational thinking often takes a backseat to instinctive reactions. This makes fear a powerful tool for controlling behavior, as people will go to great lengths to avoid threats, whether real or imagined.

One of the most effective ways fear is used to enforce obedience is through *threats of punishment*. In this context, the fear of negative consequences—such as physical harm, imprisonment, job loss, or social ostracism—acts as a deterrent, encouraging individuals to comply with authority rather than risk the penalties associated with defiance. Governments, for example, use laws and law enforcement to maintain order, with the threat of arrest, fines, or imprisonment for those who disobey. In more extreme cases, totalitarian regimes rely on the threat of violence, torture, or death to suppress dissent and ensure submission. Fear of punishment creates a psychological cost-benefit calculation, where people weigh the risk of noncompliance against the immediate dangers of disobedience, often opting for the safer, less costly option of following orders. The fear of punishment can also be more subtle, taking the form of *social consequences*. Humans are social beings, and the fear of being ostracized or shamed can be just as powerful as physical threats. In many societies, conformity to social norms is enforced through the threat of rejection or exclusion. Individuals who challenge the status quo, behave outside of accepted norms, or dissent from majority opinions may face ridicule, isolation, or damage to their reputations. This fear of losing social standing or being cast out from a group leads people to conform, even when they privately disagree with the rules or norms they are following. This form of social control can be seen in workplaces, religious communities, or political movements, where deviation from the group's ideology or practices is met with strong disapproval or ostracism.

Uncertainty is another way fear can drive obedience. People tend to fear the unknown, and this fear can paralyze decision-making and foster compliance. When faced with uncertain or unpredictable outcomes, individuals may choose to obey authority figures who offer clear directives or promises of safety. For example, during crises—such as natural disasters, economic recessions, or pandemics—people are more likely to follow government orders or expert advice, even if they have reservations about those in power. The fear of not knowing what will happen next makes obedience seem like the most rational choice, as it offers a sense of stability or control in an otherwise chaotic situation.

This fear of the unknown is often exacerbated by *propaganda* or *media manipulation*, where governments or other authorities exaggerate dangers to cultivate fear. When the media focuses on worst-case scenarios, threats of terrorism, or public health emergencies, it creates an atmosphere of fear that makes people more willing to accept stringent measures or restrictions on their freedoms. In such contexts, individuals may comply with laws or policies they would normally question, as the fear of the greater perceived threat outweighs concerns about personal autonomy or civil liberties.

Fear also plays a key role in *hierarchical structures*, where power dynamics are maintained through threats of punishment or loss. In organizations or institutions where authority is concentrated at the top, obedience is often enforced through fear of retribution from superiors. This dynamic is especially common in authoritarian regimes, militaries, or corporations with rigid hierarchies. In these environments, individuals are conditioned to obey orders, often without questioning them, because defiance could result in demotion, firing, or even imprisonment. The higher the stakes, the more powerful fear becomes as a tool of control, ensuring that those lower in the hierarchy remain compliant to avoid the consequences of disobedience.

A famous psychological experiment that demonstrates the power of fear in obedience is Stanley Milgram's *obedience to authority* experiment, conducted in the 1960s. In this experiment, participants were instructed by an authority figure to administer electric shocks to a "learner" (an actor) whenever the learner answered a question incorrectly. Despite hearing the learner's cries of pain, many participants continued to administer shocks when ordered to do so by the authority figure, even when they believed they were causing real harm. The experiment revealed the extent to which people are willing to obey authority, even when it conflicts with their moral beliefs, especially when fear of defying the authority or breaking the rules is present.

Milgram's experiment highlights the concept of *diffusion of responsibility*, which is another psychological mechanism that makes fear-driven obedience so effective. When individuals are part of a system where authority is centralized, they may feel less personally responsible for the consequences of their actions. In the case of Milgram's participants, the authority figure assured them that they would not be held accountable for harming the learner, which alleviated their fear of personal consequences. This detachment from responsibility makes it easier for people to obey harmful or unethical commands, as they are more focused on avoiding immediate threats to themselves than on the potential harm to others.

Another reason fear is so effective in enforcing obedience is that it often operates on a *subconscious level*. People may not always be aware that their actions are being influenced by fear, especially when the threat is not overt. In many cases, fear is internalized over time, becoming part of an individual's belief system or worldview. This internalization can happen through years of exposure to fear-based messages in media, political rhetoric, or cultural narratives. For example, if people are repeatedly told that a particular group is dangerous or that their safety is constantly at risk, they may develop a generalized fear that leads to automatic obedience to authority figures who promise to protect them. In this way, fear becomes a deeply ingrained motivator, shaping behavior even when individuals are not consciously aware of its influence.

Fear can also be reinforced through *repetition*. The more people are exposed to fear-inducing messages, the more they internalize that fear and respond with obedience. This is often seen in authoritarian regimes, where state-controlled media frequently broadcasts messages about external enemies, internal threats, or crises that require strong government intervention. Over time, the constant repetition of these messages creates a culture of fear, where individuals are conditioned to obey the government out of a sense of self-preservation. The effectiveness of this tactic lies in its ability to wear down resistance and normalize fear-based obedience as a way of life.

In some cases, *fear of loss*—whether of security, wealth, or status—can be just as effective in enforcing obedience as the fear of direct punishment. Individuals who feel that their livelihoods or social standing are at risk are more likely to comply with authority figures to protect what they have. For example, in corporate environments, employees may fear losing their jobs or damaging their career prospects if they speak out against unethical practices or challenge their superiors. Similarly, in social or political contexts, individuals may fear losing their social status or being excluded from important networks if they refuse to conform to the prevailing norms or ideologies. This fear of loss encourages compliance and discourages dissent, as people weigh the potential costs of defiance against the stability that comes with obedience.

However, while fear is a powerful motivator for obedience, it is not always sustainable in the long term. Fear-driven control can lead to resentment, frustration, and a loss of trust in authority figures, especially when the threats used to maintain obedience are perceived as unjust or excessive. Over time, people may become desensitized to fear or reach a tipping point where they decide that the risks of disobedience are worth taking. This dynamic can be seen in historical revolutions or social movements, where populations that have been controlled through fear eventually rise up to challenge the systems that oppressed them. When the cost of obedience becomes greater than the fear of punishment, people may choose resistance over compliance.

In conclusion, fear is an incredibly effective tool for enforcing obedience, whether through threats of punishment, social exclusion, or the fear of the unknown. Governments, institutions, and authority figures have long used fear to maintain control, knowing that people are more likely to comply when they feel that their safety, security, or social standing is at risk. The psychological mechanisms behind fear-driven obedience—such as the fight-or-flight response, diffusion of responsibility, and internalized fear—make it a powerful motivator for compliance. However, while fear can create short-term obedience, it also has the potential to backfire, leading to rebellion or resistance when people decide that the cost of submission is too high. Understanding the role of fear in obedience is crucial for recognizing when it is being used to manipulate behavior and for developing strategies to resist fear-based control.

Coercion and Compliance: The Subtle Ways We Are Controlled

Coercion and compliance are pervasive forces in everyday life, often operating in subtle and insidious ways that shape our decisions, actions, and beliefs without our full awareness. While overt coercion—such as threats of violence or punishment—is easily recognizable, much of the control we experience is far more subtle, relying on psychological manipulation, social pressure, and implicit expectations. These tactics can be found in everything from marketing and workplace dynamics to political systems and interpersonal relationships. In this chapter, we will explore the nuanced ways coercion and compliance are used to control individuals, examining the psychological mechanisms behind these forces and how they shape behavior.

One of the most effective forms of subtle control is *social pressure*. Humans are inherently social beings, and we have a deep-rooted need to belong to groups and be accepted by others. This desire for social acceptance can make us highly susceptible to compliance with group norms, even when those norms conflict with our personal values or beliefs. Social pressure works by creating a sense of *implied obligation*, where individuals feel that they must conform to the expectations of their peers, family, or community in order to maintain their social standing. This pressure can manifest in many ways—ranging from the fear of embarrassment or ridicule to the desire to avoid conflict or disapproval.

In workplaces, for example, employees may comply with company policies or cultural expectations, not because they believe in them, but because they want to avoid being ostracized or jeopardizing their career prospects. A worker might stay late at the office, adopt a specific political stance, or engage in team-building activities they dislike simply because of the subtle pressure to fit in or be seen as a "team player." This *fear of social exclusion* drives compliance, even when no explicit threats are made, because the consequences of non-compliance—such as being seen as difficult, uncooperative, or not aligned with the company's values—can damage one's reputation and prospects for advancement.

Similarly, in social or political settings, people often go along with prevailing norms or ideologies due to the fear of being labeled as outsiders or dissenters. Social movements, religious groups, and political parties often rely on group cohesion to maintain control over their members. The implied threat is not physical punishment but *social isolation* or being viewed as a "traitor" to the cause. This kind of coercion can be especially powerful in tightly knit communities where the social consequences of non-compliance are severe.

Another subtle form of control is *manipulative persuasion*, where individuals are influenced to comply with demands or expectations without realizing they are being coerced. This often involves the use of *framing* or *priming*—techniques that present choices in a way that makes one option seem far more appealing or logical than the others. For example, in marketing, companies often frame products as limited-time offers, using phrases like "act now" or "while supplies last" to create a sense of urgency. This tactic manipulates consumers into making quick decisions out of fear of missing out, rather than allowing them to make more rational, thoughtful choices.

In political contexts, governments or leaders may use similar framing techniques to push certain policies by presenting them as the only viable solution to a pressing problem. By framing the situation in a way that leaves little room for debate—such as emphasizing the urgency of a crisis or the risks of inaction—leaders can coerce citizens into compliance without making overt threats. This manipulation often plays on *fear and uncertainty*, encouraging individuals to comply because they believe there are no other realistic alternatives. In this way, people may feel that they are acting freely, even though their options have been carefully manipulated to steer them in a particular direction.

Authority figures also play a key role in shaping compliance through subtle coercion. In many situations, people are more likely to comply with requests or orders from those in positions of authority, even if those requests conflict with their own judgment or values. This phenomenon, known as *obedience to authority*, was famously demonstrated in the *Milgram experiment*, where participants were willing to administer what they believed were painful electric shocks to others simply because they were instructed to do so by an authority figure. While the experiment involved overt commands, much of the control exercised by authority figures in daily life is more subtle, relying on the implicit power dynamics between superiors and subordinates.

In workplaces, for example, employees may comply with the wishes of their bosses or managers out of a sense of deference to authority, even when they have concerns about the ethics or feasibility of a task. This compliance is often driven by the fear of negative consequences—such as losing their job, missing out on a promotion, or damaging their relationship with their superior. In these cases, the threat is implied rather than stated, and employees comply because they understand the unspoken consequences of disobedience.

Surveillance and the perception of being watched can also lead to compliance, even when no direct orders or threats are issued. The concept of *panopticism*, derived from the design of the Panopticon prison, suggests that people alter their behavior when they believe they are being observed, even if they are not sure when or how they are being watched. In modern times, the pervasive use of surveillance technology—such as cameras, online tracking, and digital monitoring—creates an environment where individuals feel they must constantly comply with rules or expectations because they fear being caught. This *self-regulation* is a form of subtle coercion, where the mere possibility of being watched leads people to conform without the need for overt control or intervention.

This phenomenon is particularly evident in the workplace, where employees know that their performance is being monitored through various tools, such as time-tracking software, email monitoring, or productivity metrics. Even if these tools are not used to punish underperformance, the knowledge that they exist leads employees to comply with expectations, often working longer hours or maintaining a certain level of productivity to avoid negative evaluations.

In more personal settings, coercion often takes the form of *emotional manipulation*. This type of subtle control is common in relationships, where individuals use guilt, flattery, or emotional appeals to influence the behavior of others. For example, a partner may guilt their significant other into complying with their wishes by implying that failure to do so would hurt the relationship or cause emotional harm. Similarly, parents may use guilt or disappointment to coerce children into behaving in certain ways, framing compliance as a way to earn approval or avoid upsetting the family. In these cases, the coercion is not overt but relies on emotional leverage to manipulate behavior.

Incentives and rewards are another subtle form of coercion, where compliance is encouraged through the promise of positive outcomes rather than the threat of punishment. In this context, individuals are motivated to conform to expectations because they believe they will benefit from doing so—whether through financial rewards, promotions, recognition, or other forms of validation. While incentives can be a healthy way to motivate behavior, they can also be used to manipulate individuals into compliance by creating a sense of dependency. For example, employees may comply with unreasonable demands or workloads because they believe it will result in a bonus or career advancement, even when the long-term effects on their well-being are negative.

The *illusion of choice* is another technique often used to create compliance. In situations where individuals are given multiple options, the choices are often framed in a way that makes one option seem overwhelmingly favorable, leading people to believe they are making an independent decision. This tactic is frequently used in politics, advertising, and negotiations, where the illusion of choice creates a sense of agency, even though the options have been carefully constructed to guide the individual toward a predetermined outcome. In reality, the individual is being coerced into compliance without fully realizing it.

Framing of social expectations is a further method of subtle control, especially in environments where cultural or organizational norms dictate behavior. For instance, in many corporate cultures, there is an unspoken expectation that employees will work long hours or prioritize the company over their personal life, even when work-life balance is emphasized in official policies. These norms are enforced not through direct orders but through a culture where deviations from these expectations are quietly discouraged or frowned upon. Employees comply with these norms because they understand the social and professional consequences of failing to align with the company's unspoken rules.

Lastly, *cognitive dissonance*—the discomfort experienced when holding conflicting beliefs or behaviors—can also lead to compliance. When individuals are coerced into acting against their own beliefs or values, they often resolve this tension by altering their internal beliefs to align with their actions. This psychological adjustment makes it easier for them to continue complying in the future, as they no longer feel the internal conflict. Over time, people may come to accept the very beliefs or practices they initially resisted, making subtle coercion a highly effective tool for long-term control.

In conclusion, coercion and compliance operate in a wide range of contexts, often in subtle and indirect ways that can be difficult to recognize. Social pressure, manipulation, authority, surveillance, and incentives all contribute to shaping behavior, guiding individuals toward compliance without the need for overt threats or force. Understanding these mechanisms is crucial for identifying when we are being subtly controlled and for developing strategies to resist manipulation. By becoming more aware of the forces that influence our decisions and actions, we can reclaim agency over our lives and make more conscious, autonomous choices.

Surveillance Technology: From CCTV to AI-Driven Control

Surveillance technology has evolved dramatically over the past several decades, transforming from relatively simple systems like closed-circuit television (CCTV) to highly sophisticated, AI-driven tools that monitor and influence behavior in real time. This evolution reflects a growing desire by governments, corporations, and other institutions to gain more control over public spaces, private activities, and even the inner workings of individual minds. Surveillance has become an omnipresent feature of modern life, affecting everything from law enforcement to workplace management, consumer habits, and political activism. In this chapter, we will explore the development of surveillance technology, its increasing reliance on artificial intelligence, and how these technologies are being used to exert control over individuals and societies.

CCTV, one of the earliest forms of modern surveillance, began as a relatively straightforward system for monitoring public spaces and securing property. Originally developed in the mid-20th century, CCTV systems allowed authorities to observe real-time footage from strategically placed cameras. Over time, these systems became ubiquitous in urban environments, particularly in public areas like streets, transportation hubs, and shopping centers. While initially seen as a tool for deterring crime, CCTV soon became a symbol of constant oversight, with critics questioning the impact of pervasive surveillance on personal privacy and freedom.

The widespread deployment of CCTV reflects a shift in how societies manage security, emphasizing the use of technology to monitor behavior and identify potential threats. However, traditional CCTV systems were limited by their reliance on human operators to review footage and detect suspicious activities. This reliance on human observation made it difficult to monitor large volumes of data effectively, leading to inefficiencies and missed opportunities for intervention.

As technology advanced, CCTV systems became more automated, incorporating features like motion detection and facial recognition. These innovations significantly expanded the scope of surveillance, allowing authorities to identify individuals in real-time and track their movements across multiple locations. Facial recognition technology, in particular, marked a major turning point in surveillance, as it enabled the automatic identification of people in public spaces. Initially developed for security purposes, facial recognition is now widely used by governments, law enforcement, and private companies, sparking widespread debate about privacy, consent, and the potential for abuse.

Facial recognition technology operates by analyzing the unique features of a person's face—such as the distance between the eyes, the shape of the nose, and the contour of the jawline—and comparing this data to a pre-existing database of images. When a match is found, the system can identify the individual in real-time, providing authorities with an unprecedented ability to monitor people's movements and activities. While facial recognition has proven effective in law enforcement—helping to identify criminals and missing persons—it has also raised significant concerns about civil liberties. Critics argue that the technology can be used to target political activists, suppress dissent, and disproportionately affect marginalized communities.

The rise of artificial intelligence (AI) has taken surveillance technology to an entirely new level. AI-powered surveillance systems are capable of analyzing vast amounts of data in real-time, recognizing patterns, and making predictions about human behavior. Unlike traditional surveillance methods, which required human operators to manually review footage, AI-driven systems can process and interpret data far more efficiently, allowing for continuous monitoring without human intervention. These systems are now being used in a variety of settings, from public safety and urban planning to workplace management and marketing.

One of the key advantages of AI-driven surveillance is its ability to *predict behavior*. Using algorithms trained on large datasets, AI systems can analyze patterns in human movement, communication, and behavior to predict potential threats or violations. For example, in law enforcement, AI can be used to identify individuals who may be at risk of committing a crime based on their previous actions or associations. This form of *predictive policing* allows authorities to intervene before a crime is committed, but it also raises concerns about profiling, discrimination, and the potential for innocent people to be unfairly targeted.

Predictive policing relies on vast amounts of data, much of which is collected through digital surveillance systems, such as social media monitoring, location tracking, and communications surveillance. AI algorithms analyze this data to identify individuals who fit certain risk profiles, potentially flagging them for further investigation or intervention. While proponents of predictive policing argue that it improves public safety, critics warn that it can reinforce existing biases in the criminal justice system. For example, if an algorithm is trained on data that reflects historical biases in policing—such as disproportionately targeting minority communities—it may perpetuate those biases, leading to unfair treatment and discrimination.

In addition to predictive policing, AI-driven surveillance is increasingly being used in *workplace management*. Many companies now use AI tools to monitor employee performance, track productivity, and ensure compliance with company policies. These systems can analyze a wide range of data, including email correspondence, internet usage, and even physical movements within the workplace. For example, some AI-powered surveillance systems use cameras equipped with facial recognition and motion detection to track when employees enter and leave the office, how long they spend on breaks, and how much time they spend at their desks.

While these systems are often justified as tools for improving efficiency and accountability, they also raise significant concerns about *privacy* and *worker autonomy*. The constant monitoring of employees can create a culture of surveillance, where workers feel pressured to conform to company expectations and avoid behaviors that could be perceived as unproductive. This can lead to increased stress, anxiety, and burnout, as employees become more focused on meeting surveillance metrics than on doing meaningful work. Moreover, the use of AI-driven surveillance in the workplace blurs the line between professional and personal life, as employees may feel that their every move is being watched and judged.

Beyond the workplace, AI-driven surveillance is also transforming *consumer behavior*. Companies use sophisticated AI algorithms to analyze online behavior, track purchasing habits, and predict consumer preferences. This form of surveillance, often referred to as *surveillance capitalism*, allows companies to target individuals with personalized advertisements and marketing strategies. While this can make shopping more convenient, it also raises concerns about data privacy and the extent to which individuals are being manipulated by invisible forces. The data collected through online surveillance can reveal intimate details about a person's life, including their interests, relationships, and even political beliefs, leading to concerns about how this information is being used, stored, and shared.

One of the most controversial uses of AI-driven surveillance is in *China's Social Credit System*, where the government monitors citizens' behavior and assigns them scores based on their actions. These scores are used to determine a person's access to various privileges, such as travel, loans, or even employment. The system is powered by a vast network of surveillance cameras equipped with facial recognition technology, as well as AI algorithms that analyze data from social media, financial transactions, and public records. While the Chinese government claims that the system is designed to promote trust and good citizenship, critics argue that it represents a dystopian form of control, where individuals are constantly monitored and judged by an all-seeing state.

The Social Credit System demonstrates the potential for AI-driven surveillance to be used as a tool of *social control*. By constantly monitoring citizens and assigning them scores based on their behavior, the government can encourage conformity and suppress dissent. Individuals who are deemed to be non-compliant or untrustworthy may face significant restrictions on their freedoms, creating a climate of fear and self-censorship. While China's Social Credit System is an extreme example, it highlights the broader trend of governments and corporations using surveillance technology to influence behavior and maintain control over populations.

As AI-driven surveillance continues to advance, the *ethical implications* of these technologies become increasingly urgent. While surveillance can undoubtedly improve security, efficiency, and convenience, it also poses significant risks to privacy, civil liberties, and human autonomy. The ability of AI to analyze and predict human behavior raises fundamental questions about consent, accountability, and the role of technology in shaping society. Without proper oversight and regulation, AI-driven surveillance could lead to a future where individuals are constantly monitored, judged, and controlled by unseen algorithms.

In conclusion, the evolution of surveillance technology—from the early days of CCTV to the rise of AI-driven systems—reflects a growing desire for control and oversight in modern society. While these technologies offer undeniable benefits in terms of security and efficiency, they also raise serious concerns about privacy, civil liberties, and the potential for abuse. As AI continues to transform the way we monitor and influence human behavior, it is essential to strike a balance between the need for security and the protection of individual rights. Without careful consideration of the ethical implications, surveillance technology risks becoming a tool of oppression, rather than a force for good. Understanding the potential dangers of AI-driven control is the first step in ensuring that these technologies are used responsibly and transparently.

The Mind Control Tactics of Authoritarian Regimes

Authoritarian regimes, throughout history and in the modern era, have employed a range of mind control tactics to maintain power, suppress dissent, and shape the thoughts and behaviors of their populations. These tactics are designed to manipulate perception, control the flow of information, and create an atmosphere of fear and conformity. By using psychological manipulation, propaganda, censorship, and surveillance, authoritarian leaders aim to ensure that citizens not only comply with the regime's rules but also internalize its ideologies. In this chapter, we will explore the mind control tactics commonly used by authoritarian regimes, examining how these methods affect individuals and society, and the long-term consequences of living under such systems of control.

One of the most effective mind control tools in authoritarian regimes is the use of *propaganda*. Propaganda serves as a way to shape the narrative, controlling how people perceive the government, society, and the outside world. Through constant exposure to state-sanctioned messages, the population is conditioned to accept certain ideas as truths while being shielded from opposing viewpoints. The goal of propaganda is not only to manipulate what people think but to control how they think—creating an environment where the regime's version of reality becomes the dominant, unquestioned narrative.

In many authoritarian regimes, propaganda is disseminated through *state-controlled media*. News outlets, television channels, radio, and even social media platforms are often either directly owned by the state or operate under strict governmental control. These media outlets present a carefully curated version of events, selectively reporting information that aligns with the regime's agenda while omitting or distorting facts that could challenge its authority. For example, in North Korea, state-run media portrays the ruling Kim family as god-like figures, capable of miraculous feats and responsible for the well-being of the nation. This narrative is reinforced through daily broadcasts, posters, and public speeches, creating an environment where dissent or questioning of the regime is unthinkable for most citizens.

Propaganda is also deeply embedded in *education systems* in authoritarian regimes. Schools and universities become instruments of indoctrination, where curricula are designed to instill loyalty to the regime from a young age. History is rewritten to glorify the regime and its leaders, while opposing political ideologies, cultures, or historical figures are vilified. This form of indoctrination creates a cycle of control, as each generation is raised with a limited and distorted understanding of the world, making it easier for the regime to maintain its grip on power. For example, in Nazi Germany, the education system was designed to promote anti-Semitic ideologies and instill loyalty to Adolf Hitler, preparing the youth to become obedient members of the state.

Censorship is another essential tool for authoritarian regimes in their effort to control minds. By restricting access to information, regimes prevent citizens from encountering alternative viewpoints or uncovering inconvenient truths about the government's actions. In countries like China, the government tightly controls the internet through the "Great Firewall," which blocks foreign websites and censors politically sensitive content.

Citizens are unable to access information about democracy, human rights abuses, or criticisms of the ruling Communist Party. This creates an *information bubble*, where the government controls the flow of knowledge and shapes the public's understanding of reality.

Authoritarian regimes also use *fear* as a powerful psychological weapon to enforce obedience and compliance. Fear of punishment—whether in the form of imprisonment, torture, execution, or social ostracism—forces people to conform to the regime's rules. In many cases, authoritarian regimes rely on *secret police* or intelligence agencies to monitor and punish dissenters, creating a climate of paranoia where individuals are afraid to speak out, even in private. In East Germany, for example, the Stasi, the state security service, maintained an extensive network of informants who reported on citizens' activities. This constant surveillance created a culture of fear, where people were unsure of who they could trust, leading to widespread self-censorship and compliance with the regime.

Surveillance plays a critical role in reinforcing the fear that drives compliance. As technology has advanced, authoritarian regimes have adopted more sophisticated methods of monitoring their populations. In China, for instance, the government has implemented an extensive surveillance system that includes facial recognition cameras, internet monitoring, and the controversial *social credit system*, which tracks citizens' behavior and assigns them scores based on their compliance with social and political norms. Those with low scores may face restrictions on travel, employment, and access to services. This constant monitoring conditions people to regulate their own behavior, knowing that any deviation from the regime's expectations could have serious consequences.

In addition to fear, authoritarian regimes often cultivate a sense of *nationalism* and *group identity* to foster loyalty and control the minds of their citizens. Leaders use national pride and the idea of an external enemy to rally citizens around the regime. By creating the perception that the nation is under threat—whether from foreign powers, ethnic minorities, or ideological opponents—the regime can justify oppressive measures and demand sacrifices in the name of protecting the country. In this environment, dissent is framed as betrayal, and citizens are encouraged to view those who criticize the government as enemies of the state.

The concept of an *external threat* is a powerful tool for mind control, as it allows authoritarian regimes to divert attention away from internal issues like corruption, economic inequality, or human rights abuses. By focusing the public's anger or fear on an outside enemy, the regime fosters a sense of unity and loyalty among its citizens, making them more willing to accept authoritarian measures. For example, during the Cold War, the Soviet Union frequently portrayed the United States and its allies as existential threats, justifying its own repressive actions as necessary to defend socialism from imperialist aggression.

The *cult of personality* is another mind control tactic commonly employed by authoritarian regimes. This involves the glorification of the leader to an almost divine status, where the leader is portrayed as infallible, heroic, and essential to the nation's survival. In North Korea, Kim Jong-un, like his father and grandfather before him, is worshipped through state-sponsored propaganda that depicts him as the "Great Leader" who is wise, powerful, and benevolent.

Through statues, portraits, and constant praise in the media, the cult of personality creates a psychological environment where loyalty to the leader is equated with loyalty to the nation itself, and any criticism of the leader is seen as an act of treason.

Authoritarian regimes also manipulate *language* to control thought. By controlling the words people use, regimes can limit how citizens think and express themselves. George Orwell famously explored this concept in his novel *1984*, where the fictional regime uses "Newspeak," a language designed to eliminate dissenting thoughts by removing the words necessary to express them. While Orwell's concept is fictional, the manipulation of language is very real in many authoritarian states. For example, in China, terms like "democracy," "freedom," and "human rights" are often censored or redefined to align with the government's version of reality. This linguistic control limits the ability of citizens to think critically or organize against the regime, as the language needed to articulate opposition is suppressed.

In some cases, authoritarian regimes use *psychological manipulation* to create a sense of learned helplessness in their populations. By constantly exposing citizens to oppression and making it clear that resistance is futile, regimes can condition people to accept their powerlessness. Over time, individuals may come to believe that no matter what they do, they cannot change the system, leading to widespread apathy and disengagement. This learned helplessness ensures that even if people recognize the injustices of the regime, they will not take action to challenge it, as they believe their efforts would be in vain.

The long-term psychological effects of living under authoritarian control can be profound. Constant exposure to fear, propaganda, and surveillance can lead to a loss of individual identity and autonomy, as people become conditioned to prioritize the needs of the state over their own thoughts and desires. The internalization of the regime's ideology can also create a sense of cognitive dissonance, where individuals struggle to reconcile the reality of their lives with the propaganda they are exposed to. In some cases, this leads to a phenomenon known as *doublethink*, where citizens simultaneously hold contradictory beliefs—accepting the regime's narrative while also recognizing its falsehoods.

However, while authoritarian regimes may succeed in controlling the minds of many, there is always the potential for resistance. Underground movements, samizdat (self-published literature), and encrypted communication methods have long been used to challenge authoritarian control and disseminate alternative viewpoints. Despite the pervasive nature of mind control tactics, history shows that no regime is entirely immune to dissent and that, over time, people can find ways to break free from psychological manipulation. Authoritarian regimes use a wide range of mind control tactics to manipulate and control their populations. Propaganda, censorship, fear, surveillance, nationalism, and the cult of personality all serve to create an environment where obedience is enforced and dissent is suppressed. These tactics shape not only how people behave but also how they think, ensuring that the regime's version of reality is the only one that most citizens know. However, while these tactics are effective in the short term, the human desire for freedom and truth often leads to resistance and, in many cases, the eventual collapse of the authoritarian system. Understanding these mind control tactics is essential for recognizing and resisting the psychological manipulation that authoritarian regimes seek to impose.

Religious Extremism: How Belief Is Twisted for Power

Religious extremism has long been a tool used by individuals and groups to consolidate power, justify violence, and control followers. While religion at its core often promotes values of peace, compassion, and community, extremist movements distort these beliefs to achieve political, ideological, or personal goals. In the hands of extremists, faith becomes a weapon, used to manipulate followers into blind obedience, dehumanize opponents, and legitimize acts of aggression that would otherwise be condemned. This chapter will explore how religious belief is twisted by extremists for power, examining the psychological, social, and political mechanisms that enable this manipulation, and the consequences it has for both individuals and societies.

At the heart of religious extremism is the *exploitation of belief*. Religion often serves as a powerful source of identity, meaning, and moral guidance for individuals, making it an ideal platform for control. Extremist leaders tap into the deep emotional and psychological connection that people have with their faith, twisting its teachings to serve their agendas. By presenting themselves as the true interpreters of religious doctrine, extremists position themselves as the only legitimate source of spiritual authority. Followers are convinced that obedience to the leader or group is synonymous with obedience to divine will, creating a sense of moral obligation that makes it difficult to question or resist the leader's commands.

One of the key tactics of religious extremists is the creation of a *binary worldview*. Extremists often frame the world in terms of an absolute battle between good and evil, where their group represents the forces of righteousness and everyone else is part of the corrupt, immoral, or even demonic opposition. This *us versus them* mentality simplifies complex social, political, or moral issues into a black-and-white narrative, leaving no room for nuance or dissent. Followers are taught that their faith is under attack, and that extreme measures are necessary to protect their religious values or community from existential threats. This creates a heightened sense of urgency and fear, making followers more willing to engage in violent or unethical behavior in the name of defending their faith.

This binary view also *dehumanizes outsiders*. By portraying those outside the extremist group as enemies of the faith, extremists can justify acts of violence, exclusion, or oppression against them. Whether these "enemies" are other religious groups, political opponents, or different ethnic or cultural groups, the process of dehumanization allows extremists to dismiss the rights and humanity of others. In this way, atrocities such as terrorism, ethnic cleansing, and religious persecution are framed as divinely sanctioned acts, necessary to protect the faith or purify society. This manipulation of religious belief allows extremists to override basic ethical principles, convincing followers that any action is permissible as long as it serves the greater goal of religious dominance or purity.

Fear is another powerful tool used by religious extremists to maintain control over their followers. Fear of divine punishment, hell, or eternal damnation is invoked to enforce obedience and discourage questioning or dissent. Extremist leaders often claim to have special access to divine truth, presenting themselves as mediators between their followers and God.

This places immense psychological pressure on followers, who may fear that questioning the leader's authority or deviating from the group's teachings will result in spiritual condemnation or personal ruin. This use of fear creates a system of control that is deeply internalized, as individuals police their own thoughts and behaviors to avoid falling out of favor with both their leader and their perceived divine mandate.

Religious extremists also frequently employ *indoctrination* as a means of twisting belief for power. Through repetitive teaching, isolation from outside influences, and the enforcement of strict dogma, extremist groups create an environment where critical thinking is discouraged and group loyalty is prioritized above all else. Members of extremist groups are often cut off from alternative sources of information, such as secular education, media, or other religious perspectives, making it difficult for them to question the group's beliefs or practices. Indoctrination can start at a young age, particularly in communities where extremist ideology is passed down through generations, ensuring that children grow up with a narrow understanding of their faith that aligns with the group's radical views.

In many cases, religious extremists also manipulate *sacred texts* to support their agendas. By selectively quoting scripture or interpreting religious teachings in a rigid, literalistic manner, extremists can create the illusion that their actions are fully supported by religious doctrine. This selective use of scripture allows extremists to claim divine authority for their violent or oppressive actions, even when these actions contradict the broader moral and ethical teachings of the religion. For example, terrorist organizations like ISIS and al-Qaeda have used distorted interpretations of Islamic texts to justify acts of terrorism, while other extremists have similarly manipulated Christian or Hindu scriptures to support acts of violence, discrimination, or political domination.

Extremists often claim that they are restoring a "pure" or "original" form of the faith, appealing to *nostalgia* for a mythic past when their religion was supposedly untainted by outside influences or modernity. This claim of returning to religious purity is particularly appealing to followers who feel that their cultural or religious identity is under threat from globalization, secularism, or modern values. By positioning themselves as the protectors of an authentic religious tradition, extremists can mobilize followers to reject any form of compromise or reform, further entrenching their radical views. This appeal to purity often goes hand-in-hand with the idea of a *glorious future*, where the group's victory will usher in a utopian era of religious dominance and moral righteousness. Followers are taught that their sacrifices, including acts of violence, are necessary to bring about this divine future.

In addition to manipulating religious texts and beliefs, extremists use *rituals and symbols* to strengthen group cohesion and reinforce their authority. Rituals, whether they involve prayer, fasting, or other religious practices, are often transformed into acts of loyalty to the group rather than expressions of individual faith. Participation in these rituals serves as a way to bond members to one another and to the cause, creating a sense of collective identity that overrides personal autonomy. Extremist groups also frequently use symbols—such as flags, clothing, or slogans—that convey the group's ideology and create a visual representation of their power. These symbols become markers of group membership, signaling loyalty to the cause and reinforcing the us-versus-them mentality.

Martyrdom is another concept that religious extremists frequently exploit to manipulate followers. Martyrdom, or the idea of sacrificing oneself for the faith, is framed as the ultimate act of devotion, offering rewards in the afterlife or ensuring the group's victory. Extremist leaders often glorify those who die for the cause, portraying them as heroes or saints who are guaranteed a place in paradise. This romanticization of martyrdom is particularly effective in convincing young, impressionable followers to commit acts of violence, such as suicide bombings, because they believe their sacrifice will be rewarded both spiritually and by the group.

Religious extremists also use *charismatic leadership* to wield power. Many extremist movements are built around a single leader who is seen as a prophet, messiah, or chosen one. This leader is believed to have a unique connection to the divine, and their authority is considered unquestionable. Followers place their trust entirely in the leader, often surrendering their own judgment and autonomy in the process. Charismatic leaders often use emotional manipulation to inspire devotion, framing their relationship with followers as one of spiritual guidance and protection. This dynamic creates a system where questioning the leader is equated with questioning God, making it nearly impossible for followers to break free from the group's control.

One of the most dangerous aspects of religious extremism is its ability to foster *violence and intolerance*. By twisting belief systems to frame violence as a moral or divine necessity, extremists can mobilize large groups of people to commit acts of terror, genocide, or civil conflict. Extremists often target those they deem as "heretics," "infidels," or enemies of the faith, fostering a culture of hate and aggression that dehumanizes others and justifies cruelty in the name of religious purity. This violence is often framed as a defensive action, with extremists claiming that they are protecting their faith from existential threats. In reality, these acts of violence are often more about consolidating power and spreading fear than about religious defense.

The consequences of religious extremism are far-reaching, both for individuals and societies. Followers of extremist movements often suffer from psychological manipulation, isolation, and the loss of personal freedom. Many are pressured into committing acts of violence or enduring hardships in the belief that they are serving a higher purpose. On a societal level, religious extremism can lead to deep divisions, civil unrest, and prolonged conflict. It can also foster a climate of intolerance, where those who do not conform to the extremist group's beliefs are persecuted or marginalized. This intolerance often leads to human rights abuses, as extremists seek to impose their version of religious law on entire populations. Religious extremism represents a dangerous manipulation of faith for the sake of power. By exploiting deeply held beliefs, extremists are able to control followers, justify violence, and create societies based on fear and intolerance.

Through tactics such as propaganda, indoctrination, dehumanization, and charismatic leadership, extremists twist religious teachings to serve their own agendas, often causing immense suffering for individuals and communities. Understanding how religious belief is twisted for power is essential for recognizing and combating extremism, both within religious communities and on a global scale. Only by exposing the tactics of extremists and promoting dialogue, tolerance, and critical thinking can societies begin to counter the dangerous influence of religious extremism.

Media Manipulation in Democracies: Subtle but Powerful

In democratic societies, the media plays a crucial role in informing citizens, shaping public opinion, and holding those in power accountable. However, even in democracies where freedom of the press is upheld, media manipulation can subtly influence public perception and behavior in ways that are not immediately obvious. Media manipulation in democracies often operates through the selective presentation of information, the framing of narratives, and the use of emotional appeals. Unlike overt propaganda in authoritarian regimes, media manipulation in democracies is more nuanced and sophisticated, leveraging commercial interests, political agendas, and psychological tactics to steer public discourse. This chapter will explore how media manipulation operates in democratic societies, the techniques used to influence audiences, and the broader implications for democratic participation and informed citizenship.

One of the most common forms of media manipulation is *agenda-setting*, where media outlets decide which topics and issues receive coverage and which are ignored. In a democracy, where media is typically not directly controlled by the state, the power to set the agenda lies in the hands of media organizations, often influenced by their ownership, advertisers, and political affiliations. By focusing on certain issues while downplaying others, media organizations shape what the public perceives as important. For example, sensational stories about crime, scandal, or celebrity culture may dominate headlines, while critical but less dramatic issues like economic inequality, climate change, or healthcare policy receive far less attention.

Agenda-setting can create a skewed perception of reality, where certain problems seem more urgent than they are, while more pressing societal challenges remain underreported. This selective coverage leads to what is known as the *media spotlight effect*, where the issues that receive the most coverage are assumed to be the most important. The result is a public discourse that may not align with the actual priorities and needs of the population. For example, extensive coverage of terrorism or violent crime can create the perception that these issues are far more common than they are, influencing public opinion and policy debates in ways that do not reflect the true scale of the problem.

Another subtle form of media manipulation is *framing*, where media outlets present information in a way that emphasizes certain aspects of a story while downplaying or omitting others. Framing shapes how audiences interpret events, issues, or policies by influencing the context in which they are understood. For example, a news outlet might frame a political protest as a "violent riot" rather than a "peaceful demonstration," leading viewers to perceive the event as more dangerous or illegitimate than it actually is. Similarly, framing can be used to highlight positive or negative aspects of a politician's actions, depending on the outlet's bias or agenda.

FRAMING OFTEN INVOLVES the use of *loaded language*—words or phrases that carry strong emotional connotations. For example, terms like "freedom fighter" versus "terrorist" or "reform" versus "dismantling" evoke very different emotional responses, even if they refer to the same actions or policies. By carefully choosing the language used to describe events or individuals, media outlets can subtly manipulate public perception, steering audiences toward specific conclusions without overtly distorting facts. This manipulation is particularly powerful because it operates at the level of language, shaping thought processes before people even realize they are being influenced.

Bias by omission is another tactic used in media manipulation, where certain facts or perspectives are deliberately left out of a story to present a skewed version of reality. This form of manipulation is especially effective because it is difficult for audiences to detect what they are not being told. For example, during an election campaign, a news outlet with a particular political affiliation might choose to focus on the scandals or failures of one candidate while ignoring or downplaying the shortcomings of another. This selective reporting creates an imbalanced narrative that can influence voting behavior without explicitly lying or fabricating information. The omission of critical context, alternative perspectives, or contradictory evidence can have a profound impact on how stories are perceived.

In addition to framing and omission, *emotional manipulation* plays a significant role in how media shapes public opinion. In democratic societies, media organizations are often driven by the need to attract and retain audiences, which can lead to an emphasis on sensationalism over substance. Stories that provoke strong emotional reactions—such as fear, anger, or outrage—are more likely to capture attention and generate engagement. This focus on emotional content can skew public discourse toward issues that are highly charged but not necessarily the most important in terms of policy or societal impact.

For example, news coverage that focuses on isolated incidents of violent crime or terrorist attacks can create a heightened sense of fear and insecurity, even if the overall crime rate is low. This *fear-based reporting* can influence public opinion, leading to support for harsher law enforcement measures, increased surveillance, or more restrictive immigration policies, even when such measures may not be proportionate to the actual level of threat. Emotional manipulation is particularly effective in shaping public attitudes because it bypasses rational analysis and taps directly into the audience's instincts and feelings.

In the digital age, *social media platforms* have become a powerful tool for media manipulation. Social media algorithms prioritize content that generates engagement—such as likes, shares, and comments—which often means that emotionally charged or sensational content is more likely to be promoted. This creates a feedback loop where the most provocative or polarizing stories rise to the top, reinforcing echo chambers and deepening political polarization. Unlike traditional media, where editorial standards and fact-checking may serve as a barrier to outright manipulation, social media allows misinformation and emotionally manipulative content to spread quickly and widely, often without the same level of scrutiny.

The *attention economy* further exacerbates the problem of media manipulation in democracies. In a highly competitive media landscape, news outlets and social media platforms compete for viewers' attention, which is monetized through advertising revenue. This creates an incentive to prioritize clickbait headlines, sensationalism, and simplified narratives that appeal to emotions rather than complex, nuanced reporting. The focus on generating engagement leads to a media environment where stories are tailored to capture attention rather than inform or educate. As a result, public discourse is shaped more by what is entertaining or emotionally compelling than by what is factually accurate or meaningful for democratic decision-making.

Media manipulation in democracies is also closely tied to *corporate ownership* and the influence of powerful interests. In many democratic countries, a small number of large corporations control a significant portion of the media landscape. These corporations often have vested interests in certain policies, industries, or political outcomes, which can shape the content and perspective of the media outlets they own. For example, media organizations owned by corporations with ties to the fossil fuel industry may downplay the significance of climate change or promote skepticism about environmental regulations. While these outlets may not engage in outright disinformation, they can subtly shape the narrative in ways that align with their corporate interests.

In addition to corporate interests, *political bias* is a key factor in media manipulation. Media outlets often have ideological leanings that influence their coverage, whether conservative, liberal, or centrist. This bias can manifest in the choice of stories covered, the framing of issues, and the selection of sources or experts featured in the news. While bias is inevitable to some degree, the problem arises when media outlets present themselves as objective or neutral while subtly advancing a political agenda. This can mislead audiences into believing they are receiving balanced information when, in reality, they are being exposed to a skewed version of events.

One of the most significant consequences of media manipulation in democracies is its impact on *public trust*. As audiences become more aware of bias, selective reporting, and corporate or political influence in the media, trust in news organizations erodes. This erosion of trust can lead to *media cynicism*, where people become skeptical of all news sources, making it difficult to discern fact from fiction. In extreme cases, media cynicism can fuel conspiracy theories or lead to disengagement from democratic processes, as citizens lose faith in the ability of the media to provide accurate and reliable information.

Another consequence of media manipulation is the reinforcement of *political polarization*. When media outlets cater to specific ideological audiences, they contribute to the creation of echo chambers, where individuals are exposed only to information that aligns with their pre-existing beliefs. This selective exposure deepens divisions within society, making it harder for people with different political views to engage in constructive dialogue. As polarization increases, democratic processes become more contentious, and the ability to find common ground on important issues diminishes.

DESPITE THE CHALLENGES posed by media manipulation, there are ways to mitigate its effects. One of the most important steps is fostering *media literacy* among the public. Media literacy involves teaching individuals how to critically evaluate news sources, recognize bias, and identify manipulative tactics. By developing these skills, citizens can become more informed consumers of media, better equipped to navigate the complexities of modern information environments.

Another approach is promoting *diverse and independent media outlets* that are not beholden to corporate or political interests. Publicly funded media, non-profit journalism, and independent news organizations can provide a counterbalance to the influence of commercial and political pressures in the media landscape. Ensuring that a wide range of perspectives is represented in public discourse helps to prevent the monopolization of narratives and promotes a more informed and engaged citizenry.

In conclusion, media manipulation in democracies operates through a range of subtle but powerful techniques, from agenda-setting and framing to emotional manipulation and corporate influence. While these tactics are less overt than the propaganda used in authoritarian regimes, they still have a profound impact on public opinion, political discourse, and democratic participation. As citizens, recognizing and understanding these tactics is essential for resisting manipulation and ensuring that the media serves its vital role as a watchdog and source of reliable information in a democracy. By fostering media literacy, supporting independent journalism, and holding media organizations accountable, societies can protect the integrity of democratic processes and promote a more informed and engaged public.

The Power of Repetition: How Ideas Become Beliefs

Repetition is one of the most powerful tools for shaping human thought and turning ideas into deeply held beliefs. Whether in advertising, politics, education, or everyday communication, repeating the same messages over time ingrains them into our minds, making them more familiar, comfortable, and ultimately accepted as truth. The power of repetition lies in its subtlety—people often don't realize how much their opinions and beliefs are shaped by the constant reinforcement of ideas they encounter. This chapter will explore the psychological mechanisms behind repetition, how it is used to influence beliefs, and the broader implications for individuals and society when repetition is leveraged for persuasion or manipulation.

At its core, repetition works because of a psychological phenomenon known as the *mere exposure effect*, or the familiarity principle. This effect refers to the human tendency to develop a preference for things simply because we are repeatedly exposed to them. The more we hear, see, or experience something, the more familiar it becomes, and with familiarity comes comfort and acceptance. This principle applies to everything from catchy advertising jingles to political slogans. What begins as a neutral or even disagreeable idea can, through repeated exposure, gradually become more palatable or agreeable, eventually becoming an accepted part of a person's belief system.

In the context of *advertising*, repetition is a cornerstone strategy. Brands use repetitive messaging to ensure that their products or services become familiar to consumers. Slogans, logos, and advertisements are repeated across various media platforms to reinforce brand recognition and loyalty. The more a consumer is exposed to a particular brand, the more likely they are to trust it and choose it over a less familiar competitor. Even if a consumer does not actively engage with an advertisement, the simple act of seeing or hearing it repeatedly increases the chances that they will remember and trust the brand when making purchasing decisions. This is why advertising campaigns are often sustained over long periods, with the same message delivered across different formats.

Repetition also plays a crucial role in *political messaging*. Politicians and political parties often repeat the same slogans, phrases, and policy points throughout their campaigns to ensure that their message sticks in voters' minds. For example, phrases like "Make America Great Again" or "Yes We Can" became ingrained in public consciousness through constant repetition during political campaigns. These slogans are designed to be memorable, simple, and easy to repeat, making them ideal vehicles for reinforcing a political narrative. By repeating key messages across speeches, debates, social media, and advertisements, political actors can shape public perception, making their ideas more likely to be accepted as valid or even inevitable. The power of repetition in politics is particularly evident in the use of *talking points*. Political parties and candidates often distribute talking points to their supporters, ensuring that the same language and arguments are repeated across various media outlets, interviews, and public appearances. This repetition creates the illusion of consensus, as audiences are exposed to the same ideas from multiple sources, reinforcing the belief that these ideas are widely accepted or true. In reality, the repetition of talking points is a deliberate strategy to manufacture agreement and suppress dissent, making it difficult for alternative viewpoints to gain traction in public discourse.

Repetition also has a profound effect on *memory* and *learning*. From an early age, people learn through repetition, whether it's memorizing the alphabet, practicing math problems, or mastering a new skill. In education, repetition is used to reinforce key concepts and ensure that they are retained over time. The more often a piece of information is repeated, the more likely it is to be stored in long-term memory. This process, known as *consolidation*, strengthens neural connections in the brain, making the repeated information easier to recall. However, the same principle that helps us learn useful skills can also be exploited to reinforce misinformation or biased perspectives.

For instance, in media and news reporting, repeating certain narratives or frames can shape how audiences perceive an event or issue. If a particular news outlet consistently frames immigration as a "crisis" or presents certain political figures as "corrupt," these repeated messages become ingrained in the audience's understanding of the issue, regardless of whether the framing reflects the full complexity of the situation. Over time, the repetition of these frames solidifies them as part of the collective belief system, making it difficult for alternative interpretations to take hold.

The *illusion of truth effect* is another psychological phenomenon that underscores the power of repetition. This effect occurs when people begin to believe false or misleading information simply because they have heard it multiple times. Even if the information is incorrect or lacks evidence, the mere fact that it has been repeated increases its perceived credibility. This is particularly problematic in the context of misinformation or propaganda, where falsehoods can become widely accepted simply because they are repeated frequently in the media or by public figures. The illusion of truth effect makes it difficult for individuals to distinguish between fact and fiction, as repetition can override critical thinking and skepticism.

Confirmation bias also plays a role in how repetition turns ideas into beliefs. When people are repeatedly exposed to ideas that align with their existing beliefs, they are more likely to accept and internalize those ideas. Repetition reinforces the bias, making individuals more confident in their views and less open to alternative perspectives. For example, someone who holds a particular political or ideological belief is more likely to seek out media sources that reinforce their views. As they repeatedly encounter the same narratives, their belief becomes stronger, even if it is based on incomplete or biased information. This feedback loop of repetition and confirmation bias creates echo chambers, where individuals are insulated from opposing viewpoints and increasingly resistant to change.

Repetition is also used to create *social norms* and enforce conformity. In both small and large social groups, certain behaviors, attitudes, and beliefs are reinforced through repetition, creating an environment where deviations from the norm are discouraged. For example, in religious communities, repeated rituals, prayers, and teachings serve to reinforce specific moral values and beliefs. Over time, these repeated practices become ingrained as unquestioned truths, shaping the behavior and worldview of individuals within the community.

Similarly, in workplace cultures or social movements, the repeated promotion of certain values or ideologies creates a sense of shared identity, making it more difficult for individuals to challenge the prevailing norms.

The power of repetition is further amplified by *media saturation* in the digital age. With the rise of social media, streaming platforms, and 24-hour news cycles, individuals are exposed to a constant barrage of information. This relentless repetition of certain ideas, memes, or narratives creates a sense of inevitability, where the most frequently encountered messages dominate public consciousness. Social media algorithms, in particular, prioritize content that has already proven popular or engaging, leading to the repeated exposure of the same ideas or stories. This creates a feedback loop where the most repeated content is also the most visible, reinforcing its influence over time.

In advertising and consumer culture, the power of repetition is leveraged to *create desire* and *shape habits*. Brands use repeated exposure to build familiarity with their products, making them more desirable in the eyes of consumers. Through constant repetition in commercials, online ads, and social media, brands can associate their products with positive emotions, experiences, or aspirations. Over time, repeated exposure to these messages creates a sense of need or desire, even for products that consumers may not have initially considered. This repetition-driven desire can lead to habitual purchasing, where consumers unconsciously choose familiar brands over competitors simply because they have been exposed to them more often.

However, the power of repetition also has its limitations. When repetition becomes too obvious or excessive, it can lead to *fatigue* or *resistance*. People may begin to tune out messages that they perceive as overly repetitive, especially if they feel that they are being manipulated or overwhelmed by the frequency of the message. This is known as the *wear-out effect*, where repeated exposure to the same idea or message loses its effectiveness over time. To avoid this, marketers, politicians, and media organizations often vary the presentation of their messages, using different formats, platforms, or emotional appeals to keep the repetition subtle and engaging.

In conclusion, repetition is an incredibly powerful force in shaping beliefs, whether in advertising, politics, education, or media. Through the mechanisms of familiarity, memory consolidation, the illusion of truth effect, and confirmation bias, repetition transforms ideas into accepted truths over time. While repetition can be used to promote positive behaviors, reinforce learning, and create social cohesion, it can also be exploited to manipulate public opinion, spread misinformation, and entrench bias. In a world where information is constantly repeated across multiple platforms, individuals must develop the critical thinking skills necessary to recognize when they are being influenced by repetition and to evaluate ideas based on evidence rather than mere familiarity. Understanding the power of repetition is key to resisting manipulation and ensuring that beliefs are formed through thoughtful reflection rather than unconscious influence.

Controlling the Masses: Techniques Used in Totalitarian States

Totalitarian states are characterized by an all-encompassing control over nearly every aspect of public and private life, employing a range of techniques to manipulate, dominate, and subdue the masses. These regimes seek absolute authority, often using psychological manipulation, violence, propaganda, and mass surveillance to create a climate of fear, obedience, and ideological conformity. The methods used to control populations in totalitarian regimes are comprehensive, aiming to suppress dissent, eliminate opposition, and shape the thoughts and behaviors of individuals to align with the regime's goals. In this chapter, we will explore the techniques used in totalitarian states to control the masses, examining how these strategies undermine personal freedom, erode individuality, and maintain a firm grip on power.

One of the most prominent tools for controlling the masses in a totalitarian state is the use of *fear and intimidation*. Totalitarian regimes maintain power by instilling a pervasive sense of fear among the population, often through the threat of violence, imprisonment, or death. The regime's security apparatus—such as secret police, military forces, and intelligence agencies—plays a central role in enforcing this climate of fear. Individuals know that any act of defiance, no matter how small, could result in severe consequences not only for themselves but for their families and communities. The fear of punishment, often arbitrary or disproportionate, leads to widespread self-censorship, as citizens internalize the risks of speaking out or opposing the regime. The result is a culture of silence, where dissent is suppressed before it can even take root.

One of the most chilling aspects of totalitarian control is the use of *show trials* and public executions to reinforce the regime's power. By making examples of perceived enemies or dissidents, the regime sends a clear message to the population: disobedience will not be tolerated, and any challenge to authority will be met with brutal retribution. These public displays of punishment serve not only to eliminate opposition but to remind citizens of the regime's absolute control over life and death. Show trials often involve forced confessions, fabricated evidence, and orchestrated spectacles designed to reinforce the legitimacy of the state while dehumanizing those who resist.

Mass surveillance is another key technique used in totalitarian states to maintain control. Modern technology has made it easier than ever for regimes to monitor the activities, communications, and movements of their citizens. Surveillance programs often operate on multiple levels, from the monitoring of phone calls, emails, and social media, to the physical tracking of individuals through cameras, facial recognition software, and informant networks. The mere knowledge that one is constantly being watched—whether by the government or by neighbors and colleagues who act as informants—creates a sense of paranoia and insecurity. People begin to self-regulate their behavior, avoiding any actions or conversations that could be interpreted as disloyal to the regime.

THIS OMNIPRESENT SURVEILLANCE is particularly effective because it blurs the line between public and private life. In totalitarian states, there is no refuge from the state's watchful eye; even in one's home, individuals may feel compelled to act as though they are being observed, for fear that their actions or words could be reported by others. This creates a deep psychological burden, as citizens must constantly second-guess their thoughts and behaviors to avoid attracting attention from the authorities.

One of the most effective techniques used by totalitarian states is the control of *information and propaganda*. In these regimes, the government often monopolizes the media, ensuring that only state-approved narratives are broadcast to the public. Independent journalism is either banned or heavily censored, and citizens are exposed to a constant stream of propaganda designed to glorify the regime, demonize its enemies, and promote its ideology. This manipulation of information creates a distorted reality, where the regime's version of events becomes the only accepted truth. By controlling what people see, hear, and read, totalitarian governments can shape public perception, making it difficult for individuals to challenge the official narrative or seek alternative perspectives.

Propaganda in totalitarian states is often relentless and all-encompassing, permeating every aspect of daily life. Schools, workplaces, entertainment, and public spaces are saturated with messages that promote loyalty to the regime and its leaders. In many cases, these messages are designed to evoke strong emotional responses, using symbols, slogans, and imagery that appeal to national pride, fear of external threats, or devotion to the leader. Over time, this constant reinforcement of the regime's ideology can wear down resistance, as individuals become conditioned to accept the state's version of reality as normal or inevitable.

Education and indoctrination are also key components of totalitarian control. From a young age, children in totalitarian states are taught to revere the regime and its leaders, often through a highly politicized curriculum that promotes the government's ideology. History is rewritten to suit the regime's narrative, while opposing viewpoints or inconvenient truths are erased from textbooks. By shaping the minds of the young, totalitarian states seek to create a generation that is loyal, obedient, and unquestioning of authority. Indoctrination extends beyond formal education, with youth organizations, state-sponsored extracurricular activities, and public ceremonies designed to instill a sense of duty and devotion to the regime.

The use of *collective punishment* is another method by which totalitarian regimes control the masses. In many cases, the regime does not punish only the individual who is accused of dissent but extends the punishment to their family, friends, or community. This tactic is designed to isolate dissidents and create a sense of communal responsibility for individual actions. By making the consequences of defiance collective, the regime discourages opposition, as individuals fear not only for their own safety but for the safety of their loved ones. This form of punishment fosters a culture of fear and mistrust, where citizens are encouraged to report on one another to avoid being implicated in acts of dissent.

THE CREATION OF A *cult of personality* around the leader is another hallmark of totalitarian regimes. Leaders in these states are often depicted as infallible, god-like figures who embody the spirit of the nation or ideology. Through constant praise and adulation, the leader is elevated above all criticism, and loyalty to the leader becomes synonymous with loyalty to the state. This cult of personality is reinforced through media, art, literature, and public ceremonies, where citizens are required to participate in demonstrations of devotion, such as chanting slogans, attending parades, or displaying portraits of the leader in their homes. The goal is to create an emotional bond between the leader and the people, making it difficult for individuals to imagine a reality without the leader's guidance.

In addition to these methods, totalitarian regimes often use *manipulation of language* to control thought. George Orwell's concept of *Newspeak* in his novel *1984* illustrates how language can be restricted and manipulated to limit the range of thought. In totalitarian states, certain words or phrases may be banned, while new terms are introduced to enforce the regime's ideology. By controlling the language that people use, totalitarian regimes limit the ability of individuals to articulate dissent or even conceive of alternatives to the existing system. When the language of resistance is stripped away, the very possibility of rebellion is diminished.

Totalitarian regimes also manipulate *psychological and emotional vulnerabilities* to maintain control. They often appeal to feelings of *nationalism* or the idea that the nation is under constant threat from external enemies. By fostering a sense of perpetual crisis, the regime can justify extreme measures, such as censorship, militarization, or the suspension of civil liberties. Citizens are led to believe that the survival of the nation depends on their complete loyalty to the state, and any dissent is portrayed as a betrayal of the nation's values. This technique is particularly effective in times of economic hardship, war, or political instability, when individuals may be more willing to sacrifice personal freedoms for the sake of security.

Totalitarian states also engage in the *rewriting of history* to control the masses. Historical events that contradict the regime's narrative are erased or altered, while past leaders or movements that challenged the regime are demonized or forgotten. This manipulation of history creates a false sense of continuity and legitimacy for the regime, as it presents itself as the rightful successor to a long tradition of governance or revolution. By controlling the past, totalitarian regimes can shape the future, ensuring that their version of history is the only one that is remembered or taught.

The psychological impact of living under a totalitarian regime is profound. Over time, individuals may experience *learned helplessness*, where they come to believe that resistance is futile and that they have no control over their circumstances. This sense of powerlessness leads to widespread apathy and disengagement, as people lose hope that change is possible. In some cases, individuals may even internalize the regime's ideology, coming to believe that the oppressive system is justified or inevitable. This internalization of control is one of the most insidious aspects of totalitarianism, as it reduces the need for overt coercion by creating a population that willingly submits to the regime's authority.

In conclusion, totalitarian regimes use a wide range of techniques to control the masses, from fear and surveillance to propaganda and indoctrination. These methods are designed to suppress dissent, create conformity, and eliminate any threat to the regime's power. By controlling information, shaping language, and manipulating psychological vulnerabilities, totalitarian states can maintain a tight grip on their populations, making resistance difficult and dangerous. While the specific tactics may vary from regime to regime, the goal is always the same: to create a society where obedience to the state is absolute, and individual freedom is crushed under the weight of totalitarian control. Understanding these techniques is essential for recognizing the warning signs of authoritarianism and defending against the erosion of democratic values.

The Psychological Consequences of Mind Control

Mind control, in its various forms, can have profound and lasting psychological consequences on individuals and society as a whole. Whether in authoritarian regimes, cults, abusive relationships, or through subtle manipulation in democratic societies, the impact of mind control techniques can reshape an individual's sense of self, alter cognitive functions, and lead to a range of mental health issues. The psychological effects of mind control are often far-reaching, leaving individuals emotionally, mentally, and sometimes even physically altered long after the initial manipulation has ended. This chapter will explore the psychological consequences of mind control, focusing on the mechanisms through which control is exerted, the emotional and mental toll it takes on victims, and the long-term impacts on both individuals and societies.

One of the most immediate psychological consequences of mind control is the loss of *individual autonomy*. Mind control techniques, whether overt or subtle, seek to strip individuals of their sense of independence, replacing their thoughts and beliefs with those of the controlling authority. In environments where obedience and conformity are enforced, individuals lose the ability to make decisions for themselves, leading to a diminished sense of personal agency. Over time, this loss of autonomy can result in a profound sense of *powerlessness*, as individuals come to believe that they have no control over their lives, their actions, or their thoughts.

This sense of powerlessness is often accompanied by *learned helplessness*, a psychological condition in which individuals, after prolonged exposure to a controlling or abusive environment, become unable to see any possibility of escape or change. Learned helplessness is a key outcome of environments where mind control tactics are used, such as in authoritarian regimes or cults, where individuals are consistently made to feel that resistance is futile. When people are repeatedly subjected to manipulation, coercion, or punishment for disobedience, they begin to internalize the belief that their efforts to resist or assert independence are pointless. This can lead to a sense of deep resignation, where victims of mind control no longer attempt to escape or challenge their situation, even when opportunities for change arise.

Mind control also has profound effects on *cognitive functions*, particularly the ability to think critically and engage in independent thought. In environments where mind control techniques are prevalent, individuals are often subjected to a constant barrage of propaganda, misinformation, and manipulation designed to shape their worldview. Over time, this repeated exposure to distorted information can lead to cognitive dissonance, where individuals struggle to reconcile conflicting ideas or experiences. To resolve this internal tension, many victims of mind control adopt the beliefs or narratives promoted by their controllers, suppressing their own doubts and accepting the imposed worldview as reality. This cognitive shift makes it difficult for individuals to engage in *critical thinking*, as they come to rely on the controlling authority for guidance on what to think and believe.

ONE OF THE MORE INSIDIOUS effects of mind control is the *fragmentation of identity*. In environments where individuals are forced to conform to a particular ideology or belief system, they may experience a split between their authentic self and the persona they are required to adopt to survive. This fragmentation occurs when individuals feel compelled to suppress their true thoughts, desires, and values in order to avoid punishment or rejection. Over time, this suppression can lead to a weakened sense of self, where individuals no longer feel connected to their own identity or values. This disconnection from the self can manifest in feelings of confusion, self-doubt, and emotional numbness, as victims struggle to reconcile their true identity with the persona they have adopted under the influence of mind control.

In extreme cases, this fragmentation can result in *dissociation*, a psychological response in which individuals disconnect from their thoughts, feelings, or sense of reality as a way of coping with trauma or intense emotional distress. Dissociation is common in victims of abusive relationships or cults, where the psychological pressure to conform and the fear of punishment are constant. Victims may mentally "check out" during moments of intense manipulation or coercion, detaching themselves from the emotional pain of the experience. Over time, this coping mechanism can become a chronic condition, where individuals have difficulty staying present or maintaining a cohesive sense of identity.

Another psychological consequence of mind control is the *emotional toll* it takes on individuals. Victims of mind control often experience intense feelings of *fear, guilt, and shame*. Fear is a primary tool used in mind control environments, whether it is fear of punishment, ostracism, or divine retribution. This constant sense of fear can lead to chronic anxiety, hypervigilance, and a heightened stress response, as individuals are constantly on guard for potential threats or consequences. Over time, the chronic activation of the body's stress response can lead to physical symptoms such as fatigue, headaches, and digestive issues, as well as mental health conditions like generalized anxiety disorder or post-traumatic stress disorder (PTSD).

Guilt and shame are also commonly experienced by victims of mind control, particularly in environments where individuals are made to feel responsible for their own suffering or the suffering of others. In cults or abusive relationships, for example, victims are often blamed for their perceived failures or inadequacies, leading to a deep sense of shame and self-blame. This emotional manipulation is designed to keep individuals compliant, as they come to believe that they are inherently flawed or deserving of the treatment they are receiving. Over time, this internalized guilt and shame can erode self-esteem and lead to feelings of worthlessness or depression.

One of the long-term psychological consequences of mind control is *trust issues.* After experiencing prolonged manipulation, victims often find it difficult to trust others, as they have been betrayed or exploited by individuals or institutions that they once believed in. This breakdown in trust can extend beyond the immediate situation, affecting relationships with friends, family, and society as a whole. Victims may become suspicious of others' motives, struggle to form meaningful connections, or isolate themselves from social interaction. This lack of trust can also make it difficult for victims to seek help or support, as they may fear being manipulated or hurt again.

Isolation is another common psychological outcome of mind control. In many cases, controlling authorities seek to isolate individuals from outside influences, preventing them from forming relationships or engaging with alternative perspectives that might challenge the imposed ideology. This isolation can be physical, such as in cults where members are cut off from family and friends, or psychological, where victims are made to feel that no one outside of the controlling group can be trusted. Over time, this isolation reinforces the controlling authority's power, as individuals become increasingly dependent on the group or leader for social, emotional, and psychological support.

One of the most destructive long-term effects of mind control is the *difficulty in breaking free* from the controlling influence. Even when individuals manage to escape a physically controlling environment, the psychological grip of mind control can persist for years. Victims may continue to struggle with feelings of guilt, fear, and confusion, as they try to rebuild their sense of identity and autonomy. The process of deprogramming—reversing the psychological effects of mind control—can be slow and painful, requiring individuals to confront the beliefs and behaviors they were conditioned to adopt. Many victims require therapy or counseling to help them process the trauma of their experiences and regain their ability to think independently.

On a broader societal level, the psychological consequences of mind control can lead to *social fragmentation and division*. In environments where large groups of people are subjected to mind control, whether in totalitarian states or through mass media manipulation, society can become polarized, with individuals divided into those who accept the imposed ideology and those who resist it. This division can create a climate of fear, mistrust, and hostility, where open dialogue and critical thinking are stifled. Over time, the effects of mind control can erode democratic values, weaken social cohesion, and make it more difficult for societies to address collective challenges.

In conclusion, the psychological consequences of mind control are profound and far-reaching. From the loss of autonomy and identity fragmentation to emotional distress and long-term mental health issues, mind control can leave lasting scars on individuals and society. The manipulation of thoughts, beliefs, and behaviors erodes personal freedom, damages relationships, and creates a climate of fear and mistrust. Understanding these psychological effects is crucial for recognizing the warning signs of mind control and supporting those who have been subjected to it in their journey toward recovery. While the process of healing from mind control can be challenging, it is possible for individuals to reclaim their sense of self, regain their autonomy, and rebuild their lives free from the influence of controlling forces.

Resisting Manipulation: How to Protect Yourself from Control

Resisting manipulation and protecting yourself from control is crucial in a world where mind control tactics are prevalent, whether through media, politics, relationships, or broader societal structures. While manipulation can often be subtle and difficult to detect, there are ways to build awareness and develop the psychological tools necessary to safeguard your independence and mental autonomy. This chapter will focus on practical strategies for recognizing manipulation, resisting control, and protecting your ability to think and act freely. By strengthening critical thinking skills, emotional resilience, and self-awareness, you can become less susceptible to manipulation and maintain control over your own beliefs, decisions, and actions.

One of the most important steps in resisting manipulation is developing *self-awareness*. Understanding your own thoughts, emotions, and motivations helps you recognize when external forces are attempting to influence or manipulate you. Self-awareness involves being mindful of how your emotions and beliefs are shaped by external stimuli, such as media messages, social interactions, or persuasive arguments. By reflecting on your reactions to information or pressure, you can better identify when your thoughts and behaviors are being influenced by manipulation rather than by your own values and judgment.

For example, if you find yourself feeling unusually angry, fearful, or anxious after consuming certain media or engaging with certain people, it's important to pause and consider whether these emotions are being artificially provoked. Manipulators often use emotional appeals—especially fear, guilt, or outrage—to bypass critical thinking and encourage compliance or acceptance of their agenda. By recognizing when your emotions are being manipulated, you can take a step back, regain control, and evaluate the situation more objectively.

Critical thinking is one of the most effective defenses against manipulation. This skill involves analyzing information, questioning assumptions, and evaluating evidence before forming conclusions. Manipulators often rely on emotional appeals, oversimplified narratives, or selective presentation of facts to influence others. By approaching information critically, you can identify logical fallacies, contradictions, and biases in the messages you receive.

To strengthen your critical thinking, practice asking questions such as:

- What is the source of this information? Is it reliable and credible?
- What evidence supports this claim, and are there any alternative explanations?
- Is this message appealing to my emotions rather than presenting facts?
- What might be the agenda or motive behind this information?

Developing the habit of questioning information and thinking critically allows you to resist manipulation by refusing to accept messages at face value. This approach helps you avoid being swayed by misleading arguments, propaganda, or emotional manipulation.

Recognizing manipulation techniques is also key to resisting control. Many manipulators use similar tactics to influence people's thoughts and behaviors, whether in personal relationships, advertising, or politics. Some common manipulation techniques include:

- **Gaslighting**: This occurs when someone makes you doubt your own perception of reality by denying or

twisting facts, leading you to question your memory, judgment, or sanity.
- **Emotional appeals**: Manipulators may use fear, guilt, shame, or flattery to manipulate your emotions, making you feel pressured to comply with their demands.
- **Framing and language manipulation**: The way information is presented can influence how you interpret it. Be mindful of how words and phrases are used to shape your perceptions or evoke emotional reactions.
- **Over-simplification**: Manipulators often reduce complex issues to simple, black-and-white terms, encouraging you to adopt a specific viewpoint without considering nuance or opposing perspectives.
- **Authority appeal**: People in positions of authority may use their power or status to push ideas or demands, expecting compliance based on their position rather than the validity of their argument.

By familiarizing yourself with these techniques, you can spot when they are being used and take steps to resist their influence. Recognizing that someone is attempting to manipulate you is the first step toward reclaiming control over your thoughts and decisions.

Setting boundaries is another essential tool in protecting yourself from manipulation, particularly in personal relationships. Manipulative people often attempt to blur the lines between your needs and their desires, pushing you to prioritize their interests over your own. By establishing clear boundaries, you can maintain control over your actions and decisions, preventing others from taking advantage of you.

When setting boundaries, it's important to communicate your limits assertively and consistently. If someone tries to pressure you into doing something you are uncomfortable with, politely but firmly state your boundaries and refuse to be swayed by guilt, coercion, or emotional manipulation. Setting boundaries reinforces your autonomy and sends a clear message that you are not easily manipulated.

In addition to setting boundaries, *cultivating emotional intelligence* is a powerful defense against manipulation. Emotional intelligence involves understanding and managing your own emotions, as well as recognizing and responding to the emotions of others. Manipulators often exploit emotional vulnerabilities, such as insecurity or fear, to control their targets. By developing emotional intelligence, you can become more attuned to your emotional triggers and less reactive to attempts at emotional manipulation.

Practicing *emotional regulation* techniques, such as mindfulness, deep breathing, or journaling, can help you maintain emotional balance and stay grounded in situations where you feel pressured or manipulated. When you are emotionally centered, you are less likely to be swayed by external influences and more capable of making decisions based on rational thought rather than emotional impulses.

Building a strong sense of identity is another important aspect of resisting manipulation. People who have a clear sense of who they are, what they believe in, and what their values are tend to be less susceptible to external pressure. When you are confident in your own identity, it becomes easier to resist manipulation because you are less reliant on others for validation or approval. To strengthen your sense of identity, take time to reflect on your core values, beliefs, and goals. Ask yourself what truly matters to you and what you stand for, independent of the opinions or expectations of others. When you have a strong internal compass, you are better equipped to navigate situations where someone may try to sway you away from your principles.

Another key strategy for resisting manipulation is *seeking out diverse perspectives*. Manipulators often create echo chambers, where only certain viewpoints are allowed, and alternative perspectives are silenced. By actively exposing yourself to a wide range of ideas, perspectives, and sources of information, you can challenge your assumptions and avoid becoming trapped in a narrow worldview. Engage in conversations with people who have different opinions or beliefs, read from a variety of news sources, and explore topics that may be outside your usual areas of interest. By broadening your understanding of the world, you can become more resilient to manipulation, as you are better able to weigh different viewpoints and recognize when someone is presenting a biased or incomplete narrative.

Self-care and maintaining mental well-being are also critical in protecting yourself from manipulation. Manipulation thrives when individuals are stressed, fatigued, or emotionally vulnerable. When you are overwhelmed or exhausted, it becomes easier for others to influence your decisions or take advantage of your weakened mental state. By prioritizing self-care—whether through rest, relaxation, exercise, or spending time with loved ones—you can build emotional resilience and maintain the mental clarity needed to recognize and resist manipulation.

Finally, one of the most important tools for resisting manipulation is *developing a support network*. Surrounding yourself with trusted friends, family, or colleagues can provide a valuable source of perspective and encouragement. When faced with situations where you feel manipulated or pressured, reaching out to your support network can help you regain clarity and confidence. Others can offer insight, advice, or simply a listening ear, helping you to see the situation more objectively and empowering you to make decisions that align with your own values. Resisting manipulation requires a combination of self-awareness, critical thinking, emotional intelligence, and a strong sense of personal identity. By recognizing common manipulation techniques, setting clear boundaries, cultivating emotional resilience, and seeking diverse perspectives, you can protect yourself from control and maintain your autonomy in a world where manipulation is often subtle but pervasive. Through these practices, you can reclaim control over your thoughts, decisions, and actions, ensuring that you live in alignment with your own values and beliefs, rather than being swayed by external influences.

The Role of Fear in Religious Control Systems

Fear plays a central role in religious control systems, serving as a powerful tool to enforce obedience, shape behavior, and maintain authority over followers. Throughout history, religious institutions and leaders have leveraged fear—whether of divine punishment, eternal damnation, or social ostracism—to control the thoughts and actions of believers. While many religions are built on positive messages of hope, compassion, and community, some religious systems manipulate fear to reinforce their power, compel compliance, and suppress dissent. This chapter will explore the role of fear in religious control systems, examining how it is used to maintain authority, shape belief, and influence individual behavior.

At the heart of fear-based religious control systems is the concept of *divine punishment*. Many religions posit the existence of a higher power or moral law that governs human behavior, with severe consequences for those who disobey or stray from prescribed beliefs. In such systems, fear of divine wrath—whether in the form of eternal punishment in an afterlife, natural disasters, or personal suffering—becomes a primary motivator for compliance. Individuals are taught that their actions are constantly observed and judged by a higher power, and failure to adhere to religious laws or commandments can result in severe, often eternal, consequences.

One of the most well-known examples of this fear is the concept of *hell* or *eternal damnation*, present in many major religions. In Christianity, for instance, the idea of hell as a place of eternal torment for sinners has been a powerful means of enforcing moral behavior. The fear of spending eternity in suffering for failing to live a virtuous life or for rejecting religious teachings instills a deep psychological dread that influences the decisions, actions, and beliefs of followers. In Islam, the fear of divine judgment on the Day of Resurrection similarly motivates believers to follow the prescribed path of righteousness, with the threat of eternal punishment in the afterlife serving as a deterrent to sin.

This use of fear can also be found in other religious traditions, where specific actions or failures are believed to invite divine retribution in the form of bad fortune, illness, or suffering. By framing negative life experiences as the result of divine disfavor, religious leaders can manipulate fear to control not only behavior but also thoughts and beliefs. Believers may come to view suffering as a sign of their own moral or spiritual shortcomings, reinforcing a cycle of fear-driven obedience as they strive to earn favor and avoid further punishment.

Fear is also used to reinforce *social control* within religious communities. Religious control systems often rely on the fear of *ostracism* or *excommunication* to keep followers in line. In tightly-knit religious groups, deviating from the accepted doctrine or questioning the authority of religious leaders can result in being shunned, cast out, or rejected by the community. This fear of isolation or losing one's place in the religious group can be a powerful motivator for compliance, as social belonging is a fundamental human need. For many people, the prospect of being ostracized by their religious community—whether through formal excommunication or informal social rejection—is as terrifying as divine punishment itself.

Religious control systems may also use *rituals* and *symbols* to reinforce fear. Rituals that emphasize the consequences of sin, such as confessions, prayers of repentance, or public acts of penance, are often used to remind followers of the ever-present threat of divine judgment. These rituals serve as constant reminders that failure to conform to religious teachings carries significant spiritual risks. Similarly, religious symbols—such as images of hell, the crucifixion of

Christ, or the scales of divine judgment—are often employed to evoke fear and reinforce the need for submission to religious authority.

In many cases, fear is used in combination with the promise of *salvation* or *redemption*. While religious systems may instill fear of divine punishment or social rejection, they also offer the possibility of deliverance for those who obey the rules and live in accordance with religious teachings. The fear of punishment is balanced by the hope of reward—whether that reward takes the form of eternal life in heaven, spiritual enlightenment, or acceptance within the community. This combination of fear and hope creates a powerful psychological mechanism for control: followers are motivated to obey not only to avoid punishment but also to achieve the promise of salvation. Religious leaders often position themselves as the intermediaries who can guide followers toward this salvation, reinforcing their authority and control over the spiritual lives of believers.

Fear of the *unknown* also plays a significant role in religious control systems. For many people, religion provides answers to existential questions about life, death, and the afterlife. In systems where religious authorities claim exclusive knowledge of these mysteries, fear of uncertainty can drive individuals to submit to religious teachings in search of comfort and reassurance. Fear of what lies beyond death—whether eternal damnation, reincarnation, or some other form of existence—can compel people to adhere to religious doctrines that promise protection from these unknowns. By presenting themselves as the gatekeepers of salvation or spiritual truth, religious leaders exploit the human fear of uncertainty, creating dependency and control over their followers.

The role of *guilt* and *shame* is another crucial aspect of fear-based religious control. Many religious systems instill a strong sense of guilt for perceived moral failings or shortcomings, leading followers to internalize feelings of unworthiness or sinfulness. This guilt is often reinforced through religious teachings that emphasize the inherent flaws or sinful nature of humanity, requiring constant repentance or spiritual work to remain in good standing with the divine. The fear of being unworthy of divine love or redemption creates a cycle of self-criticism and shame, where individuals feel compelled to seek forgiveness and atone for their sins, often through rituals, donations, or acts of service. Religious leaders can use this guilt to control behavior, encouraging followers to submit to authority or participate in religious practices as a way of alleviating their internalized feelings of shame.

Another common tactic in religious control systems is the use of *apocalyptic warnings* or *prophecies* to create a sense of urgency and fear among believers. Predictions of impending doom—whether in the form of divine retribution, the end of the world, or a coming apocalypse—can generate a heightened sense of fear and obedience among followers. The belief that the end is near or that divine judgment is imminent creates an atmosphere where individuals are more likely to conform to religious demands, abandon critical thinking, and follow leaders who claim to offer salvation or protection. By leveraging the fear of an uncertain and terrifying future, religious leaders can consolidate power and maintain control over the actions and beliefs of their followers.

Cults are an extreme example of how fear is used in religious control systems. In many cults, fear is a primary mechanism for maintaining control over members. Cult leaders often manipulate fear to keep members isolated, dependent, and obedient. Fear of punishment, both spiritual and physical, is commonly used to suppress dissent and prevent members from leaving the group. Cults also frequently rely on fear of the outside world, convincing members that leaving the group will result in dire consequences—whether spiritual damnation or physical harm. This fear-based control creates an environment of psychological dependency, where members feel trapped and unable to escape the influence of the group.

The psychological effects of fear-based religious control can be devastating. Over time, individuals subjected to constant fear may develop *anxiety disorders*, *depression*, and other mental health issues. The chronic stress of living under the threat of divine punishment or social rejection can take a heavy toll on emotional well-being. Additionally, the internalization of guilt, shame, and fear can erode self-esteem and lead to a sense of powerlessness and helplessness. In extreme cases, individuals may experience *trauma* or *post-traumatic stress disorder* (PTSD) as a result of prolonged exposure to fear-based religious control.

In conclusion, fear plays a central role in many religious control systems, acting as a powerful tool to enforce obedience, shape behavior, and maintain authority over followers. Through the fear of divine punishment, social rejection, guilt, shame, and the unknown, religious leaders can exert significant control over the thoughts and actions of believers. While fear-based control can create a sense of order and compliance, it often comes at the cost of individual autonomy, critical thinking, and emotional well-being. Understanding the role of fear in religious control systems is crucial for recognizing when religious teachings or practices are being used to manipulate rather than uplift, and for empowering individuals to reclaim their spiritual agency.

How Propaganda Creates Enemies: Us vs. Them

Propaganda is a powerful tool in mind control, particularly when it comes to creating the perception of enemies and establishing an "us vs. them" mentality. Throughout history, regimes, political movements, and even religious institutions have used propaganda to divide societies, fostering hostility toward an external or internal group labeled as the enemy. This tactic plays on deep-seated psychological needs for identity, belonging, and security, as well as the instinct to protect one's in-group from perceived threats. By demonizing the "other," propaganda not only reinforces loyalty and obedience but also justifies aggressive actions, discrimination, and even violence. This chapter will explore how propaganda creates enemies through the "us vs. them" dynamic, examining its psychological impact and how it is used to manipulate societies.

At the core of this strategy is the creation of a clear distinction between the *in-group* ("us") and the *out-group* ("them"). Propaganda often presents the in-group—whether it is a nation, religious group, political party, or cultural identity—as inherently virtuous, righteous, and deserving of protection. The out-group, by contrast, is portrayed as dangerous, immoral, or fundamentally opposed to the values of the in-group. This *dichotomy* simplifies complex social and political realities into a binary framework, where all positive attributes are assigned to "us," and all negative attributes to "them." In this way, propaganda encourages individuals to identify with their in-group while simultaneously cultivating fear, suspicion, and hatred toward the out-group.

One of the most effective ways propaganda creates enemies is by *dehumanizing the out-group*. Dehumanization is the process of stripping people of their humanity, portraying them as less than human—often as animals, monsters, or soulless entities. This psychological tactic makes it easier to justify hostile or violent actions against the out-group because they are no longer seen as deserving of empathy, rights, or moral consideration. Historical examples of dehumanization in propaganda include the portrayal of Jewish people as rats in Nazi Germany, the depiction of Tutsis as cockroaches during the Rwandan genocide, and the labeling of political dissidents as subversive or traitorous in authoritarian regimes. By reducing the out-group to something subhuman, propaganda encourages aggression and indifference toward their suffering.

Fear is a critical element in creating the "us vs. them" divide. Propaganda often exaggerates or fabricates threats posed by the out-group, portraying them as existential dangers to the in-group's security, culture, or way of life. This fear-mongering taps into the basic human instinct for self-preservation, triggering a fight-or-flight response that overrides critical thinking and rational decision-making. Fear-based propaganda encourages individuals to view the out-group not merely as opponents or competitors but as enemies who must be defeated or neutralized for the survival of the in-group.

FOR EXAMPLE, DURING wartime, governments frequently use propaganda to instill fear of foreign enemies, emphasizing the threat they pose to national security. By depicting the enemy as ruthless aggressors or as plotting to destroy the in-group's values, propaganda rallies public support for military action or harsh policies. This fear-driven narrative unites the population against a common foe, often leading to widespread support for actions that might otherwise be seen as unethical or extreme, such as internment camps, civilian casualties, or prolonged warfare. In the Cold War era, for instance, both the United States and the Soviet Union used propaganda to paint the other side as a mortal enemy, cultivating fear and mistrust on both sides of the ideological divide.

Propaganda also frequently employs *scapegoating*, where the out-group is blamed for a society's problems. By framing the out-group as responsible for economic hardship, social instability, or moral decline, propagandists deflect blame from those in power and create a convenient target for public frustration and anger. This technique is particularly effective during times of crisis, when people are more susceptible to seeking simple explanations for complex issues. In Nazi Germany, for example, Jews were scapegoated for the country's economic struggles and the perceived moral decay of society, which helped justify the atrocities of the Holocaust. Similarly, in authoritarian regimes, political dissidents or marginalized groups are often blamed for the country's difficulties, leading to their persecution under the guise of protecting national stability.

Repetition is another key factor in how propaganda creates enemies. By consistently and relentlessly repeating the same negative messages about the out-group, propaganda reinforces the belief that they are dangerous, inferior, or morally corrupt. Over time, these messages become ingrained in the public consciousness, even if they were initially met with skepticism or doubt. The more often a message is repeated, the more familiar and accepted it becomes, eventually shaping public opinion and behavior. This repetition desensitizes people to the out-group's humanity, making it easier to justify discrimination, violence, or exclusion.

In addition to repetition, *visual imagery* plays a powerful role in reinforcing the "us vs. them" dynamic. Propaganda often uses stark, emotional images to evoke visceral reactions, making the out-group appear menacing or grotesque. Posters, cartoons, and films have historically been used to depict enemies in exaggerated, stereotypical ways, tapping into deep-seated prejudices and reinforcing the dehumanization process. Visual propaganda is particularly effective because it bypasses logical reasoning and appeals directly to emotions, leaving a lasting impression on the viewer.

Language is another powerful tool in the creation of enemies through propaganda. The way the out-group is described—using derogatory terms, slurs, or euphemisms—can have a profound impact on how they are perceived. Language shapes thought, and by controlling the vocabulary used to discuss the out-group, propagandists can influence public attitudes toward them. For instance, labeling political dissidents as "terrorists" or "traitors" immediately frames them as threats to the state, justifying harsh crackdowns or repressive policies. Similarly, using language that evokes fear, such as calling immigrants "invaders" or "criminals," primes the public to see them as dangerous outsiders rather than fellow human beings.

The creation of enemies through propaganda also involves the *construction of myths* and *narratives* that shape collective memory. Propaganda often relies on historical grievances, real or imagined, to stoke resentment against the out-group. By presenting the out-group as the perpetual antagonist in a larger historical struggle, propagandists can tap into cultural or nationalistic pride, framing the in-group as the righteous defender of its legacy. This narrative often includes stories of past betrayals, invasions, or atrocities committed by the out-group, which are used to justify current hostility and reinforce the idea that the out-group is an enduring threat.

Polarization is the ultimate goal of propaganda that creates enemies. By fostering an "us vs. them" mentality, propaganda divides societies into opposing camps, making dialogue, compromise, or understanding increasingly difficult. Once people are convinced that the out-group is the enemy, any attempts at bridge-building or negotiation are framed as betrayal or weakness. This polarization not only strengthens the power of the propagandists but also leads to the breakdown of social cohesion, as individuals become more isolated within their ideological echo chambers.

The psychological impact of this polarization is significant. People who have internalized the "us vs. them" mentality often experience *cognitive dissonance* when confronted with information that contradicts the propaganda they have been exposed to. Instead of questioning the propaganda, they may double down on their beliefs, rationalizing or dismissing conflicting evidence. This deepens the divide between the in-group and out-group, further entrenching hostility and reducing the likelihood of meaningful communication or reconciliation.

The consequences of propaganda-driven polarization can be devastating for society. It fosters an environment where *violence* and *discrimination* against the out-group are not only tolerated but encouraged. In extreme cases, this can lead to acts of genocide, ethnic cleansing, or widespread persecution, as history has tragically shown. Even in less extreme circumstances, the social fabric is eroded as trust between different groups deteriorates, leading to long-term divisions and instability.

In modern times, the role of social media in amplifying propaganda and the "us vs. them" dynamic cannot be overlooked. Algorithms that prioritize sensational, emotionally charged content create echo chambers that reinforce pre-existing beliefs and biases, making it easier for propaganda to spread. In these digital spaces, misinformation and conspiracy theories about the out-group are often shared and amplified, further polarizing communities and deepening the "us vs. them" divide.

In conclusion, propaganda is a powerful tool for creating enemies through the "us vs. them" dynamic, fostering division, fear, and hostility between groups. By dehumanizing the out-group, manipulating language and imagery, and using fear and repetition, propaganda shapes public perception and behavior, often leading to polarization and conflict. The psychological and social consequences of this manipulation are profound, as individuals become more entrenched in their beliefs, and societies become more fragmented and divided. Understanding how propaganda creates enemies is essential for resisting manipulation, promoting critical thinking, and fostering a more inclusive and compassionate society. By recognizing the tactics used to create the "us vs. them" mentality, individuals can challenge the narratives that seek to divide and build bridges toward understanding and unity.

Breaking Free from Brainwashing: Deprogramming the Mind

Breaking free from brainwashing and deprogramming the mind is a complex and often difficult process, but it is possible with awareness, support, and the right techniques. Brainwashing, also known as coercive persuasion or thought reform, is a psychological manipulation technique that seeks to strip individuals of their autonomy and replace their beliefs, values, and sense of identity with those imposed by an external authority. This can happen in cults, abusive relationships, authoritarian regimes, and even through subtler forms of media and societal manipulation. The process of deprogramming involves dismantling the beliefs instilled through brainwashing and reclaiming personal autonomy. In this chapter, we will explore how brainwashing works, the psychological challenges of breaking free, and practical strategies for deprogramming the mind and restoring critical thinking.

At the core of brainwashing is the *manipulation of identity and belief.* Brainwashing targets an individual's sense of self, stripping away their prior beliefs, values, and connections, and replacing them with a new set of ideas that serve the controlling group or individual. This process often involves isolation from outside influences, repetitive indoctrination, emotional manipulation, and the use of fear or guilt to suppress dissenting thoughts. Over time, individuals subjected to brainwashing may lose their ability to think critically, becoming dependent on the authority that controls their thoughts and behavior.

The first step in breaking free from brainwashing is *recognizing that it has occurred.* This can be one of the most challenging aspects of deprogramming because brainwashing often creates a deep sense of loyalty to the controlling entity. Victims may initially resist the idea that they have been manipulated, as the indoctrinated beliefs may feel like their own. However, recognizing that external forces have shaped these beliefs is crucial for reclaiming mental autonomy. This awareness often comes when individuals are exposed to alternative perspectives, begin to experience cognitive dissonance, or when they face moments of crisis that force them to question their current belief system.

Once a person begins to acknowledge that they have been subjected to brainwashing, the next step is *challenging the indoctrinated beliefs.* This requires a process of self-reflection and critical thinking, where the individual examines the beliefs and values they have been taught and asks whether they truly align with their own understanding of the world. Critical thinking exercises, such as evaluating evidence, identifying contradictions, and questioning the motivations of the controlling authority, are essential in this stage. By actively questioning the validity of the brainwashed beliefs, individuals can begin to dismantle the false narratives that have been imposed upon them.

It's important to recognize that the process of deprogramming is not immediate—it often takes time and persistence. One of the reasons for this is the deep emotional investment that individuals may have in the belief system they've been indoctrinated into. Brainwashing often involves emotional manipulation, such as fear, guilt, or shame, to create strong psychological bonds with the controlling entity. Deprogramming requires individuals to confront these emotions and untangle their feelings of loyalty or fear from their critical evaluation of the beliefs themselves.

Therapeutic support is often crucial in the deprogramming process, especially for individuals who have been subjected to prolonged or intense brainwashing. Professional therapists or counselors who specialize in trauma, cult recovery, or psychological abuse can help individuals navigate the emotional and mental challenges of breaking free from brainwashing. Therapy provides a safe space for individuals to explore their doubts, fears, and identity, offering tools to rebuild self-esteem and independence. Group therapy or support groups made up of others who have experienced similar forms of brainwashing can also be invaluable, as they offer a sense of community and shared understanding.

One of the most important aspects of deprogramming is *rebuilding a sense of identity* that is independent of the controlling entity. Brainwashing often strips individuals of their personal identity, replacing it with a group identity that is entirely dependent on the controlling authority. To break free, individuals must reconnect with their authentic selves—rediscovering their values, beliefs, and sense of purpose outside the confines of the brainwashing experience. This may involve reconnecting with old hobbies, friends, and family, as well as exploring new interests and experiences that reinforce a sense of personal agency and freedom.

Detoxing from the controlling environment is another key element of deprogramming. In many cases, breaking free from brainwashing requires physical and emotional distance from the people, places, or media that reinforced the manipulated belief system. This could mean leaving a cult, ending an abusive relationship, or disengaging from harmful media sources. The goal is to create a safe space where individuals can begin to think independently without the constant pressure of the controlling entity. During this time, individuals can explore alternative viewpoints, engage with new sources of information, and rebuild social connections that support their recovery.

Education and knowledge are powerful tools in the deprogramming process. Brainwashing often thrives on misinformation, oversimplified narratives, and the suppression of critical thinking. By exposing oneself to a wide range of perspectives, knowledge, and evidence-based information, individuals can broaden their understanding of the world and regain the ability to make informed decisions. This might involve reading books, attending seminars, or engaging in discussions that challenge the ideas instilled through brainwashing. The process of learning and self-education not only helps dismantle false beliefs but also empowers individuals to reclaim control over their own thoughts.

Challenging cognitive distortions is another important step in deprogramming. Brainwashing often relies on cognitive distortions—irrational or exaggerated patterns of thinking that reinforce the controlling narrative. For example, black-and-white thinking (seeing things as all good or all bad) is a common tactic in brainwashing, as it eliminates nuance and forces individuals into an "us vs. them" mindset. In deprogramming, individuals must learn to recognize and challenge these distortions, replacing them with more balanced, nuanced, and evidence-based thinking. Cognitive-behavioral therapy (CBT) techniques can be particularly helpful in this regard, as they teach individuals to identify and correct distorted thinking patterns.

Rebuilding social connections is critical for individuals who have been isolated as part of the brainwashing process. Isolation from family, friends, and outside perspectives is a common tactic used by controlling groups to strengthen their hold on individuals. Reconnecting with trusted relationships outside the controlling environment can provide emotional support, perspective, and validation during the deprogramming process. It also helps individuals regain a sense of normalcy and belonging, counteracting the isolation and dependency created by the brainwashing experience.

Another crucial part of deprogramming is *addressing trauma*. Brainwashing often involves psychological or emotional abuse, which can leave deep scars on an individual's mental health. Trauma-informed therapy is essential for helping individuals process the fear, guilt, shame, and confusion that are often a result of long-term manipulation. By addressing the emotional trauma associated with brainwashing, individuals can begin to heal and rebuild their mental and emotional well-being.

One of the final steps in deprogramming is *reclaiming personal autonomy*. Brainwashing often involves the gradual erosion of an individual's ability to make decisions for themselves. In the process of deprogramming, individuals must actively practice making their own choices, even in small, everyday matters. This might involve setting personal goals, asserting boundaries, or making decisions without the influence of the controlling entity. By practicing autonomy and self-determination, individuals can rebuild their confidence and sense of agency, empowering themselves to live according to their own values and beliefs.

It's important to note that deprogramming is not a linear process—it may involve setbacks, moments of doubt, and periods of intense emotional struggle. Some individuals may feel conflicted about leaving the belief system they were indoctrinated into, particularly if it provided a sense of purpose or community. It is essential for those undergoing deprogramming to be patient with themselves and to seek out supportive networks or professionals who can guide them through this difficult journey.

In conclusion, breaking free from brainwashing is a challenging but achievable process that involves recognizing manipulation, challenging indoctrinated beliefs, rebuilding personal identity, and reclaiming autonomy. Through critical thinking, emotional healing, support networks, and education, individuals can dismantle the psychological control that has been imposed on them and regain their ability to think, feel, and act independently. Deprogramming is not just about rejecting a set of beliefs—it's about rediscovering one's authentic self and taking back control of one's life and mind.

Political Polarization: How Division Is Manufactured

Political polarization—the deepening divide between opposing political viewpoints—is often perceived as a natural consequence of differing ideologies. However, in many cases, polarization is deliberately manufactured by those in power, media organizations, political parties, and interest groups to control the public, maintain loyalty, and advance specific agendas. Manufactured polarization exploits fears, biases, and identity politics to create division, reinforcing an "us vs. them" mentality. This division leads to a breakdown in constructive dialogue, heightened emotional responses, and the erosion of social cohesion, making it easier for those who benefit from polarization to maintain control. In this chapter, we will explore how political polarization is manufactured, the techniques used to create and deepen division, and the impact this has on democratic societies.

One of the most effective tools for manufacturing political polarization is the use of *identity politics*. By framing political issues in terms of identity—whether based on race, religion, nationality, gender, or social class—political actors can tap into deep-seated emotions and personal beliefs, making individuals feel as though their identity is under attack. This tactic encourages people to view political disagreements not as differences in opinion but as existential threats to their very being. When political affiliations become tied to personal identity, individuals are more likely to defend their position aggressively, view opponents as enemies, and resist compromise. This emotional investment makes polarization deeply entrenched, as it shifts political discourse away from policy debates and toward identity-based conflicts.

Manufactured polarization often relies on *fear-mongering* to escalate division. Political actors, particularly populists or authoritarian-leaning leaders, use fear to frame the opposing side as a dangerous threat to the nation, its values, or its security. This fear-mongering can take many forms, such as warnings about economic collapse, the loss of cultural identity, or external threats like immigration or terrorism. By amplifying fears of the "other," political leaders create an atmosphere of anxiety and distrust, where voters feel that they must choose a side to protect themselves from the perceived threat. In this climate of fear, people become more rigid in their beliefs, less willing to engage with opposing viewpoints, and more susceptible to the idea that compromise is equivalent to surrender.

Media manipulation plays a significant role in manufacturing political polarization. Media outlets—particularly those aligned with specific political interests—often present news in a way that reinforces division, using emotionally charged language, selective framing, and biased reporting to stoke outrage and loyalty among their audience. Polarizing media narratives emphasize the most extreme elements of each side, magnifying conflicts and portraying the opposition as not just wrong, but morally corrupt or dangerous. Sensationalist headlines, fear-inducing coverage, and inflammatory commentary create a feedback loop, where viewers are continually exposed to messages that confirm their biases and fuel their sense of grievance.

The rise of *social media* has further accelerated political polarization by creating echo chambers, where individuals are primarily exposed to content that aligns with their pre-existing beliefs. Algorithms on platforms like Facebook, Twitter, and YouTube prioritize content that generates high engagement—often emotionally charged or sensationalist posts—leading users to see more of what they already agree with and less of opposing viewpoints. As individuals are repeatedly exposed to content that reinforces their views and vilifies the opposition, their beliefs become more entrenched, and their willingness to engage in dialogue with the other side diminishes. This phenomenon, known as *confirmation bias*, deepens polarization by creating a false sense of consensus within ideological bubbles and fostering hostility toward those outside of it.

Political actors also manufacture polarization through *disinformation campaigns*, spreading false or misleading information to sow confusion and distrust. Disinformation is often designed to amplify existing divisions by exaggerating or distorting facts, framing the opposing side as malicious or incompetent. This tactic was evident in the 2016 U.S. presidential election, where foreign actors used social media platforms to spread divisive messages and stoke racial, political, and cultural tensions. By creating a sense of chaos and confusion, disinformation erodes trust in institutions, fuels anger, and makes it difficult for individuals to discern truth from propaganda. In this environment, political factions become more isolated, and the middle ground—the space for compromise and constructive dialogue—shrinks.

Another technique used to manufacture political polarization is the *exaggeration of differences*. Political actors, particularly in highly partisan environments, often present policy disagreements as being more extreme than they actually are. By framing the opposing side's policies as radical or dangerous, political leaders can rally their base by casting themselves as defenders of the status quo or protectors of the nation. This tactic creates the perception that the stakes are incredibly high, leading voters to believe that any victory for the opposition would result in catastrophic consequences. As a result, political discourse becomes more adversarial, and the possibility of finding common ground diminishes.

Framing political opponents as enemies is another powerful method for manufacturing polarization. Rather than engaging in policy debates, political actors often resort to *ad hominem attacks*, character assassination, or fear-based rhetoric that dehumanizes the other side. This tactic encourages voters to see political opponents not as fellow citizens with different views but as dangerous adversaries who must be defeated. By vilifying opponents, political leaders foster a climate where dialogue is replaced by hostility, making it easier to dismiss the legitimacy of the other side's concerns or arguments. This dehumanization of political opponents further entrenches division and makes reconciliation or cooperation seem impossible.

POLITICAL PARTIES ALSO contribute to polarization through *gerrymandering* and *strategic political tactics* designed to cement power by exploiting divisions. Gerrymandering—the manipulation of electoral district boundaries to favor one party—creates environments where politicians are more concerned with appealing to their partisan base than reaching across the aisle. In heavily gerrymandered districts, candidates often adopt more extreme positions to secure their party's nomination, contributing to a political landscape where moderation is punished and extremism is rewarded. This leads to the election of more ideologically extreme candidates, who are less willing to compromise or work with the opposition, further deepening polarization.

Interest groups and *lobbyists* also play a role in manufacturing polarization by pushing political leaders to adopt more extreme positions on specific issues. These groups, often funded by wealthy donors or corporations, exert significant influence on political campaigns and policy decisions. By promoting divisive issues, such as gun rights, abortion, or climate change, interest groups can polarize the electorate and mobilize specific voting blocs. Politicians who rely on these groups for campaign funding or support may feel pressured to adopt more extreme positions, further fueling division within the political landscape.

The psychological impact of manufactured polarization is significant. As individuals become more polarized, they are more likely to engage in *black-and-white thinking*, where they view their own side as entirely good and the opposing side as entirely evil. This binary thinking reduces the complexity of political issues and discourages nuanced understanding or compromise. Polarized individuals are also more likely to experience *confirmation bias*, where they seek out information that confirms their existing beliefs and reject information that challenges them. This creates a feedback loop of reinforced beliefs, making it difficult for individuals to change their views or engage with opposing perspectives.

The social consequences of political polarization are profound. Polarized societies experience a breakdown in *social cohesion*, as trust between individuals from different political backgrounds erodes. Friendships, families, and communities can become divided along political lines, leading to increased tension, conflict, and alienation. In extreme cases, polarization can lead to *political violence*, as individuals become so entrenched in their beliefs that they are willing to take aggressive action to defend their side or attack the opposition. The breakdown of civil discourse also makes it more difficult to address collective challenges, such as economic inequality, healthcare reform, or environmental protection, as political actors are more focused on defeating their opponents than on finding solutions.

Manufactured polarization also undermines *democratic institutions*. In deeply polarized environments, trust in government, the media, and other democratic institutions is weakened, as each side perceives these institutions as biased or corrupt. This erosion of trust makes it easier for authoritarian figures to rise to power by promising to "fix" the system or by exploiting the divisions for their own gain. When polarization becomes so extreme that political opponents are seen as illegitimate or treasonous, the foundations of democracy—compromise, dialogue, and the peaceful transfer of power—are at risk.

Despite the challenges posed by political polarization, there are ways to resist and reduce its impact. One of the most important steps is *promoting media literacy* and critical thinking. By teaching individuals how to identify bias, analyze information, and seek out diverse perspectives, societies can reduce the influence of manipulative media narratives and disinformation. Encouraging dialogue and debate in schools, workplaces, and communities can also help bridge divides, allowing individuals to engage with different viewpoints in a constructive and respectful manner.

Reforming electoral systems to reduce the influence of gerrymandering and partisan politics is another important step in combating polarization. By creating fairer and more representative electoral districts, political leaders can be encouraged to adopt more moderate positions and work across party lines. Additionally, supporting independent and nonpartisan media outlets can provide a counterbalance to the sensationalist and polarized reporting that dominates much of the media landscape.

Finally, *individuals can take personal steps* to resist polarization by engaging with people who hold different views, seeking out information from a variety of sources, and being mindful of their own cognitive biases. By practicing empathy, curiosity, and openness to dialogue, individuals can help counter the manufactured divisions that fuel polarization.

In conclusion, political polarization is often manufactured by political actors, media organizations, and interest groups that exploit identity, fear, and bias to divide societies and maintain control. The techniques used to create polarization—fear-mongering, media manipulation, disinformation, and the dehumanization of opponents—are designed to deepen divisions and make compromise and cooperation difficult. The consequences of polarization are profound, affecting social cohesion, trust in democratic institutions, and the ability to address collective challenges. However, by promoting critical thinking, media literacy, and dialogue, individuals and societies can resist polarization and work toward a more inclusive and cooperative political environment.

The Future of Mind Control: Emerging Technologies and Dangers

As technology continues to evolve at a rapid pace, so too does the potential for mind control to become more sophisticated and pervasive. While traditional methods of manipulation, such as propaganda, fear, and psychological coercion, remain powerful, emerging technologies open new avenues for influencing thoughts, behaviors, and beliefs. From artificial intelligence (AI) and brain-computer interfaces (BCIs) to virtual reality (VR) and social media algorithms, the future of mind control could be shaped by tools that allow unprecedented access to the human mind. These technologies carry both promise and peril, as they have the potential to enhance human capabilities but also pose significant dangers if used for manipulation or control. In this chapter, we will explore the emerging technologies that could reshape the landscape of mind control, examining their potential uses, ethical implications, and the risks they pose to personal autonomy and freedom.

One of the most significant emerging technologies with the potential for mind control is *artificial intelligence* (AI). AI-driven algorithms already play a major role in shaping how people consume information, particularly through social media platforms. These algorithms are designed to maximize engagement by analyzing user behavior and serving content that is likely to capture attention, reinforce biases, or provoke emotional responses. As AI continues to improve, its ability to tailor content to individual preferences will become even more precise, allowing for more effective manipulation of thoughts and behaviors. This personalized manipulation, often invisible to users, can deepen political polarization, promote consumerism, or influence public opinion on critical issues without individuals fully realizing the extent to which they are being influenced.

The danger of AI in mind control lies in its ability to *create echo chambers* and *reinforce cognitive biases*. As AI algorithms increasingly deliver content that aligns with a user's pre-existing beliefs, individuals are less likely to encounter diverse perspectives, making it harder to engage in critical thinking or question their own assumptions. This process not only entrenches polarization but also leaves individuals more vulnerable to targeted misinformation or propaganda campaigns. In the future, AI could be used by governments, corporations, or other entities to subtly influence large populations, shaping beliefs and behaviors on a mass scale.

Another emerging technology with mind control implications is the development of *brain-computer interfaces* (BCIs). BCIs allow direct communication between the human brain and external devices, enabling users to control technology with their thoughts. While BCIs have the potential to revolutionize fields such as healthcare—allowing people with disabilities to regain mobility or communicate more effectively—they also raise profound ethical concerns regarding privacy, autonomy, and control over one's own thoughts. As BCIs become more advanced, the possibility of *manipulating or altering brain activity* through external devices becomes a real concern.

IN THE FUTURE, BCIS could be used not only to read brain signals but also to influence them. Theoretically, BCIs could be employed to *implant thoughts, emotions, or suggestions* into a person's mind, blurring the line between personal autonomy and external control. Such technologies, if used maliciously, could allow for unprecedented forms of mind control, where individuals may not even be aware that their thoughts are being shaped or manipulated by an external source. This raises serious ethical questions about consent, control over one's own mental states, and the potential for abuse by authoritarian regimes, corporations, or other entities seeking to exert influence over individuals or populations.

Virtual reality (VR) and augmented reality (AR) are other emerging technologies that hold potential for both enhancing human experience and enabling new forms of mind control. VR and AR can create immersive environments that simulate reality, offering users the ability to experience and interact with digital worlds in ways that can profoundly influence perception, emotion, and behavior. While VR and AR offer tremendous opportunities for education, entertainment, and therapy, they also present risks if used to manipulate or condition users.

One of the primary concerns with VR and AR is the potential for *immersive indoctrination*. By creating highly realistic and emotionally charged virtual environments, VR technology could be used to reinforce specific ideologies or beliefs. In a virtual world, users could be exposed to carefully crafted scenarios that provoke fear, anger, or loyalty, shaping their attitudes and behaviors in ways that mirror real-world propaganda but with far greater emotional impact. For example, VR could be used in educational or training contexts to condition individuals to adopt specific political or social viewpoints, making it easier to manipulate or control their thoughts over time.

The *psychological impact* of spending extended periods in immersive virtual environments is also an area of concern. As VR technology becomes more advanced and integrated into daily life, the lines between reality and virtual experience could blur, making it more difficult for individuals to distinguish between genuine beliefs and those shaped by digital environments. The potential for VR to create *false memories*, reinforce behavioral conditioning, or desensitize users to certain experiences raises important ethical questions about the use of this technology for mind control purposes.

Neurotechnology—technologies that directly interact with the nervous system—also presents new possibilities for influencing the human mind. Advances in neuroscience have led to the development of tools that can monitor, stimulate, or alter brain activity with increasing precision. Technologies like *transcranial magnetic stimulation (TMS)* or *deep brain stimulation (DBS)* are already used in clinical settings to treat mental health conditions like depression or epilepsy by altering brain function. However, the ability to manipulate brain activity also opens the door to the potential for *external control of thoughts and emotions*.

WHILE NEURO-STIMULATION technologies offer promising therapeutic benefits, they could also be used to *suppress dissent*, manipulate behavior, or control populations. For example, in authoritarian regimes, neuro-technologies could theoretically be employed to reduce resistance, encourage conformity, or enforce obedience by targeting specific brain regions associated with motivation, fear, or pleasure. The ethical implications of using such technologies for mind control are vast, as they challenge the very concept of free will and personal autonomy.

The role of *biometric surveillance* in mind control is also likely to expand as technology becomes more advanced. Biometric data—such as facial expressions, eye movements, heart rate, and brain activity—can provide detailed insights into an individual's emotional and cognitive state. Governments and corporations are increasingly using biometric data to monitor behavior, detect emotions, and predict actions, raising concerns about the potential for *behavioral manipulation*.

In the future, biometric data could be used to deliver highly personalized and emotionally manipulative content. For instance, a social media platform could monitor a user's facial expressions and heart rate to determine when they are most susceptible to influence, then serve them content designed to exploit that emotional vulnerability. This form of *psychographic targeting* would allow for an unprecedented level of control over individuals' thoughts and actions, as the content they consume would be tailored to their emotional states in real time.

Algorithmic manipulation through data collection is already shaping public opinion and consumer behavior, but as AI and machine learning continue to evolve, these technologies will become even more sophisticated. Algorithms could be designed to detect and exploit individuals' emotional, psychological, and behavioral patterns, delivering content that subtly shapes their beliefs and actions without their awareness. This form of algorithmic control could be used by political parties, corporations, or governments to influence elections, drive consumer behavior, or suppress dissent.

One of the most profound risks posed by these emerging technologies is the potential for *totalitarian surveillance states*. As governments and corporations gain access to more data about individuals' thoughts, emotions, and behaviors, the ability to exert control over entire populations becomes more feasible. Technologies like facial recognition, AI-driven surveillance, and neuro-monitoring could be used to create a society where dissent is detected and suppressed before it even manifests, and where individuals are conditioned to conform to the expectations of those in power. In such a future, the very concept of personal freedom could be redefined, as individuals may no longer have control over their own thoughts, emotions, or actions. This dystopian vision of mind control represents the ultimate danger of emerging technologies if they are not regulated and used ethically. The future of mind control is likely to be shaped by emerging technologies such as AI, brain-computer interfaces, virtual reality, neuro-technology, and biometric surveillance. While these technologies hold the potential to improve human life in many ways, they also present significant risks if used for manipulation or control. As technology advances, it is essential to consider the ethical implications of these developments and to establish safeguards that protect individual autonomy and prevent abuse. The future of mind control will depend on how societies balance the potential benefits of emerging technologies with the need to preserve freedom, privacy, and the integrity of the human mind.

Mind Control in the Digital Age: The New Frontier

Mind control in the digital age represents a new frontier where technology intersects with psychological manipulation, influencing individuals on a scale and with a precision that was unimaginable in the past. With the rapid rise of social media, artificial intelligence (AI), big data, and algorithm-driven content, the ways in which people are influenced and controlled have evolved significantly. This digital landscape allows for unprecedented access to the minds of individuals, as their behavior, preferences, and even emotions are constantly being monitored, analyzed, and manipulated. This chapter will explore how mind control operates in the digital age, the technologies that enable it, and the challenges it presents for individual autonomy and democratic societies.

At the heart of digital-age mind control is the ability to *gather massive amounts of personal data*. Through social media platforms, search engines, smartphones, and various digital services, vast amounts of data are collected on individuals—ranging from their browsing history and purchase patterns to their political beliefs and emotional states. This data provides a detailed profile of each user, allowing algorithms to predict their preferences, vulnerabilities, and behavior. By analyzing these data points, digital platforms can create personalized content designed to capture attention, reinforce biases, and subtly shape thought patterns.

Social media algorithms are among the most powerful tools for influencing individuals in the digital age. These algorithms are designed to maximize engagement by delivering content that users are most likely to interact with, based on their past behavior. While this personalization enhances the user experience, it also creates a form of digital echo chamber where individuals are continuously exposed to content that aligns with their existing beliefs and interests. This can reinforce biases, deepen political polarization, and prevent exposure to alternative viewpoints, thereby narrowing a person's perspective and making it easier for them to be influenced by manipulative narratives.

One of the most concerning aspects of social media manipulation is the use of *emotional engineering*. By analyzing how users react to certain types of content—whether through likes, shares, comments, or even pauses in scrolling—algorithms can determine which emotions drive the most engagement. Content that evokes strong emotional responses, particularly fear, anger, or outrage, tends to be prioritized because it increases user interaction. This emotional manipulation can be exploited by political actors, corporations, or interest groups to push specific agendas, as emotionally charged individuals are more likely to make decisions based on impulse rather than reasoned thought.

This emotional manipulation is further amplified by the phenomenon of *virality*. In the digital age, content that generates a strong emotional response can spread rapidly across social networks, reaching millions of people in a matter of hours or days. This can create a *viral feedback loop*, where emotionally charged content is amplified by users and algorithms alike, shaping public discourse and opinion. This rapid dissemination of content allows for the spread of misinformation, propaganda, or sensationalized narratives that manipulate public sentiment on a large scale.

Another form of digital-age mind control comes from *targeted advertising*, which leverages big data to deliver highly personalized and persuasive marketing messages. Unlike traditional advertising, which broadcasts a single message to a broad audience, digital ads can be tailored to the specific interests, behaviors, and psychological profiles of individual users. This level of personalization allows advertisers to craft messages that appeal to users' subconscious desires, fears, and motivations, making them more likely to engage with the product or service being promoted.

This *psychographic targeting* goes beyond traditional demographic segmentation, allowing advertisers to reach users based on their emotional and psychological traits. For example, a user who has shown signs of anxiety through their online behavior may be targeted with ads for products that promise stress relief, while a politically conservative user might be shown ads that emphasize law and order themes. The ability to tailor messages to an individual's emotional state makes digital advertising a powerful tool for shaping consumer behavior and influencing decision-making.

Artificial intelligence (AI) is another key player in the digital mind control landscape. AI algorithms are used not only to deliver personalized content but also to generate content that is designed to manipulate users. *Deepfake technology*, for instance, uses AI to create hyper-realistic but entirely fabricated images, videos, or audio clips. These deepfakes can be used to spread misinformation, manipulate public opinion, or damage the reputations of political figures or other influential individuals. As AI becomes more sophisticated, the line between reality and manipulation will continue to blur, making it increasingly difficult for users to distinguish between truth and deception.

AI is also used in *bots* and *automated accounts* that can flood social media platforms with specific messages, creating the illusion of widespread support or opposition for a particular idea or cause. These bots can be programmed to engage in coordinated campaigns of disinformation, amplifying false narratives, conspiracy theories, or divisive content to sway public opinion. The use of bots allows for the manipulation of online discourse on a massive scale, influencing elections, social movements, and even international relations.

Surveillance capitalism is another key concept in understanding mind control in the digital age. This term refers to the business model in which companies profit from the collection and analysis of personal data. Tech giants like Google, Facebook, and Amazon use the data they collect from users to build predictive models that can anticipate behavior, allowing them to sell targeted advertising and other services. However, this same data can be used to subtly influence users' thoughts and behaviors without their awareness, shaping their perceptions and decisions in ways that serve corporate interests. This form of manipulation, though less overt than traditional propaganda, is no less powerful, as it operates invisibly in the background of everyday digital interactions.

The rise of *filter bubbles*—the result of algorithms that show users content they are likely to agree with—also plays a significant role in mind control in the digital age. Filter bubbles isolate individuals from information that challenges their beliefs or introduces new ideas, leading to a more polarized and fragmented society.

When individuals are repeatedly exposed to content that reinforces their existing worldview, they become more resistant to alternative perspectives and less likely to engage in critical thinking. This narrowing of information streams makes it easier for those in control of the algorithms to subtly shape public opinion, as individuals are unaware of the broader context or diversity of viewpoints that exist outside their bubble.

Behavioral nudging is another subtle but effective form of digital manipulation. Behavioral science has shown that small "nudges" in the digital environment—such as the design of a website, the placement of a button, or the framing of a choice—can significantly influence decision-making. Tech companies, governments, and other organizations can use these nudges to steer users toward certain behaviors, whether it's purchasing a product, voting for a candidate, or adopting a particular belief. While nudging is not inherently malicious, it becomes a form of mind control when used to manipulate individuals without their informed consent.

The potential for *government surveillance* and control in the digital age is another critical issue. Many governments around the world are leveraging digital technologies to monitor and influence their populations. For example, China's *social credit system* uses data collected from citizens' online activity, financial behavior, and social interactions to assign scores that can determine access to services, jobs, and even travel. This system not only monitors behavior but also conditions it, as citizens are incentivized to conform to government-approved norms to avoid punishment or gain rewards. This form of digital surveillance represents a new level of state control, where the behavior, thoughts, and choices of individuals are shaped by a constant and invisible system of monitoring.

The combination of *biometric data* and digital surveillance also poses significant risks for mind control. With advances in facial recognition, emotion detection, and neurotechnology, governments and corporations may soon be able to track and influence emotional responses in real-time. This capability would allow for even more precise manipulation, as content or interventions could be delivered at the exact moment when individuals are most vulnerable to influence.

In addition to individual manipulation, the digital age has also given rise to the concept of *mass mind control*. Social media platforms and digital technologies enable the rapid dissemination of ideas, allowing for the manipulation of entire populations or demographics at once. Political campaigns, disinformation efforts, and social movements can be orchestrated and amplified through digital means, shaping public opinion on a grand scale. This ability to manipulate large groups of people at once, often without their awareness, represents a significant shift in the balance of power between individuals and those who control the digital platforms. Mind control in the digital age represents a new and complex frontier where technology, psychology, and data converge to influence thoughts, behaviors, and beliefs. The rise of social media algorithms, AI, surveillance capitalism, and behavioral nudging has created an environment where individuals are constantly being monitored and manipulated in subtle but powerful ways. As digital technologies continue to evolve, the potential for both personal and mass manipulation will only increase. Understanding how these systems operate, and developing the tools to recognize and resist digital manipulation, will be critical in preserving individual autonomy and ensuring that the digital age does not become an era of unseen control over the human mind.

Mass Manipulation in the Age of Information Overload

In the modern world, individuals are constantly bombarded with information from an overwhelming number of sources: social media, news outlets, advertisements, emails, and more. This era of information overload has created a unique environment for mass manipulation, where controlling the flow and interpretation of information can lead to significant influence over public opinion, behavior, and beliefs. The sheer volume of information can be disorienting, leaving people vulnerable to manipulation techniques that exploit cognitive biases, emotional reactions, and the desire for simplicity in a chaotic information landscape. In this chapter, we will explore how mass manipulation is carried out in the age of information overload, the strategies used to influence large groups of people, and the psychological and societal effects of living in a world where too much information can paradoxically make it easier to control the masses.

At the heart of mass manipulation in the age of information overload is the concept of *information saturation*. In today's digital world, individuals are exposed to far more information than they can realistically process. This saturation often leads to *cognitive overload*, where the brain's capacity to filter, prioritize, and critically evaluate information is overwhelmed. When individuals feel inundated with information, they are more likely to rely on cognitive shortcuts or heuristics to make sense of the world, which can leave them vulnerable to manipulation.

One such shortcut is the *availability heuristic*, where people tend to judge the likelihood or importance of events based on how easily they can recall examples from recent memory. In the context of information overload, stories that are sensational, emotional, or repeated frequently tend to stand out and shape perception, even if they are not the most accurate or important. For example, repeated media coverage of isolated incidents of violence or terrorism can create the impression that such events are far more common than they actually are, leading to heightened fear and support for policies that address these perceived threats. By flooding the information space with specific types of content, manipulators can direct public attention and shape beliefs without needing to suppress alternative viewpoints outright.

Selective framing is another key tactic in mass manipulation during information overload. Framing refers to how information is presented, emphasizing certain aspects while downplaying others. In an oversaturated information environment, the way a story is framed can have a profound impact on how it is understood. For example, the framing of an economic downturn as a result of "incompetent leadership" rather than "global market forces" shifts public perception and blame, influencing political attitudes and voting behavior. In this way, framing allows manipulators to guide interpretations and narratives, effectively controlling how people perceive and respond to the information they receive.

Repetition plays a critical role in manipulation during information overload. In an environment where information is overwhelming, repetition becomes a powerful tool for ensuring that certain messages rise above the noise. Research has shown that people are more likely to believe something if they have heard it multiple times, even if it is false.

This is known as the *illusion of truth effect*. When the same message is repeated across multiple platforms—on social media, in the news, in advertisements, and by influencers—it can create the perception that the message is widely accepted or unquestionably true, regardless of its accuracy. Repetition is particularly effective in shaping public opinion on complex or controversial issues, as it simplifies the narrative and reinforces certain beliefs.

The use of *emotionally charged content* is another manipulation strategy that thrives in the age of information overload. Emotionally driven stories, images, and videos are more likely to capture attention and go viral, as humans are hardwired to respond to emotional stimuli. Manipulators often exploit this tendency by crafting content that provokes fear, anger, outrage, or sympathy, encouraging emotional reactions rather than rational analysis. In a world where people are constantly scrolling through endless streams of information, emotional content cuts through the noise and leaves a lasting impression. This emotional manipulation can be used to sway public opinion, promote political agendas, or drive consumer behavior.

Echo chambers—digital spaces where individuals are exposed only to information that aligns with their existing beliefs—amplify the effects of manipulation in the information overload era. Social media platforms and personalized algorithms often reinforce these echo chambers by curating content based on users' preferences and past behavior. As a result, people become trapped in feedback loops where they are repeatedly exposed to the same ideas, perspectives, and narratives, which reinforces their beliefs and makes it more difficult to encounter alternative viewpoints. This isolation from dissenting opinions makes individuals more susceptible to manipulation, as their understanding of the world becomes increasingly one-dimensional and unchallenged.

Disinformation and *fake news* have become pervasive tools for mass manipulation in the information overload era. Disinformation refers to the deliberate spread of false or misleading information with the intent to deceive. In an environment where information is overwhelming, it becomes difficult for individuals to fact-check or verify every piece of information they encounter, making it easier for disinformation to spread and take hold. Social media platforms, in particular, are breeding grounds for disinformation, as users can easily share false stories without scrutinizing their sources. Once disinformation goes viral, it can influence public opinion, create confusion, and undermine trust in legitimate sources of information.

One of the most insidious forms of manipulation in the information overload era is *context collapse*, where information is presented without the necessary background or context needed for full understanding. This often happens on social media, where complex issues are reduced to bite-sized headlines, memes, or tweets that lack nuance. Without context, individuals are more likely to misinterpret information or draw simplistic conclusions. This can lead to the spread of misinformation or reinforce polarized thinking, as people rely on incomplete narratives to form their opinions. Context collapse also makes it easier for manipulative actors to distort reality, as removing or altering context can change the meaning of a message entirely.

Another tool of mass manipulation is *algorithmic control*. Social media platforms, news websites, and search engines use algorithms to determine which content users see, and these algorithms are often designed to maximize engagement, not accuracy or truth. Algorithms prioritize content that generates strong reactions—whether positive or negative—because such content keeps users on the platform longer. As a result, sensationalist or emotionally charged content is more likely to be promoted, while more balanced or nuanced information may be buried. This creates a distorted information landscape where users are more likely to be exposed to content that manipulates their emotions and reinforces their biases.

Algorithmic control also allows for *personalized manipulation*. By analyzing user data, algorithms can deliver content that is tailored to individual preferences, behaviors, and vulnerabilities. For example, someone who has shown an interest in conspiracy theories might be shown more content that aligns with those beliefs, deepening their involvement in fringe ideas. This personalized manipulation creates a feedback loop where users are fed content that reinforces their existing beliefs, making it more difficult for them to escape the cycle of misinformation and manipulation.

Confirmation bias—the tendency to search for, interpret, and remember information in a way that confirms one's pre-existing beliefs—further exacerbates the effects of information overload and manipulation. In an environment where individuals are overwhelmed by information, they are more likely to gravitate toward sources and content that align with their existing views. Manipulative actors exploit this bias by creating or promoting content that resonates with specific ideological groups, knowing that people are more likely to accept information that aligns with their worldview. This reinforces division and makes it harder for individuals to engage in critical thinking or seek out alternative perspectives.

The psychological impact of information overload and mass manipulation is significant. Individuals exposed to a constant stream of emotionally charged, repetitive, and polarized content may experience *decision fatigue*, where the sheer volume of information makes it difficult to think critically or make informed choices. Decision fatigue can lead to disengagement, where individuals become apathetic or indifferent to the information they encounter, making them more vulnerable to manipulation by those who offer simple, emotionally satisfying solutions to complex problems.

Mass manipulation in the information overload era also has profound *societal implications*. The constant bombardment of information, much of it designed to manipulate emotions and reinforce biases, contributes to increasing polarization and the breakdown of civil discourse. As people retreat into echo chambers and become more resistant to alternative viewpoints, it becomes harder to engage in constructive dialogue or find common ground. This fragmentation of society makes it easier for manipulative actors to exploit divisions, whether for political, ideological, or commercial gain.

MOREOVER, THE SPREAD of disinformation and the collapse of trust in traditional institutions and media have led to a *crisis of authority*. As individuals are increasingly unable to distinguish between reliable and unreliable sources of information, they may lose faith in experts, governments, and the media. This erosion of trust creates fertile ground for conspiracy theories, populist movements, and extremist ideologies, further destabilizing democratic institutions and social cohesion.

In conclusion, the age of information overload has created a unique environment for mass manipulation, where the sheer volume of information, combined with cognitive biases and emotional manipulation, makes it easier to influence public opinion and behavior. Through tactics like selective framing, repetition, emotional content, disinformation, and algorithmic control, manipulative actors can shape the way individuals perceive and respond to the world. The consequences of this manipulation are profound, leading to increased polarization, the breakdown of civil discourse, and a crisis of trust in democratic institutions. To resist mass manipulation, individuals must develop critical thinking skills, seek out diverse perspectives, and be mindful of the psychological traps that arise in a world of information overload.

The Ethics of Mind Control: Where Should We Draw the Line?

The ethics of mind control raises profound and challenging questions about the boundaries of influence, autonomy, and consent. As technologies and techniques for influencing human thoughts and behaviors become more sophisticated—whether through media, advertising, neurotechnology, or artificial intelligence—understanding where to draw the line between acceptable persuasion and unethical manipulation becomes increasingly important. The debate around mind control touches on issues of free will, privacy, psychological autonomy, and the balance of power between individuals, institutions, and governments. In this chapter, we will explore the ethical implications of mind control, the different forms it can take, and the critical question: Where should we draw the line?

At its core, the ethical debate over mind control hinges on the issue of *consent*. Consent is a fundamental principle in ethical decision-making, particularly when it comes to influencing another person's thoughts or actions. In situations where individuals are fully informed and voluntarily agree to be influenced, such as in education, therapy, or self-improvement, there is generally no ethical concern. However, when influence is exerted without a person's knowledge, or when manipulation crosses the threshold into coercion or deception, ethical concerns arise.

One of the key ethical challenges of mind control lies in the distinction between *persuasion* and *manipulation*. Persuasion is a legitimate form of influence that relies on reason, evidence, and voluntary agreement. It respects the autonomy of the individual by providing them with information and allowing them to make their own choices. Manipulation, on the other hand, seeks to control or alter a person's thoughts, emotions, or behavior in ways that bypass or undermine their ability to make informed, autonomous decisions.

For example, advertising can be seen as a form of persuasion when it presents factual information about a product and leaves the decision to the consumer. However, when advertising uses psychological manipulation, such as exploiting emotional vulnerabilities, fear, or social pressure, it becomes ethically problematic. This line is particularly blurred in the digital age, where advertisers can use data-driven techniques to target individuals with highly personalized messages that exploit their subconscious biases and emotional states.

The use of *subliminal messaging* is a clear case of unethical mind control. Subliminal messages are designed to influence individuals without their conscious awareness, often by embedding messages in media that are below the threshold of perception. Because individuals cannot consciously reject or evaluate subliminal messages, they are considered a form of covert manipulation that violates the principle of consent. Most ethical frameworks agree that attempts to influence individuals without their knowledge or ability to resist are inherently unethical.

IN ADDITION TO SUBLIMINAL messaging, *emotional manipulation* raises ethical concerns, particularly when it involves exploiting vulnerabilities such as fear, guilt, or shame. Emotional appeals are common in political campaigns, advertising, and media, but when these appeals are designed to bypass rational thought and provoke automatic emotional responses, they can undermine an individual's autonomy. For example, fear-based propaganda that exaggerates threats or demonizes an out-group to influence political behavior raises serious ethical questions. While emotional appeals can be effective, they become unethical when they distort reality or exploit psychological weaknesses to manipulate behavior.

In the context of *neuro-technology* and *brain-computer interfaces* (BCIs), the ethical questions around mind control become even more complex. BCIs, which allow direct communication between the brain and external devices, have the potential to enhance human capabilities, but they also raise concerns about *mental privacy* and *cognitive liberty*. As neuro-technology advances, the ability to read or even influence brain activity could become a powerful tool for manipulation, blurring the line between external influence and internal thought processes.

Ethicists have expressed concern that if neuro-technologies are used to influence or control thoughts without explicit consent, it could lead to unprecedented forms of mind control that infringe on an individual's right to mental autonomy. For example, the ability to implant suggestions or alter emotional responses through neuro-stimulation raises questions about how much control individuals will have over their own minds. In such cases, the ethical principle of *informed consent* must be strictly enforced, ensuring that individuals are fully aware of the effects of the technology and have the ability to opt out.

Similarly, the rise of *artificial intelligence (AI)* and *algorithmic manipulation* presents new ethical challenges. AI algorithms used by social media platforms, search engines, and digital advertising can shape users' thoughts and behaviors by curating the information they see. This form of influence, while not inherently unethical, becomes problematic when it operates invisibly or without the user's awareness. When algorithms are designed to prioritize content that provokes emotional responses or reinforces existing biases, they can manipulate users in ways that distort their understanding of reality.

The ethical question here is whether it is acceptable for technology companies, governments, or other actors to use AI to subtly influence people's beliefs or behaviors without their explicit consent. Should there be limits on how much control algorithms can exert over what information people are exposed to? And how can individuals be empowered to resist these forms of manipulation when they are largely invisible and difficult to detect?

Another area of ethical concern is the use of *biometric data* to influence behavior. Biometric surveillance, such as facial recognition or emotion detection, can be used to monitor people's reactions and tailor content to their emotional states. While this technology has potential benefits, such as enhancing customer experiences or improving public safety, it also raises concerns about *invasive manipulation*. For example, using biometric data to detect when someone is feeling anxious and then delivering ads or messages designed to exploit that anxiety could be considered unethical, as it takes advantage of a person's emotional vulnerability.

In the political realm, the use of *disinformation* and *propaganda* to control public opinion presents one of the clearest ethical violations. When political actors deliberately spread false information or manipulate facts to sway public opinion, they undermine the foundation of informed democratic participation. The ethical issue here is not just about the intent to deceive, but about the broader consequences for society, including the erosion of trust in institutions, the spread of polarization, and the weakening of democratic processes.

The ethical problems associated with *mass surveillance* and *social control*, such as those seen in authoritarian regimes, represent some of the most dangerous forms of mind control. Systems like China's *social credit system*, which monitor and reward or punish citizens based on their behavior, raise fundamental questions about the balance between security and individual freedom. In such cases, mind control extends beyond psychological influence to the realm of direct behavioral control, where the state or other entities use surveillance, data collection, and punishment mechanisms to enforce compliance and obedience. In considering the ethics of mind control, it's important to recognize that *intent* plays a crucial role in determining whether a form of influence is acceptable or not. When influence is exerted with the goal of helping individuals make informed decisions, such as in education or mental health care, it is generally seen as ethical. However, when the intent is to control or manipulate individuals for the benefit of the influencer, it crosses into unethical territory.

The question of *where to draw the line* in mind control depends on several key principles:

1. **Consent**: Is the individual aware of the influence being exerted, and have they given their informed consent?
2. **Autonomy**: Does the influence respect the individual's ability to think and act independently, or does it undermine their autonomy?
3. **Transparency**: Is the influence being exerted in an open and transparent manner, or is it hidden or deceptive?
4. **Harm**: Does the influence cause harm to the individual or to society, either by distorting reality, exploiting vulnerabilities, or undermining trust?
5. **Intent**: Is the goal of the influence to benefit the individual and support their decision-making, or is it primarily for the benefit of the influencer?

In conclusion, the ethics of mind control is a complex and evolving issue, particularly as new technologies and techniques emerge that can subtly or overtly influence human thought and behavior. The line between ethical influence and unethical manipulation depends on factors such as consent, autonomy, transparency, harm, and intent. As the potential for mind control grows with advances in neuro-technology, AI, and biometric surveillance, it is crucial to establish clear ethical guidelines that protect individual freedom and mental autonomy. The challenge for societies moving forward is to balance the benefits of persuasive technologies with the need to safeguard the integrity of the human mind from manipulation and control.

The Psychology of Belief: Why We Fall for Mind Control

The psychology of belief plays a critical role in understanding why people fall for mind control. Human beings are inherently wired to seek patterns, form beliefs, and trust authority figures, all of which can make them susceptible to manipulation. Mind control techniques exploit these psychological tendencies, using persuasion, emotional appeals, cognitive biases, and social influences to shape thoughts, beliefs, and behaviors. To truly grasp why mind control is so effective, it is essential to delve into the cognitive and emotional mechanisms that drive belief formation, how they can be manipulated, and why even rational individuals can fall victim to manipulation. This chapter will explore the psychology of belief and how it makes people vulnerable to mind control.

One of the most fundamental reasons people fall for mind control is the *human need for certainty*. The world is complex, unpredictable, and often overwhelming, and people naturally seek stability and order in their lives. When faced with uncertainty, individuals are more likely to latch onto beliefs or ideologies that provide clear answers or explanations for the world around them. This desire for certainty is particularly strong in times of crisis, fear, or insecurity. Mind control techniques often offer simple, comforting narratives that eliminate ambiguity, promising security and control in exchange for submission to the ideology or authority.

For example, cults and authoritarian regimes frequently use clear-cut, black-and-white ideologies to attract followers. These systems offer a sense of purpose and certainty, often by presenting the world as a struggle between good and evil, where the follower's role is clearly defined. The appeal of such systems lies in their simplicity—followers are given a straightforward framework for understanding the world, which reduces the anxiety of ambiguity. Once individuals become invested in these systems, they may be more willing to accept manipulation or control, as the alternative—returning to uncertainty—is perceived as more threatening.

Cognitive biases also play a key role in why people fall for mind control. Cognitive biases are mental shortcuts that help the brain process information more quickly but can lead to errors in judgment. One of the most powerful cognitive biases that manipulators exploit is *confirmation bias*—the tendency for people to seek out and interpret information in a way that confirms their preexisting beliefs. Once a belief is formed, individuals will often ignore or reject information that contradicts it, while giving more weight to information that supports it. This makes it easier for manipulators to reinforce existing beliefs through selective framing or repetition, deepening an individual's commitment to the manipulated narrative.

The mere exposure effect is another cognitive bias that contributes to the success of mind control. This psychological phenomenon refers to the human tendency to develop a preference for things simply because they are familiar. The more often people are exposed to a particular idea, symbol, or message, the more likely they are to accept it as true or normal.

Repetition is a key tactic in propaganda, advertising, and other forms of mind control because it exploits the mere exposure effect, gradually making manipulated ideas feel familiar and accepted. Over time, even initially skeptical individuals may start to adopt beliefs or attitudes that they have been repeatedly exposed to, especially if those ideas are presented in authoritative or emotionally engaging ways.

Social conformity is another powerful psychological factor that makes people susceptible to mind control. Humans are inherently social creatures, and the desire to belong to a group can heavily influence beliefs and behaviors. In many cases, individuals adopt the beliefs or attitudes of their social group to avoid standing out or being ostracized. This is known as *normative social influence*, where people conform to fit in with the expectations of others. Cults, totalitarian regimes, and even political movements use this social pressure to create environments where dissent is discouraged, and individuals are encouraged to adopt the dominant narrative to maintain social harmony.

Additionally, *informational social influence* comes into play when individuals look to others, particularly authority figures, for guidance on what is true or correct. When people are uncertain about how to interpret a situation or event, they tend to rely on the opinions and behaviors of those around them, particularly those who appear knowledgeable or confident. This is why charismatic leaders, whether in political movements, cults, or religious organizations, can exert such powerful control over followers. Their confidence and certainty can make their ideas seem more credible, even if those ideas are unfounded or irrational.

Emotional manipulation is one of the most effective tools in mind control, as emotions often override rational thought. Fear, in particular, is a powerful motivator that can be used to control behavior and shape beliefs. When people are afraid—whether of an external enemy, social rejection, or personal failure—they are more likely to seek protection in the form of authority or ideology. Fear-based propaganda, for instance, exaggerates threats and presents the manipulator's agenda as the only solution to avoid catastrophe. The emotional intensity of fear makes people less likely to critically evaluate the information they are presented with and more likely to accept the narrative offered by the manipulator.

Guilt and *shame* are also frequently used to manipulate beliefs and behavior. These emotions are particularly potent in controlling environments like cults or abusive relationships, where individuals are made to feel responsible for their own suffering or for the well-being of the group. By inducing guilt, manipulators can convince individuals that they must conform to certain behaviors or beliefs to redeem themselves. Over time, this emotional manipulation can erode an individual's sense of self-worth, making them more dependent on the controlling authority for validation and guidance.

Another psychological factor that contributes to susceptibility to mind control is the concept of *cognitive dissonance*. Cognitive dissonance occurs when individuals experience a conflict between their beliefs and their actions, leading to psychological discomfort. To resolve this discomfort, people often adjust their beliefs to align with their behavior, rather than changing their behavior to match their beliefs.

Manipulators exploit cognitive dissonance by gradually leading individuals to engage in behaviors that conflict with their previous values or beliefs. Once individuals take action that supports the manipulated belief system—such as participating in a rally, making a donation, or publicly supporting a cause—they are more likely to internalize that belief to reduce the discomfort of cognitive dissonance.

Authority bias is another important factor in why people fall for mind control. Authority bias refers to the tendency to obey or trust authority figures, especially in situations of uncertainty or fear. Manipulators often position themselves as legitimate authorities, whether through charisma, knowledge, or power, to gain the trust and obedience of their followers. Once an individual sees the manipulator as a legitimate authority, they are more likely to accept the manipulator's ideas without question, believing that the authority figure knows best. This is particularly effective in hierarchical structures like cults or authoritarian regimes, where dissent is discouraged, and loyalty to the authority figure is demanded.

Scarcity and urgency are also psychological triggers that can be exploited in mind control. When people believe that something is scarce or that they must act quickly to avoid missing out or suffering harm, they are more likely to comply with requests or adopt beliefs without critically evaluating them. This tactic is commonly used in high-pressure sales tactics, political campaigns, and cult recruitment, where individuals are made to feel that time is running out or that opportunities for salvation or success are limited. By creating a sense of urgency, manipulators can bypass rational decision-making and push individuals toward immediate compliance.

The *illusion of invulnerability* also plays a role in why people fall for mind control. Many individuals believe that they are immune to manipulation or that mind control only affects other people. This sense of invulnerability can lead people to underestimate the influence of subtle manipulation techniques, making them more susceptible to those very techniques. The reality is that everyone is vulnerable to manipulation to some degree, especially when cognitive biases, emotional triggers, and social influences are at play. Acknowledging this vulnerability is the first step toward developing the critical thinking skills necessary to resist manipulation.

In conclusion, the psychology of belief is deeply intertwined with why people fall for mind control. Human cognitive biases, emotional responses, and social influences all create opportunities for manipulation, allowing skilled manipulators to shape thoughts, beliefs, and behaviors. Techniques like exploiting uncertainty, reinforcing cognitive biases, inducing emotional reactions, and leveraging social conformity are all powerful tools that can be used to control individuals and even entire populations. Understanding the psychological mechanisms that make people vulnerable to manipulation is essential for recognizing and resisting mind control. By cultivating self-awareness, critical thinking, and emotional resilience, individuals can protect themselves from falling victim to manipulative forces and maintain control over their own beliefs and decisions.

The Human Cost of Mind Control: From Personal Lives to Society

The human cost of mind control is profound, affecting individuals on both personal and societal levels. While mind control techniques—whether through propaganda, manipulation, or more direct forms of coercion—can achieve control over thoughts, behaviors, and beliefs, they leave behind significant damage. The effects can range from personal suffering, loss of autonomy, and emotional trauma to widespread societal consequences like the erosion of trust, social polarization, and the undermining of democratic institutions. This chapter will examine the human cost of mind control, exploring how it impacts individuals in their personal lives, how it affects families and communities, and the broader consequences for society as a whole.

On an *individual level,* the most immediate and devastating consequence of mind control is the *loss of personal autonomy*. When someone falls under the influence of a controlling entity—whether it's a cult, an abusive partner, a political regime, or a manipulative organization—they gradually lose their ability to think independently. Their thoughts, decisions, and even their identity become subordinated to the will of the manipulator. This loss of autonomy is not only psychologically damaging but also robs individuals of their sense of self, agency, and freedom. Over time, they may come to question their own beliefs and values, or worse, forget who they were before they fell under the manipulator's influence.

This can lead to a profound sense of *disconnection* and *alienation*. Individuals who are subjected to mind control often feel isolated, either because they are physically cut off from loved ones or because they are mentally disconnected from their former lives. This isolation is often intentionally engineered by manipulators, as it makes individuals more dependent on the controlling entity for validation, direction, and purpose. In extreme cases, this isolation can result in total estrangement from friends and family, leading to profound loneliness and emotional despair.

Another cost of mind control is the *psychological trauma* it often inflicts. The manipulation and coercion used in mind control can result in long-lasting mental health issues, such as anxiety, depression, post-traumatic stress disorder (PTSD), and dissociation. Individuals who have been manipulated often experience feelings of guilt, shame, and worthlessness, especially if they are made to believe that they are responsible for their own manipulation or suffering. This emotional manipulation can have severe effects on self-esteem and mental well-being, leading to years of psychological recovery even after the individual has escaped the controlling situation.

For many individuals, mind control also results in *financial and social loss*. Those who fall victim to cults, scams, or manipulative organizations often lose money, property, and even careers as they devote resources to the controlling group or person. In some cases, individuals are coerced into giving up their savings, homes, or businesses, leaving them financially destitute. Socially, the damage can be equally severe, as victims may lose important relationships, suffer reputational harm, or find it difficult to reintegrate into society after escaping mind control. The stigma associated with having been manipulated can also lead to feelings of shame and social exclusion, further compounding the emotional damage.

In *family and community dynamics*, the effects of mind control are often deeply disruptive. When one member of a family falls under the influence of a manipulative entity, it can strain or even sever relationships with other family members. Families may struggle to understand the behavior of their loved one, especially if they adopt beliefs or practices that are radically different from those they held before. This can lead to heartbreak, conflict, and division within families, as they try to rescue their loved one from the influence of the manipulator. Parents may feel powerless to help their children, siblings may grow distant, and spouses may face the painful reality of losing a partner to manipulation.

Children who grow up in environments where mind control is present, such as in authoritarian regimes, religious cults, or abusive households, can experience lasting psychological and emotional harm. These children may be indoctrinated from a young age, which can stunt their emotional development, distort their understanding of the world, and make it difficult for them to form healthy relationships as adults. The trauma of growing up under constant psychological control can leave deep emotional scars, contributing to mental health struggles that persist well into adulthood.

On a *societal level*, mind control has far-reaching consequences that can undermine the fabric of entire communities, institutions, and nations. One of the most damaging effects is the *erosion of trust* in both personal and public spheres. In environments where mind control is practiced on a large scale—whether through state propaganda, corporate manipulation, or disinformation campaigns—people become less able to trust the information they receive, the institutions they rely on, and even their fellow citizens. This breakdown in trust makes it difficult for society to function cohesively, as people grow more suspicious, cynical, and polarized.

Mind control also contributes to *social polarization*. When large segments of the population are subjected to manipulative messaging that creates an "us vs. them" mentality, it leads to divisions that can fracture communities, political systems, and nations. Polarization makes it harder to have constructive dialogue, as people are more likely to view those with differing opinions as enemies rather than as fellow citizens. This erosion of civil discourse can lead to increased conflict, social unrest, and even violence, as groups become more entrenched in their beliefs and less willing to compromise or cooperate.

In the political realm, mind control can have devastating effects on *democratic institutions*. Authoritarian regimes, for example, often use propaganda, censorship, and psychological coercion to control public opinion and suppress dissent. When citizens are manipulated into supporting undemocratic leaders or policies, the foundations of democracy—such as free speech, pluralism, and the rule of law—are weakened. In extreme cases, mind control can contribute to the rise of totalitarian governments, where freedom of thought and expression is entirely suppressed, and citizens are conditioned to obey without question.

THE RISE OF DISINFORMATION in the digital age has further exacerbated these societal impacts. As people are increasingly exposed to false or manipulated information through social media, news outlets, and political actors, it becomes harder for society to agree on basic facts. This proliferation of disinformation erodes the common ground necessary for democratic decision-making, making it easier for manipulative actors to sow division, undermine public trust, and manipulate elections or public policy.

Mind control also has *economic implications*. On an individual level, victims of manipulation may experience financial losses due to scams, fraud, or coerced donations. On a broader level, societal manipulation can influence economic policies, consumer behavior, and market trends in ways that benefit a few while harming the majority. Corporations that engage in manipulative advertising, for example, may drive consumers to make irrational purchasing decisions, leading to economic inefficiencies and consumer harm. Similarly, political manipulation that influences economic policy can result in decisions that favor the wealthy or powerful, exacerbating inequality and undermining social welfare.

In extreme cases, mind control can lead to *social collapse*. When large portions of a society are manipulated into believing dangerous ideologies or engaging in destructive behaviors, the consequences can be catastrophic. Examples from history, such as Nazi Germany or the Rwandan genocide, show how mass manipulation can lead to widespread violence, persecution, and the destruction of communities. These tragedies illustrate the potential human cost of mind control on a societal scale, where manipulation is used to dehumanize, divide, and destroy.

In conclusion, the human cost of mind control is immense, touching every aspect of life—from individual mental health and personal relationships to the stability and cohesion of entire societies. On a personal level, mind control strips individuals of their autonomy, causes psychological trauma, and often leads to financial and social losses. Families and communities are torn apart by the effects of manipulation, as loved ones struggle to reconnect or rescue those under the control of manipulative forces. On a societal level, mind control erodes trust, fuels polarization, undermines democratic institutions, and can even lead to social collapse. Understanding these costs is essential for recognizing the dangers of mind control and developing strategies to resist its influence, both on an individual and collective level. By promoting critical thinking, emotional resilience, and social cohesion, societies can work to mitigate the human cost of mind control and protect the freedoms and well-being of their citizens.

Remedies and Change: What can we do to Eliminate Manipulation and Control?

Restoring humanity and eliminating manipulation and control in a world where mind control is becoming increasingly sophisticated requires a multifaceted approach that addresses both individual and societal vulnerabilities. While it may not be possible to completely eradicate manipulation, we can take steps to reduce its impact by fostering critical thinking, promoting transparency, protecting personal autonomy, and creating systems that discourage manipulation. This chapter will explore potential remedies and changes that can help individuals and societies resist manipulation, protect freedom of thought, and restore a sense of humanity in an era where control tactics are pervasive.

One of the most important remedies for reducing manipulation is to *foster critical thinking skills*. Manipulation often succeeds because individuals are not equipped with the tools needed to critically evaluate the information they receive. By promoting education that emphasizes logical reasoning, media literacy, and skepticism, we can help people develop the ability to question narratives, evaluate evidence, and resist being swayed by emotional or manipulative tactics. Educational programs, both in schools and for adults, should focus on teaching individuals how to identify cognitive biases, spot disinformation, and critically assess the credibility of sources.

Media literacy is a key aspect of this critical thinking approach. In an age where information overload and disinformation are rampant, it's essential for individuals to learn how to navigate the digital landscape safely. Media literacy programs should teach people how to recognize manipulative content, distinguish between legitimate and misleading sources, and understand how algorithms shape what they see online. Equipping individuals with these skills will help them become more discerning consumers of information and less vulnerable to mind control tactics used by governments, corporations, and interest groups.

Another crucial remedy is to *promote transparency and accountability* in the systems and institutions that have the potential to influence thought and behavior. Social media platforms, tech companies, and governments should be held to higher standards of transparency in how they collect data, deliver content, and use algorithms to influence public opinion. By making these processes more transparent, individuals can better understand how their behaviors and beliefs are being shaped and take steps to resist unwanted manipulation.

For example, tech companies should be required to disclose how their algorithms prioritize content and whether they are using personal data to manipulate user behavior. Additionally, governments should establish regulations that prevent the misuse of data for political or commercial manipulation. Public pressure and legal frameworks can help ensure that the systems designed to connect and inform us are not being used to covertly control or influence our beliefs and actions.

PROTECTING PERSONAL autonomy is another critical component of resisting manipulation and restoring humanity. This means safeguarding individuals' right to make their own decisions and form their own beliefs without interference from manipulative forces. One way to do this is by ensuring that people have access to diverse and unbiased information. In many cases, manipulation thrives because people are only exposed to narrow or distorted views of reality. By promoting independent journalism, supporting diverse media sources, and ensuring that all citizens have access to uncensored information, societies can create an environment where individuals can make more informed and autonomous decisions.

On an individual level, *mindfulness and emotional awareness* can be powerful tools for resisting manipulation. Manipulative actors often exploit emotional vulnerabilities such as fear, guilt, or anger to control behavior. By practicing mindfulness—becoming more aware of one's emotional states and reactions—individuals can learn to recognize when their emotions are being manipulated and take steps to regain control. Emotional intelligence training, which teaches individuals how to manage their emotions, understand others' emotions, and maintain emotional balance, can help people resist being swayed by manipulative tactics that seek to exploit their feelings.

Creating *support networks and community resilience* is also an essential remedy for reducing the impact of manipulation. Isolation is one of the key factors that makes individuals more vulnerable to mind control. When people feel disconnected from their families, friends, or communities, they are more likely to seek validation and guidance from external sources, including manipulative figures. By fostering strong social connections and supportive communities, individuals can develop a sense of belonging and security that reduces their susceptibility to manipulation. These networks provide alternative perspectives, emotional support, and a sense of accountability that can counterbalance the influence of controlling entities.

Community-based initiatives that promote open dialogue, empathy, and mutual understanding can help combat social fragmentation and polarization, which are often fueled by manipulative tactics. Encouraging civil discourse—where individuals from diverse backgrounds and belief systems can engage in meaningful conversations—can create an environment where manipulation is less effective, as people are exposed to multiple perspectives and learn to critically evaluate their own beliefs.

On a broader societal level, *reforming political systems and reducing the influence of money and power* can help prevent manipulation in governance. Many forms of mind control, particularly propaganda and disinformation, are used by political actors to maintain power and control over populations. By reducing the role of money in politics, enacting campaign finance reform, and increasing transparency in political processes, we can create systems where manipulation for political gain is less viable. Promoting accountability for political leaders and institutions that use deceptive tactics to sway public opinion is crucial for maintaining the integrity of democratic systems.

ETHICAL GUIDELINES and oversight for emerging technologies are also critical in preventing the misuse of new tools that could enable manipulation. As artificial intelligence, neurotechnology, and biometric data become more advanced, there is an increasing need for ethical frameworks that govern their use. These technologies have the potential to enhance human capabilities, but they also carry the risk of being used for mind control and behavioral manipulation. Governments, tech companies, and international organizations must work together to establish ethical standards and regulations that protect individuals' autonomy and privacy while ensuring that these technologies are used responsibly.

For example, regulations could require informed consent for the use of neurotechnological devices that influence brain activity, transparency about how AI algorithms are designed and applied, and limits on the use of biometric data for surveillance or manipulation. Ethical oversight bodies could be established to monitor the use of these technologies and ensure that they are not being exploited for harmful purposes.

Finally, *restoring trust in institutions* is essential for reducing the influence of manipulation on a societal level. In an age where trust in governments, media, and other institutions has eroded, people are more susceptible to conspiracy theories, disinformation, and manipulative actors who claim to offer the "truth." Restoring trust requires these institutions to be more transparent, accountable, and responsive to the needs and concerns of the public. Rebuilding trust in institutions will not only reduce the impact of manipulation but also foster a sense of social cohesion and collective responsibility.

Public institutions, including governments and media organizations, should commit to higher standards of truthfulness, transparency, and integrity in their communication with the public. Fact-checking initiatives, open-access data policies, and participatory decision-making processes can help restore public confidence in these institutions. Additionally, media organizations should work to reduce sensationalism and bias in their reporting, focusing instead on providing balanced, accurate, and thoughtful coverage of important issues.

In conclusion, while mind control and manipulation are difficult to fully eliminate, there are numerous steps that individuals, communities, and societies can take to resist and reduce their impact. By fostering critical thinking, promoting transparency and accountability, protecting personal autonomy, and creating supportive networks, we can restore humanity and empower people to think and act freely. As technology and society evolve, it is crucial that we continue to develop ethical standards and systems that protect individuals from manipulation while promoting the values of empathy, understanding, and freedom of thought. Only by addressing both the individual and systemic factors that enable manipulation can we hope to create a world where humanity is respected, and manipulation is minimized.

I hope you liked this book. If you did, please leave a review where you bought it. Thank you from the author.

About the Author

Andrew Parry is a writer whose fascination with the great thinkers, philosophers, and the nature of reality deeply influences his work. His writing is shaped by an enduring curiosity about the fundamental questions of existence—what it means to be human, how we understand the world around us, and the intricate relationships between thought, perception, and reality. Through his exploration of these themes, Andrew seeks to provoke thoughtful reflection and open new pathways of understanding for his readers.

Read more at https://lonetrail.blog.